International African Studies' Perspective

THE NEW AFRICAN CIVIL-MILITARY RELATIONS

Edited by

Martin Rupiya

Gorden Moyo

Henrik Laugesen

The African Public Policy and Research Institute (APPRI) wishes to acknowledge the support provided by the Danish Royal Defence College for this project.

Published by APPRI, 357 Visagie Street, Pretoria 0001

© APPRI 2015

ISBN 978-0-620-61527-3

First published 2015

Editing by Hilda Hermann

Cover by Henrik Laugesen

Production by Bronwen Dachs Muller

Printed by MegaDigital, Cape Town

Table of Contents

Page

List of Contributors

Dr Martin R. Rupiya, Executive Director of the African Public Policy and Research Institute (APPRI), is a Research Fellow at the Institute for African Renaissance Studies and Programme Facilitator of Management of Democratic Elections in Africa (MDEA) at the University of South Africa (UNISA). He is also a visiting fellow at the Institute for Peace and Security Studies at the University of Addis Ababa. Before establishing APPRI, Lieutenant-Colonel (retired) Rupiya had been the Director of Research: Africa at Cranfield University, United Kingdom; Senior Researcher and MilAIDS Project Manager at the Institute for Security Studies, Pretoria, South Africa; Associate Professor in the Department of International Relations, University of the Witwatersrand, South Africa; Visiting Fellow in the Department of Politics and International Studies, Rhodes University, Grahamstown, South Africa; and Senior Lecturer and Director of the Centre for Defence Studies at the University of Zimbabwe. His recent publications include Zimbabwe's Military: Examining its Veto Power in the Transition to Democracy, 2008-2013 (Ed.) (APPRI, 2013) and "South Africa's Security Intervention in Africa: Libya, Cote d'Ivoire and Zimbabwe" in State of the Nation 2012-2013 (HSRC, 2012).

Dr Gorden Moyo is a former Minister of State Enterprises and Parastatals in Zimbabwe. He is currently a policy advisor to the Public Policy and Research Institute of Zimbabwe (PPRIZ). His research interests include public leadership, public participation, public institutions, developmental states, civil-military relations and conflict resolution. He holds a PhD in African Leadership Development from the National University of Science and Technology (Zimbabwe) and a Master of Arts degree in Peace Studies from the University of Bradford (UK).

Henrik Laugesen is a Major in the Royal Danish Defence College and is a PhD candidate at the University of Copenhagen. He has an MA in African Studies and his experience and interests are in security dynamics in East Africa; foreign military assistance and professionalisation of the armed forces in Kenya; democracy and democratisation; and civil-military relations in East Africa.

Dr Simon Adetona Akindes is an Associate Professor in the Department of Politics, Philosophy and Law at the University of Wisconsin-Parkside in the United States. He previously taught at Cleveland State University, and Ohio University where he earned his Ph.D in Education (Instructional Technology.) Dr Akindes also has a Masters' degree in International Affairs, a D.E.A. (Diplôme d'Etudes Approfondies) in African Literatures and Civilizations and English from Ohio University, and a B.Sc. in Political Science from Ibadan University in Nigeria. From 2012 to 2014, he was the Education and Professional Development Lead of the Managing Peace and Security in Africa Executive Masters Programme at the Institute for Peace and Security Studies at Addis Ababa University in Ethiopia. He has published educational books, academic articles, book chapters, and essays on democratisation and elections, politics and music, education, sports and culture. Among his recent publications are "An Aficionado's Perspectives on the Complexity and Contradictions of Rooting for a Team in the 2010 World Cup" in Alegi P. & Bolsmann, C., (Eds.), *Africa's World Cup: Critical reflections on play, patriotism, spectatorship, and space,* Ann Arbor: University of Michigan Press; and "Elections in Côte d'Ivoire: The Contrasting Colors of Democratization" in N'diaye, B., Houngnikpo, M. & Saine, A. (Eds.), *West Africa's Quest for Democracy: Lessons in Elections, Liberalization and Democratization, 1990-2009,* Africa World Press: Trenton, NJ.

Dr Elena Igorevna Doroshenko holds a PhD in Linguistics, specialising in Sociolinguistics. From 2001 to 2010 she worked as an Associate Professor in the Moscow State Pedagogical University, teaching a wide variety of subjects related to Language Theory and Practice. At present she is working in the sphere of analytical journalism, contributing articles to Russian scientific journals (such as *Asia and Africa Today*) and other academic editions. Her main interests include issues of security, policy and defence in the Middle East and North Africa. Among her recent works are "Target Gaddafi: 'Libyan Campaign' in the Mass Media" (*Asia and Africa Today*, October 2014) and "Arab East After a Violent Democratisation" (book review, *Asia and Africa Today*, November 2014).

Irene Limo is the Senior Programme Officer in the Peacekeeping Unit at African Centre for the Constructive Resolution of Disputes (ACCORD). She is responsible for the development of detailed implementation plans for programmes in the Peacekeeping Unit and its strategic direction. She is also responsible for supporting gender mainstreaming within the unit through training, policy development and applied research. Limo holds a Master's degree in International Studies from the University of Nairobi, Kenya, and a Bachelor of Business and Management degree from Moi University, Kenya.

Kealeboga J. Maphunye is the inaugural WIPHOLD-Brigalia Bam Research Professor and Chair in Electoral Democracy in Africa at the University of South Africa. He holds a doctoral degree in Government from the University of Essex (UK). Among others, he has worked for the School of Government, University of the Western Cape, Human Sciences Research Council (HSRC), Department of Public Service and Administration and the Electoral Commission of South Africa (IEC). Currently, he conducts research on elections, governance and democracy in Africa but his broader research interests include post-independence bureaucratic reform in developing countries, comparative politics and public administration, and gender and human rights issues in public sector organisations.

Mpho K. Mothoagae is a lecturer and programme manager/facilitator, Management of Democratic Elections in Africa (MDEA), at the University of South Africa (UNISA). The topic of the thesis of the MA degree he is pursuing is Dimo le Tselane: Rape in the Context of an African-Cultural Justice System.

Wilson Kamau Muna is a project management consultant and an expert on issues of public policy and development. He holds a Master's degree of Social Sciences in Policy and Development Studies and is currently enrolled as a doctoral candidate at the University of KwaZulu-Natal, South Africa. His recent publications include co-authored articles, "Monetary Clout and Electoral Politics in Kenya: The 1992 to 2013 Presidential Elections in Focus on governance in Kenya" in *Journal of African Elections*, 13(2) in 2014 and "Leadership and Political Corruption in Kenya: Analysis of the 2010 Constitutional Provisions on the Presidency" in *Journal of Social, Political, and Economic Studies* 38 (3) in 2013.

Dr Sunday Angoma Okello is Assistant Professor at the Institute for Peace and Security Studies, Addis Ababa University, Ethiopia. He obtained his PhD in Public Policy from the University of Birmingham, UK. His interest and involvement in peace and security issues in the Great Lakes and Horn of Africa regions spans more than 25 years. He has recently published, among others, a book mapping community conflicts in South Sudan.

Preface

The New African Civil-Military Relations is a new publication on Africa's civil-military relations and it is a valuable addition to the literature in this critical area of study and practice. It presents valuable opportunities for civilians and those associated with the military such as the army, navy, and air force to reflect on the issues involved. Thus is especially so since the inter-relationships between civil-military relations and democratisation in Africa remain under-researched or under-emphasised.

The chapters in this book raise awareness on the complex, and often difficult, dimensions of the context in which African civil-military relations affect the continent's democratisation processes. These chapters also bring forward some suggestions on how each nation and region should respond. In addition, African polities, which are now hostage to partisan or politicised militaries surrounding the long-reigning "stable coups and third term and beyond aspirants in power" should be assisted to find remedy to correct the situation. This is in contrast to the expectations of the post-Cold War era which was supposed to have ushered African nations into a new era of nation building and state formation without the intrusion of external powers and the emergence of a politico-military elite that lacked a national vision. Such vision would be expected to be aligned to the African Union's (AU) Agenda 2063 in terms of the continental unification ideals of the erstwhile Organisation of African Unity (OAU). Currently, the new era demands that we begin to invest in research that is relevant to the challenges facing Africa's civil-military relations, collaborate with experts in this and other related fields, and collaborate with university multidisciplinary faculties. Such collaboration will ensure that the work done will promote and enhance the relevant Research Agendas and appropriate notions to become policy within the emerging democratic states especially in Africa.

Sadly, when the multiparty democracy era of the 1990 was ushered in, in Sub-Saharan Africa, only 47 countries conducted competitive elections and, within months, 38 regimes had succumbed to military coups or refusal by the incumbent to leave office when their constitutionally-enshrined term limits were over. From these adverse developments, new trends have emerged that are associated with civil-military relations as Africa proceeds towards the AU's Agenda 2063. Martin Rupiya calls one of these trends 'stable coups system', which sometimes also masks the Presidential Third Term phenomenon. What distinguishes this system is the fact that it is widely accepted, almost with resignation by the international community, the sub-regional bodies and even some constituencies within a particular state.

To enhance African civil-military relations, the military or armed forces must be disarmed and the security sector should be reformed; the main reason being to avoid the phenomenon of military machines that are not subjected to civilian oversight through parliament or civilian oversight bodies. In addition, there should be extensive political reform to dissuade politicians from authorising gangs, assassins or bandits to carry out assassinations with impunity on political opponents.

One of the major challenges facing Africa is that most arms of war and military supplies are manufactured outside the continent, mostly by arms manufacturers who stand to benefit immensely from political instability and internecine conflict. Yet, it is common knowledge that the machinations of such arms manufacturers could easily be outwitted by African countries if they all worked together towards common socio-economic, political, military and other goals that can benefit the entire continent's people. Key among such goals will, necessarily, be the need to rein in the military– not only through civilian control or oversight – but also through concerted efforts by Africa's politicians towards greater democratisation through committing to free, fair and internationally accepted democratic elections.

The highlights of each chapter in the book's Introduction provide valuable hints in this study and this will benefit researchers, military personnel and executives, policy-makers working in civil-military relations, students, academics and political advisors.

Professor Phalandwa A. Mulaudzi
Institute for African Renaissance Studies, University of South Africa

Chapter 1

International African Studies' Perspectives: The *new* African civil-military relations phase in African states' development

by Martin Rupiya, Gorden Moyo and Henrik Laugesen

INTRODUCTION

Since the 1648 Treaty of Westphalia suggested the notion of the nation state system in central Europe, the phenomenon of centralised, sovereign and territorially distinct nations has become widely evident. The modern nation state, as we know it today, wrested the monopoly over security as a public good in the hands of the monarchies to locate this within parliaments, the constitution and funding support from national taxation with representation. This was a violent, sometimes messy phase, including the 1789 French Revolution in which most rulers were guillotined. In the same period, the tradition of hiring out national territorial security from the Colonels Regiments was transformed, to be replaced by the innovative Prussian example of standing armies, and supported and controlled parliaments within constitutional frameworks, spurred by the Industrial Revolution and technological discoveries. In war, it was the late 19th Century invention of the Maxim machine gun, among others, that revolutionised warfare, and the launch of air power during World War II.

Underlying the rapid transformation in the evolution of the nation state and developments towards stable civil-military relations, which we shall define shortly, were the questions: What was/is the purpose of the state? What is it organised for? Theoretically, it was to provide public goods, education, security, health and welfare; thus it required the bureaucracy to be organised in order to achieve the set goal(s).

The international interest of these emerging states, in their interaction with the African continent's state formation, has shaped and influenced the latter's civil military relations. For purposes of this chapter, which focuses on the nature, evolution and context of African civil military relations, the departure point was the era of mercantilism characterised by the search for labour and the enslavement of prime African males. Merchants were not

1

concerned with investing in sustainable bureaucracies; instead, during this predatory era, merchants sought to supply cheap labour to the plantations and the New World of the Americas, leaving a legacy on the continent of slave raiding parties.

The next epoch, represented by a transition between the fading mercantilist era and territorial imperialism, was the most important, creating lasting civil-military relations' platforms and linkages. The era opened with the now-famous Berlin Conference, hosted by Chancellor Otto von Bismarck from November 1884 until February 1885, at the behest of the Portuguese. The latter had raised complaints of unwarranted intrusion by other powers in its territorial areas of interest and called for a recognised operational framework.

It is instructive to note that it was also the Portuguese who were the last colonial power to depart from the continent, in a chaotic and unceremonious manner some nine decades later, in 1974. The reasons for disengagement in Cape Verde, São Tomé and Príncipe, Guinea Bissau, the then Portuguese East Africa (Mozambique) and Angola, was more to do with the armed forces' Carnation Revolution in Lisbon, rather than a deliberate strategy to decolonise.

The Berlin Conference, attended by 14 European powers, and including the USA, established territorial borders/boundaries and gave authority to expeditionary forces employed by the Chartered Companies to begin the effective territorial acquisition of Africa. Again, the colonial authorities, operating through the Chartered Companies, had no interest in establishing modern armies on the continent. They continued to rule by contracting the machine-gun wielding Expeditionary Forces, later supported by locally raised askaris, such as the King's African Rifles in West and East Africa. The purpose of civil-military relations was to provide security to the governor or his representative and other commercial players for extracting value from the continent to the metropolis. This phase only came to an end as part of the 'Winds of Change' speech delivered by the then British Prime Minister, Harold Macmillan, on 3 February 1960 in Cape Town, South Africa.

However, it must be acknowledged that, long before this assertion, the international security system was already victim to the post 1950s Cold War. This witnessed former World War II allies enter into a global rivalry between East and West that only ended with the economic collapse of the United Soviet Socialist Republic (USSR) in 1991. It is also true that, in that era, some African states became sites of superpower rivalry to the detriment of the natural development of local civil-military relations.

Southern Europe started its politically unshackling process during the mid-1970s, followed by Latin American in the late 1970s, the East and Southeastern Asian region by the mid-1980s, followed by former Communist Eastern Europe, also in the 1980s.

In identifying related work that inspired this volume, Muthiah Alagappa's *Coercion and Governance: The declining political role of the military in Asia* has also examined what he calls the Asian civil-military relations key developments and explanations. In a discussion of civil-military relations in the new African context, whose dual purpose is to raise awareness while inviting African intellectual investment in better understanding our context and therefore provide the skills to develop appropriate options, the immediate discoveries in Eastern Europe are also instructive. In that region, because of the overwhelming presence of the Soviet Union, countries discovered that they had not participated in the civil-military relations dimensions of their countries. Instead, everything had been taken care of by the occupying power. In casting the way forward for a redefinition of civil-military relations and its intellectual study, Anthony Forster puts it succinctly when he argues that 'the challenge is to redefine our understanding ... and ... more generally ... with civil society ... how to study it'.

Africa became the last region to experience relief, with the continent's political transformation only beginning in February 1990, manifest in a national convention in Benin, following the new ethos of political deregulation that also witnessed the release of Nelson Mandela in South Africa during the same month. The southern African closure of the Cold War came from a series of multi-stakeholder meetings held on Angola, Namibia and apartheid South Africa between Portugal, the USA, the USSR and Cuba, and representatives of the liberation movements.

More interestingly, even when the Cold War had ended, global economic imperatives continued to make a major impact on how African state security and resources were allocated and organised. The 'last fling' was the Washington Consensus, put forward by John Williams and later regretted, in which officials from the World Bank, the International Monetary Fund and United States Treasury made ten recommendations that essentially talked about economic liberalism laced ideological underpinnings as a framework to guide developing world progress within market economies after the Cold War.

Soon, Williamson had the courage to issue a *mea culpa*, reneging on what Ravi Kanbur has termed 'The Washington Consensus: Mutation of Meanings'. The importance of the Washington Consensus for Africa's civil-military relations was that it occurred at the peak of the search for alternatives to the perennial fragile African state. Operating under the auspices of this ideologically charged idea, the key recommendations to African states was to abandon all public sector support, including drastically reducing military and defence expenditure.

The end of colonialism and the freedom experienced by post-colonial states has revealed mixed reactions in the civil-military relations arena. In the former Francophone regions, a different reaction was noted – one of residual French influence in the areas foreign policy, economic and monetary policy, strategic minerals policy, and defence and security policy, as well as the actual command, control, composition, ethos, and equipping and training of these institutions.

DEFINITIONS

Power relations in modern, industrialised states were equitably shared between the corporates and the periodically and therefore transient elected executive and parliament. Technical authority was delegated to institutions responsible for maintaining the monopoly of force, finely balanced between diplomacy and intelligence, supporting territorial defence and foreign policy on the one hand, and those responsible for internal security, in the form of policing, on the other.

In a democracy, the sacrosanct civil-military lesson is that the state's coercive forces are subordinate to the elected civilian authority. It is also significant to note that the epochs in which one witnesses political and civil-military relations changes are closely associated with the economic waves – in this period, coinciding with Samuel Huntington's 'Third Wave', which Africa missed. The first was a slow wave, from 1828 until 1926, followed by some reverses that began around 1922 and peaked in 1942. The second appeared to be spurred by war production and alliances from 1943 until 1962, again witnessing 'reverse waves' from 1961 to 1975, when the third and final wave took off, coinciding with the end of the Cold War.

> [The] civil-military relations field has been subject to three major challenges which are in the process of dramatically redefining our understanding of how the armed services interact with civilian authorities and more generally with civil society ... the epistemological challenge is developing new understandings ... a second ontological challenge is leading to new foci of research, as scholars retarget attention on issues previously overlooked.

WHAT IS NEW?

Because the African continent has always been a client state in civil-military relations, the occupying forces managed to force into the ghetto its proper study, comfortable with a narrow focus on education, health and other disciplines. The practice was no different. For example, in Francophone Africa, even as France's 5th Republic of General Charles de Gaulle provided almost wholesale independence to its former colonies, Paris retained responsibility for those countries' foreign affairs, defence matters, economic and monetary issues, and strategic minerals policy. Implementation was also a French affair, as witnessed in the Central African Republic between 1980 and 1993. The skewed nature of state formation on the continent becomes clearer when confronted with the contemporary security challenges in the Central African Republic. In the parallel era post-Cold War, although initially confused by the tenets of the Washington Consensus, the opportunity for African states and the continent's civil society to engage in a comprehensive study and application of civil-military relations is upon us. Again, it is important to recognise the wide-ranging nature and plurality of 'new' civil-military relations methods, rather than a single theoretical method, depends on a multidisciplinary approach that encompasses diplomacy, law, economics, geopolitics, science, history, anthropology and psychology.

POST-1990S AFRICA AND ITS CMR DUAL CHALLENGES OF THE STABLE COUP AND THIRD TERM ASPIRANTS

Much has been written on the African state and attempts to introduce political deregulation and competition through multiparty democratisation alongside the liberal economic suggestions of the Washington Consensus. For purposes of brevity, this introduction will concentrate on only two surviving tendencies against the background of almost continent-wide failure to embrace the new ethos. The first point to note in the discussion on civil-military relations is the phenomenon that emerged post the 1960s, in the vacuum created by the Cold War era of the dominant one-party state system. This early post-colonial trend privatised civil-military relations in the hands of the presidency, his party and a pliant public sector, including the armed forces. While we have seen the post-1990s national conventions in Benin and other Francophone states as the route to democratisation, similar processes were also taking place in former Anglo colonies – for example in Tanzania, where the country decreed a one-party state under Chama Cha Mapinduzi on 1 September 1964, created a new force, and following the January mutinies with owed allegiance to the party.

The military had also been placed within Chama Cha Mapinduzi structures as one of its political regions. In the Arusha Declaration of 1967, the Presidential Commission on the Single Party or Multiparty System in Tanzania, was established, led by Chief Justice Francis Lucas Nyalali to handle the political transitional question. The reflection on Tanzania, Chama Cha Mapinduzi and the transformed role of the military before and after the 1990s represents what was true of all other situations on the continent.

In the civil military arena, now that the continent was able to begin to look after its own security interests, the African Union (AU) was launched in 2001 and embarked on the innovative African Peace and Security Architecture (APSA) predicated on the five geographical Regional Economic and Security Communities (RECs) pillars motivated to establish separate brigades of the African Standby Force (ASF). After ten years of operation, a review was undertaken by the AU to measure its level of operational efficiency and preparedness. The results, however, were disappointing. In some cases, regional member states were still fighting each other and had not embraced the sub-regional characteristics. In the Maghreb, the North African countries appeared swayed between the Arab League and even the Mediterranean and European security architectures rather than the AU and APSA. In the area of democratisation, the AU had some interesting observations as part of its balance sheet. For example, the *At Ten: Problems, Progress and Prospects of 2012* report noted that, between 1960 and 1990, during the one-party state era, not a single ruling party lost 'elections' or political power, supporting the view that 'African leaders have a startling propensity for perpetual rule'.

However, when multiparty democracy was ushered in in Sub-Saharan Africa, 47 countries hosted competitive elections and, within months, 38 regimes had succumbed to military coups or refusal by the incumbent to leave office. One of the most dramatic was the 1991 annulment of elections and a military coup in Algeria by one of Africa's first liberation movements, the Front for the Liberation of Algeria (FLN). By 2014-15, military coups and violence had returned with a vengeance in Egypt, Mali, the Central African Republic, Guinea-Bissau, South Sudan, Burundi and Madagascar. The hand of the military has been identified as the decisive factor in the politics of Madagascar. According to the International Crisis Group, in 2002 the political stalemate between Didier Ratsiraka and Marc Ravalomanana was resolved when the military shifted and stood behind Ravalomanana. In the March 2009 Andre Rajoelina and Ravalomanana crisis, the latter admitted, in texts available on Wikileaks, that it was the military who put a gun to his head and ordered him to hand over power. Finally, when Rajoelina put together his administration on the departure of Ravalomanana, his choice of Minister of Defence was vetoed by the military. Their influence continues to this day. The malaise of fragile, weak and unstable states was succinctly captured in 2014 at the AU's Ending Conflict and Building Peace in Africa: A Call to Action: High Level Panel, chaired by President Ellen Johnson Sirleaf of Liberia.

Two trends have emerged from these adverse developments, which are associated with civil-military relations going forward. The first is what I call the stable coup system, which sometimes masks the presidential third term phenomenon. What distinguishes the stable coup system is the fact that it is widely accepted, almost with resignation, by the international community, sub-regional bodies and even some constituencies within particular states – for example Egypt. Mohammed Morsi, supported by the Muslim Brotherhood, won the presidential election with 51.7% of the votes in June 2012. However, this did not go down well with the military and secular section of the population, resulting in General Abdel Fattah el-Sisi seizing power, suspending the constitution and placing Morsi under house arrest.

In conclusion, African polities have not had the opportunity to engage in nation building and state formation without the intrusive attention of external powers and the emergence of a politico-military elite lacking national vision. The result is the obvious state failures which have been witnessed on the continent. It is therefore the dual purpose of this study to raise awareness on the complex and difficult dimension of the context in which African civil-military relations finds itself in, and to what and how each nation and region should respond. For African polities now hostage to partisan militaries surrounding the long-reigning stable coups and third term and beyond aspirants in power, the new era demands that we begin to invest in research, experts and multidisciplinary university faculties whose task is to begin work on research agendas and appropriate notions to become policy within democratic states.

***

The African Public Policy and Research Institute (APPRI) prides itself as one of the leading, African civil-military relations-focused civil society organisations on the continent. Sometime in 2013, I met with Professor Vladimir Shubin from the Russian Academy of Sciences, who invited me to submit an abstract and prepare to lead a session on African Civil-Military Relations during the bi-annual 13th International Conference of Africanists: Session on the New African Civil-Military Relations Panel 3, held on 29 May 2014.

From this meeting, colleagues working on the theme agreed to submit abstracts for a book facilitated by APPRI. One of the participants, Major Henrik Laugesen agreed to lead on fundraising, and succeeded in securing support for the publication of the book from the Royal Danish Defence Academy, for which we are grateful, as this may become the catalyst for African research akin to the process we have witnessed with the EU.

***

Simon Akindes' chapter on civil-military challenges of ideological location in Benin has alluded to the two epochs – the earlier, 1972-1990, 'Marxist-Leninist Wandering' and the post-1991 'Return to Barracks'. The case study on one of Africa's leading multiparty democracies appeared to benefit from the a large pool of former French soldiers, who he describes as 'politically astute', going back to the 1950s and numbering some 54 000, who were allowed voting rights in the old Dahomey, now Benin. The discussion also reveals the organised residual French presence in the administrative structures, and technical and logistical elements of the state that continued to depend on largesse and policy influence from Paris, even after independence. The 26 October 1972 coup attempt appeared to disrupt some of the linkages but benefited Kerekou's June 1973 intervention and notions of restoring the state relationship with the army. It offers the reader a better understanding of the nature, context and challenges of civil-military relations as part of the state formation in Benin since independence.

Henrik Laugesen's research on Kenya, focusing on external support for the armed forces as part of a wider agenda for the institution to lead and deepen democratization, has produced interesting ambiguities, emerging from the interviews undertaken as part of the research methodology he addresses in the chapter. Resources from the Military Assistance Programme have been targeted widely to include socio-economic challenges, but the level of greed and corruption among officials responsible for implementation has dented the potential and positive impact of the initiative. The result has been unbalanced or lopsided democratic development that is strong on liberalisation but weak on participation. The role and function of state coercive instruments, and their relationship with the public, is not stable. Instead, the environment – gleaned from the perceptive and frustrated respondents in the interviews who see the political system as an extractive system – is one in which political actors and state officials get in for what they can get out, for personal gain rather than serving national interests. The same see the political elite as lacking in national vision and even willing and able to steal from the recently launched Constituency Development Fund initiative.

Conclusively and interestingly, Laugesen argues that the Kenyan Defence Forces role has been reduced to that of a colonial occupation force, concerned only with power retention in support of the political elite and not acting as an instrument of change. This is an important research contribution and reflection on Kenya's civil-military relations for those intending to right the wrongs as the country proceeds to consolidate its democracy and strengthen its attendant institutions, especially those responsible for the monopoly of force that appears to have been abused by the political elite.

Irene Limo and **Williams Muna** have researched the paradox of the consequences of Kenya's new foreign policy supported by the defence establishment in Operation Linda Nchi, which saw that country deploy 5 500 forces in Somalia long after other sub-regional states had done so, purportedly in support of two elements: the international war on terror and its domestic tourism industry threatened by the abduction and murder of tourists in Mombasa.

Instead of going into hiding, Somalia's former Islamic Courts Union youth wing, Al Shabaab, has reacted with fury, launching devastating attacks within Kenya and in Nairobi, the capital. The 21 September 2013 Westgate Mall attack was the most brazen, sending out a message of invincibility and even forcing the Kenyan people to begin to argue for their forces to be withdrawn from Somalia. Al Shabaab also showed its Al-Qaeda associates that it has the capacity to use violence for political and religious purposes.

Buoyed by its success, Al Shabaab has moved out to attack other soft targets, such as boarding schools and outlying government posts, including police stations on the porous border with Somalia. The Kenyan government has responded with even more determination, planning to build a fence along the border. More recently, it has shut down the perceived widely abused banking system based in Nairobi that serviced the entire East African region, including Somalia.

External deployment is not cheap as Kenya discovered in its short intervention in Somalia. Hence, the two researchers have sought to assess the balance between external deployments versus its socio-economic impact, amid questions about exit strategy. Taken together – Limo and Muna's work, and that of Laugesen – one begins to appreciate the many dimensions that research perspectives can take in examining a country's civil-military dimensions.

Elena Doroshenko tackles one of the areas in which civil-military relations, external interests and democratisation continue to offer challenges in state formation and nation building in the North African Maghreb. After the violent dismantling of what was perceived to be the undemocratic state of Muammar Gaddafi, Libya now boasts several contesting centres under the aegis of armed groups that are claiming sovereignty. At hand is the ideological competition between secular tenets and Islamic Sharia law, as well as the continued and now deepening external hand witnessed in the attempts to parachute into state house by Khalifa Hathar, a former Gaddafi general, in order to stabilise the fast disintegrating polity. The centre, not only in Libya but also across the MENA regional states, is not holding, and part of the challenge is the nature of traditional and monarchical civil-military relations as they relate to modernity informed by liberal democracy. Written early into the crisis in Libya, Elena's work and conclusions have been confirmed in the continuing milieu and conflict matrices still prevalent in that region.

Martin Rupiya has examined the impact of a string of six military rules in Bangui since independence, when Emperor Bokassa was first removed from power by David Dacko. The impact this had on the *Forces Armees Centrafricaines* (FACA) has continued to be devastating. With FACA owned and paid for by the French, and with a secret service officer, Lieutenant Jean Claude-Mantion as the sole representative of the Ministry of Defence from 1980 until 1993, the International Crisis Group's charge that the Central African Republic is not even a quasi-state but a 'phantom state' is confirmed. The absence of local political authority in foreign affairs, fiscal policy and exploitation of the country's minerals also support the view the post-colonial state in the Central African Republic was and perhaps continues to be nothing but a reference point and location for two French independent bases that operate beyond the sovereignty of the local state. Worse, in the post-Francis Bozize military coup by Michel Djotodia, further elements of Islamisation of the protracted conflict emerged, fuelled by the robust participation of anti-Balaka, purportedly Christian militia and Seleka forces from Chad. To further complicate matters, French response to the conflict in Bangui has also included its interests in the volatile Mali conflict, resulting in Paris establishing the Sahel G+5 security umbrella in the region. The Sahel G+5, made up of the now collapsed Burkina Faso, Chad, Mali, Niger and a presence in Senegal, has its headquarters in Nouakchott, Mauritania. It has not only undermined the Economic Community Of West African States (ECOWAS) sub-regional focus but also the wider AU, further reflecting competing vestiges of former colonial and contemporary stable-coup interests in the region. An example is Chad, where Idris Derby removed Hissene Habre from power in

December 1990 and has been in office ever since. The same is true of the situation in Mauritania. Without addressing the fundamental weaknesses of the state in the Central African Republic's civil-military relations, there is little hope of stability for its future government.

Gorden Moyo's chapter looks at the deepening political crisis in Zimbabwe, post-2000, against the increasing role of the military in politics. His focus in the civil-military relations debate is on how senior political and military elites and officers have colluded to work the state patronage system, and expand their roles and reach in a rapidly contracting economy. Made responsible for managing state enterprises in a context where professionals and investors are leaving, the primitive accumulation nature of management has reduced many to bankruptcy, spawning corruption and increased inefficiencies. This contradiction forms the basis for political instability and is an important observation on the development that depicts the negatives seen in the post-colonial, one-party state syndrome. Given the longevity of the president, in power since 1980, a shadowy group has emerged to guide national issues in the interests of the incumbent. This, in Moyo's view, is detrimental to public accountability and principles of democracy. Furthermore, with a president clearly advanced in age, at over 90 years old, the country's civil-military relations have now been caught up in the third term presidential term limits debate.

Moyo's further contribution is around what he terms a democratic developmental state, which he hopes will be the panacea from the crisis of the absence of leadership and looting of state assets and mismanagement by those both in uniform and retired. This valid research forces us to reiterate on the basic question that must be lost on the continent in the area of civil-military relations as we embark on the complex and difficult effort of state formation in the future: What is the purpose of the state that we are building?

Martin Rupiya and **Mpho Mothoagae** look at Lesotho's sixth coup since independence, which occurred on 30 August 2014, and confirm that countries that have experienced coups remain coup-prone, and that *putschists* have become convince that, if you cannot succeed through the political route, there is always the military and more direct method. The background to the coup was internal ructions within the ruling LCD party between 2010 and the elections of May 2012, which produced the first wafer-thin coalition in Lesotho. Within a year, it was in trouble, reacting negatively to Tom Thabane's dual anti-corruption drive and state reform agenda. What soon became clear was the unreformed nature of the public service, particularly those institutions dealing with defence and security. As Muthiah Alagappa has pointed out, a government that has no control over the armed forces has its trust evaporate immediately. With the evidence of corruption not hard to find, the political elite, who also constituted key coalition members and parties, attempted to block the process that was now angling for prosecution. When this was blocked through the suspension of parliament, soon followed with the dismissal of CDF leader, Kennedy Tlali Kamoli, this was the last straw and catalyst for a coup. In three stages, Kamoli has transformed the LDF. First it was on the night of the coup when the Mounted Lesotho Police Service was captured, disarmed and dismantled. Next, when the Southern African Development Community (SADC) responded with moderate criticism during the tense September to October negotiations period, Kamoli took the military intelligence and special commandoes units, as well as 200 infantry soldiers, mobile and armed with artillery, mortars, machine guns and small arms and ammunition into the Sedibeng Mountains, where he established a fortress defensive and offensive position. Requested to assist and disarm the renegade force, the SADC, through the South African Department of International Relations and Co-operation, pointed out that the region preferred dialogue to military operations. Finally, the DC and LDC won the 28 February 2015 elections and reinstated Kamoli while demoting Mahao. The new government and Kamoli soon reverted to their old ways, banishing the political opposition, launching special operations on an unsuspecting 56 officers, and physically, kidnapping, torturing and incarcerating the same in a process similar to the Soviet-Stalin purges of the Officers Corps in 1938. On 25 June 2015, units of the LDF shot and killed Mahao, resulting in outrage at the UN, AU and SADC, with the latter issuing an unprecedented *communiqué* whose import has all but relegated the sovereignty of the new regime. In place is a legitimated military coup politico-military group that is in office for the next five years and responds to our criteria of stable coup regimes. In future, correcting Lesotho's civil-military relations must begin with disarmament, security sector reform and extensive political reform to dissuade politicians from authorising gangs to carry out assassinations of political opponents. However, the factionalised LDF has tasted blood and this may be a phenomenon hard to repress in future.

Sunday Okello's chapter on the events surrounding 'Dark Sunday' in the short life of the government of South Sudan, and the long search for constitutional order within the SPLM, is work that is contemporary, rich and aimed at providing a better understanding of where and how civil-military relations played a role in that crisis. The SPLM and its army, the SPLA, has failed to transform since independence on 9 July 2011 from a liberation movement to a national government, guided by consensus and the need to act as the centre of stability and development. Again, we are hoping the political and military elite in

South Sudan asked themselves the major question as the protracted armed struggle came to an end: What was the purpose of the State that they were going to establish come freedom and political independence? Even bestowed with huge natural and mineral resources from inception, eight million South Sudanese continue to be mired in deep and endemic poverty, with the leadership appearing bereft of a national vision designed to uplift the masses. Sunday provides a succinct four points to explain his discussion, beginning with the challenges around the transition itself; the culture of violence as part of the political intercourse among the sub-regional and ethnic groups who are still to be forged into a national identity; the tendency towards secession and balkanisation, even of the tiny state of South Sudan; and, finally, the philosophy of division gripping the leadership. The work of civil society groups calling for increased and sustained research on adequate, affordable, accountable and representative civil-military relations in the state and nation-building projects in Africa remains valid and urgent.

NOTES

1. Robinson, 2002.

2. Ibid.

3. Forster, 2001; Cottey, Edmunds & Forster, 2000. Ably supported by the European Union, the academics have spurred a cottage industry around the issue of better understanding the history, context and possible way forward on CMR in the former Central, Eastern and Southern European countries.

4. Diamond, 1997.

5. Forster, 2001.

6. In the Nyalali Commission Report, there is a full discussion of the old and new CMR of the Tanzania People's Defence Force.

BIBLIOGRAPHY

African Union. 2010. *Moving Forward: The African Peace and Security Architecture (APSA) 2010 Assessment Study,* November 2010.

African Union. 2014. 'Ending Conflict and Building Peace in Africa: A Call to Action High Level Panel'. AU Report funded by the African Development Bank.

Agger, K. 2014. *Behind the Headlines: Drivers of violence in the Central African Republic.* Enough Project. Available at http://www.enoughproject.org. Accessed 30 July 2015.

Alagappa, M. 2001. *Coercion and Governance: The declining political role of the military in Asia.* California: Stanford University Press.

Cammaert, P. 2013. 'The UN Intervention Brigade in the Democratic Republic of Congo'. Issue Paper. International Peace Institute.

Centre for Conflict Resolution. 2012. *The AU at Ten: Problems, progress and prospects.* 30-31 August 2012. Cape Town: CCR.

Cibane, B. 2013. 'Elected Monarchs: Presidential term limits and democracy in Africa', 20 June 2013. Available at (blog): Thought leader and thinking the law. Accessed 30 July 2015.

Cottey, A., Edmunds, T. & Forster, A. 2000. 'Civil-Military Relations and Defence Planning: Challenges for Central and Eastern Europe in the New Era', Conference Report, Working Paper 09/00, March 2000, Sussex University, UK.

Diamond, L. 1997. 'Is the Third Wave of Democratization Over? An empirical assessment'. Working Paper #236. Kellogg Institute for International Studies.

Feaver, P.D. & Seeler, E. n.d. 'Before and After Huntington: The methodological maturing of civil-military relations studies'. Available at http://users.polisci.wisc.edu/kmayer/904/Seeler-Feaver%20Before%20 and%20After%20Huntington.pdf. Accessed 30 July 2015.

Feaver, P.D., Huntington, S. & Janowitz, M. 1996. 'US civil-military relations debate over civilian control' in *Armed Forces & Society,* 23(2), Winter 1996.

Forster, A. 2001. *The New Civil-Military Relations and its Research Agenda.* Available at http://www. connections-qj.org/system/files/01.2.06_forster.pdf. Accessed 30 July 2015.

Janik, R. n.d. 'Putting Security Council Resolution 2098 on the Democratic Republic of Congo in Context: The long way of peacekeeping'. Available at http://www.usak.org/tr/images_upload/files/makale4%20 (1).pdf. Accessed 30 July 2015.

Kanbur, R. 2008. 'The Co-evolution of the Washington Consensus and the Economic Development Discourse'. Available at http://www.people.cornell.edu/pages. Accessed 30 July 2015.

London, S. 1993. 'Samuel P. Huntington: The Third Wave of Democratization in the late Twentieth Century'. Available at http://www.scottlondon.com/reviews/huntington.html.

Martin, P.G. 1997. 'France's Africa Policy in Transition: Disengagement and redeployment.' *Coeccion Edision Especial.*

Omotola, J.S. 2011. 'Unconstitutional Changes of Governments in Africa: What implications for democracy?' Discussion Paper 70. Uppsala: Nordiska Afrikainstitutet.

Robinson, J.A. 2002. 'States and Power in Africa: Jeffrey Herbst: A review essay' in *Journal of Economic Literature,* Vol. XL (June 2002).

Vencovsky, D. n.d. 'Presidential term limits in Africa' in *Conflict Trends.* Available at http://www.africafiles. org/printableversion.asp? = 17065. Accessed 30 July 2015.

Williams, J. 2004. 'The Washington Consensus as policy prescription for development'. World Bank lecture. 13 January 2004.

Chapter 2

The Process of Democratisation and the Main Military Challenges to Nation Building in Libya

by Elena Doroshenko

The Arab Spring, or the tide of uprisings that engulfed the region of the Middle East and North Africa (MENA) in 2010 and 2011, triggered a number of historic processes, ranging from a relatively peaceful transformation of political system in Tunisia and Egypt, to violent regime change and ensuing chaos in Libya and Yemen. Most importantly, it cut at the root of the decades-old sets of relationships that were firmly established in every sphere of societal life, not only in the countries immediately affected by the uprisings, but also in the region as a whole.

In the aftermath, the vast majority of MENA states had to reconsider their political and social standing, and adjust to the new realities created by the Arab Spring; some, of which Libya appears to be the most representative, still need to reconstruct the very idea of state and nation.

In this chapter, the nation-building process is viewed as an inseparable part of creating a state from scratch, and is thought to consist of two intertwined issues: first, building a new authentic governmental system, with its institutions fitting the unique socio-political landscape of the country, developed along the lines of its historical course; second, forging popular unity based on a new national idea to which every citizen of the country could easily subscribe, and thus extend his or her identity to the state, beyond the immediate surroundings of a family, a clan, a tribe, or a sect.

However, in *de facto* failed states, such as Libya, this process is seriously impeded by numerous challenges, most of which are directly related to security/military challenges. As this chapter seeks to demonstrate, civil-military relations (CMR), as well as the official Libyan security forces and the army, are still in a forming phase. Since the destruction of the Jamahiriyan Army by NATO-aided rebels in 2011, CMR in Libya has largely been eclipsed by the ever-reproducing and spreading pattern of terror by armed militias of ex-revolutionaries against civilians.

It stands to reason that the situation in Libya is complex and multifaceted, and it is hardly possible to single out a particular set of major defining factors and build on them. Each detail seems to have its own meaning. Moreover, the factors and details are as important as the connections between them. The first part of this chapter briefly reviews the most common Arab Spring-related themes, placed in the Libyan context and draws some historical parallels – its meaning, supposed orientation towards democracy, and the possibility of bloodshed avoidance. The second part presents post-Gaddafi Libya, where the real power belongs to former rebels rather than the official authorities. The main issues addressed are the new state ideology and resulting civil society strife, the rise of radical Islamism, and ideological and racial persecution and its ramifications for the society, the state and the region. The third part singles out and describes separatist tendencies, observed in every sphere of Libyan life; separatism is treated as the main cause and the characteristic indication of the failed state. The fourth part offers some explanation and analysis of the reasons behind the deteriorating condition of the state in Libya, including the erroneous actions of the new ruling elites (forming alliances with militias) and NATO's intervention.

The conclusion presents readers with some opinions and prognoses related to the country's future. While the position of the author is easily discernible, final inferences are left to the reader. Developments occur in the country on a daily basis, which is why there can be no universal approach to or estimation of the ongoing processes.

Libya remains one of the countries whose transformations will never cease to be breathtaking, for better or worse, and will always serve as a case-study for historians and political and social scientists.

THE ARAB SPRING'S MANY FACES

The sweeping sandstorm of 2010 and 2011 Arab Spring uprisings was initially welcomed by the world media, who advertised it as 'an epic battle pitting the enlightened forces of democracy and dignity against the dark powers of dictatorship and despotism' (Diab, 2011).

The core idea conveyed by this, and similar statements broadcast by numerous sources, was that the revolt was a politically mature action undertaken by the people, with a clear vision of their objectives and future. Both the political maturity and the clarity of vision were linked to the general concept of democracy. The need to achieve it immediately legitimised the use of arms by the rebels, as was the case of Libya, Yemen and Syria. Thus, the armed rebellion was eventually regarded as the only instrument fit to do away with old regimes that would not easily surrender to the opposition, namely the revolutionary forces fighting for an unquestionably noble cause.

Outside the MENA region, this transition, no matter how violent, was considered an evolutionary and revolutionary step forward. Probably the most appealing point of the issue was that the political basis for state-building, democracy, was to be Western-style by default. A memo released by the European Commission on 16 December 2011 demonstrates how seriously the Arab Spring was taken abroad. The document stated that the European Union (EU) was 'ready to support the democratic and constitutional reform processes' and stressed that the EU 'recognised the need to adopt a new approach to relations with its southern neighbours'.

Even the term 'Arab Spring', or 'awakening', presumably coined by *Foreign Policy* (*see* Keating, 2011), evokes highly positive emotive associations with a 'new beginning' and a 'major change for the better'.

However, several years on, it has become quite obvious that the political and social content of the Arab Spring has shifted from the intended outcome to the initial expectation. In other words, this notion now relates more to what should have been achieved than to what is unfolding. The first results of this tectonic shift vary greatly from country to country, making it impossible to arrive at a generalised conclusion or to have a unified outlook on events, even in simple terms of 'positive' or 'negative'.

Assessing what went wrong, it is useful to start with two crucial points seemingly overlooked by the local makers of the revolution and their Western allies from the very onset of the Arab Spring. The first point is that, historically in the MENA region, very few borrowed or imposed Western political concepts could be implemented fully and directly without radical adaptation. The second is that the concept of democracy does not immediately guarantee law, order and prosperity to the state undergoing reform. In other words, the mere existence of democratic institutions and instruments, such as elections, does not mean that from the moment they are introduced, the state will start functioning properly and completely in accordance with the assigned principles.

The first factor is partly attributable to Sharia or Islamic law, the viable indigenous alternative to any imported political concept, and the decades-long opposition between secular 'modernity' and religious 'tradition' inherited from the era of colonialism and national liberation movements. Thus, in the 1950s and 1960s, the search for the original policy resulted in the emergence of two authentic phenomena which greatly influenced the then Third World countries: Islamic socialism and the Non-Aligned Movement (NAM). Those in combination with the larger Arab nationalist agenda have played their role in shaping the present-day MENA political landscape, and it would be incorrect to discard them now, even though the traces may not be immediately obvious.

The second factor is rooted in the need for a clearly defined political programme – something the 'revolutionary forces' lacked from the beginning. As already mentioned, the word 'democracy' is not a universal spell against the political, economic and other ills the state might be suffering; a well-designed action plan should have been established by those responsible for the change of the long-standing status quo before they made their first move. For a party that has succeeded in replacing the old regime and committed itself to the task of rebuilding the state, it is a natural duty to come up with a detailed description of the goals and practical ways of achieving them in a programme that answers the questions: 'Why the revolution?' and 'What next?'. However, the 'post-revolutionary regimes have not to date shown any clear idea, beyond the neoliberal orthodoxy ... about how they will deliver meaningful growth' (Dodge, 2012). As it turns out, the 'structural' sense of democracy (as a system of government) was almost completely replaced by the 'ideological' one (the expected inspirational freedoms), and the latter, as will be demonstrated, was eventually overrun by Islamism.

On a more general level, revolutionary transformation cannot be limited to a simple change of regime and dealing with those who represent the old order. It is vital that all spheres of state functioning undergo restructuring, otherwise the revolution deteriorates into a mere witch-hunt, and, as a result, creates a power vacuum.

Unfortunately, this was exactly the case of Libya, where the urge to eliminate Gaddafi and those associated with his government became the apparent defining goal of the revolution. The multiple murders that took place, including that of the long-standing leader, seem to have been recognised as the legitimising ground for the new authorities. It goes without saying that the ensuing discourse and actions of hatred and vengeance, leading to the country's disunity and imminent fracturing, cannot serve as a solid ideological and political foundation of a new state.

Another surprising insight revealing the forces riding the tide of the Arab Spring, was that a number of affected countries ended up with Islamist-dominated governments instead of the expected arrival of modernity-oriented democrats.

In Libya, the official announcement of Sharia law as the main source of law occurred about a week after Gaddafi's death. It came as a shock both to the Western countries that played a crucial role in the regime change, and locally to Libyan women who felt that they were losing the democratic 'revolutionary' battle for equal rights.

In Egypt, the devastating year-long rule of the Muslim Brotherhood, even though the party was brought to power through free and democratic elections, triggered yet another round of Tahrir Square protests and a new revolution.

As these two cases demonstrate, the direct implementation of Western-style democracy proved inappropriate. Two possible political solutions presented themselves: The first was developing and introducing a totally new indigenous political model, which would be a combination of traditional and modern trends, such as Islamic democracy (like Islamic socialism beforehand). The second was deep reforms, designed and carried out in full accordance with the historical course of each country, starting with the reinvention and possible reconstruction of the existing institutes of power – in other words, giving them a new meaning and function in the new state system.

Both ways are highly debatable; the former would be posing the inevitable question of how big the Islamic role should be, and the latter may force the present-day governments out of existence due to potentially grave contradictions between their policies and the general historical course of their respective states. Devising something that ambitious is also extremely time-consuming, but still worth it, as it offers a liable means of terminating the social insecurity and political instability caused by the 'Islamist Winter' in the aftermath of the Arab Spring (see Schenker, 2012).

There is also the question of whether the Arab Spring in Libya, Yemen and Syria was doomed to be that bloody. It should be taken into account that, during an uprising, much depends on the military taking sides, either with the regime or with the opposition, and 'the results of the [Arab Spring] events were determined by the willingness or lack thereof of the military to support the incumbent' (Segell, 2013).

However, it is incorrect to regard the bloodshed as an unavoidable side-effect of regime change and the imposition of 'popular will'. In this respect, a meaningful parallel can be drawn with the chain of uprisings induced by Gamal Abdel Nasser's revolution in Egypt in 1952. There are a few similarities: the scale and the all-encompassing nature of the change which terminated the political and social order, then common for most MENA countries – but this is where the semblance ends.

The revolutions of the 1950s and 1960s happened to be the peak of peoples' struggle for independence and freedom from the occupying colonial powers and the puppet regimes at their disposal, de facto serving foreign interests. Unlike the Arab Spring uprisings, the core of those revolutions was getting rid of something imposed from the outside, rather than overthrowing authentic governments with the assistance of foreign military force, as took place in Libya. That seems to explain why most of the mid-20th century MENA revolutions were bloodless. For example, unlike the rebels of 2011, Gaddafi's coming to power did not entail any bloodshed, or even heavy fighting. This circumstance points to the high degree of accord existing among military and civilian actors alike. There were no high-profile political murders; much as the new authorities, most from a military background, might have hated the ousted monarch, his rule ended in exile, not an internationally broadcast lynching. Thus, back in 1969, such an arrival in the political arena could be considered, at the very least, more democratic than that of the present-day Libyan government.

The enemy that Nasser and the followers of his Free Officers Movement all over the region had to face, arguably had posed a more serious threat than that which the present-day rebels stood against. Then, unlike in 2011, the colonial powers were very likely to defend the habitual order of things than take sides with the insurgents. The tripartite aggression of France, Britain and Israel against Egypt following Nasser's nationalisation of the Suez Canal in 1956 (just four years after the revolution) is clear proof of this.

Some experts characterise the regimes toppled by the Arab Spring as pro-Western and thus deserving their fate at the hands of patriotic rebels (see, for example, Cook, 2011). From this perspective, the 2011 events appear to have an anti-colonial agenda, not unlike the Arab nationalist revolutions of 1950s and 1960s. Following this logic, however, it is unclear why Western powers would so whole-heartedly, yet selectively, support the forces whose aim was to overthrow their alleged allies.

While the entire MENA region was affected in one way or another, the Arab Spring didn't happen in Morocco, Saudi Arabia, Oman or Qatar. Whatever protests there were in Bahrain, there was no audible support from the West, let alone military aid, and here is why:

> As the base for the US Fifth Fleet, Bahrain is important to Washington, which values [King] Hamad's bellicose attitude towards Tehran ... For most observers, the lesson is clear: western and Arab governments alike badly need the Gulf region's energy and financial resources. That's why Bahrain's spring is already over. (Black, 2011)

In a number of countries, where the change from dictatorship to democracy has been decided by certain foreign states, it seems more natural for them to install democracy through friendly proxies and by means of reforms. It remains a mystery as to why the King of Morocco was given the chance to reform his state, but Gaddafi's Libya had to be unconditionally destroyed.

NATO's now obvious intervention in Libya had multiple negative consequences, of which some are already visible and others are yet to surface. One of the gravest is found in the sphere of CMR: the population demands security and the army still seems unable to provide it, overpowered by myriad feuding ex-rebel militias. Furthermore, neither the new political authorities, nor the military, are capable of virtually holding the country together, and eventual partition is looming over Libya's future.

Overall, the Arab Spring and NATO's involvement in Libya triggered violent rearrangement, not only of the established political order, but also the state's integrity, including its borders. With the basic needs of the population still unmet, the question remains whether it was indeed humanitarian considerations that defined NATO's agenda in early 2011, or some broader geopolitical interests?

LIBYA UNDER THE REBEL'S RULE

Analysing the ongoing process of democratisation in Libya and the forming CMR, one should consider the basic question of whether the dictatorial regime and its downfall alone can be blamed for the resulting set of problems? The answer will vary depending on whether priority is given to the pro-security or the pro-social liberties view; however, a more immediate concern is that the armed militias made up of former revolutionaries (*thuwars*) are the *de facto* rulers of Libya. Instead of putting down their weapons, the rebels have been using them to terrorise civilians and underscore their presence in the most vital spheres of the country's life. Tactics include pressing the government into passing laws, kidnapping the prime minister, and attempting to make independent economic decisions related to oil exports.

In post-Arab Spring Libya, the media-incited narrative of hatred calling for vengeance against the 'dictator', eventually evolved into a new state ideology. The official process of sweeping 'degaddfination'[1] reached its highest point in the form of an anti-glorification law, which challenged freedom of speech by criminalising any expression of support for Gaddafi, his children or his ideas.[2] Though the law was later revoked by the Libyan Supreme Court – most likely under mounting pressure from international human rights organisations – it was soon replaced by another similar piece of legislation, the Political Isolation Law (PIL), effectively banning all former officials from power.

The obvious outcome of the legally defined lustration was the disruption of major political processes and activities of the new state. Gaddafi-era professionals, whose much-needed experience could have been utilised, found themselves isolated and expelled, regardless of their actual role in the uprising. The same applied not only in the sphere of politics, but also in that of national security and defence, wherein the purges in the army and the police have undoubtedly contributed to lawlessness and ongoing chaos. An interesting example attesting to this is the case of Khalifa Haftar, a former Gaddafi-era general who defected decades ago to the USA, but returned to Libya in 2011 to fight against Gaddafi. In May 2014 he started a military campaign, Operation Dignity, 'aiming to stamp out the militias who were increasingly controlling Libya's public institutions.'[3] The militias, in turn, 'denounced Haftar as a Gaddafi loyalist who is trying to stage a counter-revolution with other officials of the former regime'[4] – a serious accusation from the Arab Spring veterans.

Needless to say, more military action, this time partially conducted from the air, did not aid stability in Libya. If the 'Gaddafi loyalist' issue had been put to rest, Haftar and others with a similar background could have been successfully integrated instead of being forced to take part in the fight for power, adding to the crisis.

The confrontational attitude projected onto society at large 'legally' set Libyans against each other. This deepened divisions and resentment, which made national dialogue and reconciliation virtually impossible.

Yet another issue, the unlawful killing of dissidents, previously associated solely with the former dictatorial regime, did not end with the arrival of the new authorities. In only two years after the Arab Spring in Libya, some 1 200 people fell victim to political assassinations and overwhelming violence; on 19 September 2014, 'Black Friday' in Benghazi alone took the lives of at least 10 people in about 24 hours. Worse still, Facebook and Twitter activists, who played a major role in bringing people to the streets in 2011 and were to become prominent members of the new civil society, became targets of extremists. Sami al-Kawafi and Tawfik Bensaud, 17 and 18 years old respectively, described as 'giants of Libya's nascent civil society', were among those murdered on 'Black Friday'. In general, civil society activists seem to have become the most vulnerable social category in the new Libya, as the 'civil society is extremely disorganised and activists usually have nothing to fall back on when their lives and livelihoods are being threatened' (Eljarh, 2014).

By now, arguably more people have been detained, tortured and executed by the former rebels than in the 42 years of Gaddafi's rule, although the exact numbers remain unknown.

Under deteriorating security conditions, Libyans were forced to protect themselves. It goes without saying that, in such an environment, it is hardly possible for anyone to concentrate on democratic perspectives, as the low turnout at successive elections shows.

However, it is now clear that the government's early attempts to integrate the militias into state security and military forces have failed, which is another indication of the new officials' isolation and lack of political will and authority. Eventually, it was not the government that neutralised the militias, but the militias who reinforced the split in central power by taking sides either with the internationally recognised parliament in Tobruk, or with the 'unofficial' Islamist one in Tripoli. The population at large is clearly against the militias, as numerous demonstrations prove, but it appears that the militias are there to stay.

The most common pretext of militias' attacks on civilians is support – real or deemed – of the previous regime. This 'ideological' reason can be clearly traced in the situation in Sirte, Gaddafi's birthplace. According to a 2012 BBC report:

> The city has been destroyed, there are tens of thousands of refugees, and hundreds of lives have been lost; citizens of Sirte allege they are the victims of arbitrary arrest, torture, and theft. The culture of revenge is strong here, and many Sirtis argue that militias from places like Misrata and Derna came seeking payback for the crimes of the Gaddafi years. (Urban, 2012)

At present, not only the residents of a certain area, but also whole tribes are persecuted on similar grounds:

> The Warshefana are a tribe often seen as having been loyalists to Moammar Gadhafi's regime. …The militias now besieging the tribe see its members as traitors to Libya's revolution, which they claim to be upholding. [At the beginning of September 2014] a part of a militia coalition that took effective control of Tripoli … have been heavily shelling Warshefana from their surrounding positions and have … killed more than 70 residents, including at least 12 children. An additional 140 are believed to be injured. (Stevenson, 2014).

Racial bias, coupled with the abovementioned ideological claim, is obvious in the situation unfolding in Tawergha, the place made into a 'ghost town' by the militias from the neighbouring city of Misrata:

> For two years most of [Tawerghans], nearly all black-skinned, have camped on building sites strewn across Libyan cities, since the Arabs who ousted Colonel Muammar Qaddafi drove them out as punishment for supporting him. ... Few Misratans acknowledge the atrocities – and the ethnic cleansing of Tawergha – perpetrated in revenge. Misratan militiamen still hold over a thousand Tawerghans ... in prisons that remain outside Libya's official judicial system.[5]

The internal displacement and persecution of Tawerghans has been monitored and reported by human rights organisations such as Amnesty International (2012).

The next case clearly demonstrating the regional ramifications of Libyan militias' policy against the ideologically, ethnically and racially differing groups of the inherited society, is the issue of the Touaregs. Labelled 'black-skinned Gaddafi mercenaries' (Thurston, 2011), they were forced out of Libya in 2011; their options were few – either to starve, having lost the jobs and every source of income they used to enjoy under Gaddafi, or try to create their own state. In this vein, Azawad, the short-lived dream of an independent Touareg country came into being in Northern Mali in 2012. However, it was doomed when Al-Qaeda intervened, seeking to establish an emirate at that territory. French military involvement was necessary to help the official Malian government bring the situation under control.

This is but one example of the destabilising effect the post-Arab Spring state of Libya has had on the MENA region. Moreover, the country's position in the centre of the northern part of the African continent and its proximity to Europe (Italy), make Libya a very important strategic gain for Al-Qaeda and, potentially, ISIS. Not surprisingly, the presence of radical Islamists in the country is being clearly felt. There have been recurring attempts at creating an Islamic emirate in Derna, eastern Libya, with the active involvement of Al-Qaeda-associated militant group, Ansar al-Sharia (blacklisted by the United Nations (UN) in late 2014). Now, as ISIS's influence has spread throughout the region, Derna's status as an Islamist emirate is confirmed.

Concluding, these four cases of ideological and racial persecution – the plight of the people of Sirte and Tawergha, Touaregs and the tribe of Warshefana – were selected to define the character of the current relationship between the civilian population of Libya and armed militias. None of these cases should be considered isolated incidents, contradicting the general pattern. On the contrary, all of them reveal the highly alarming trends that have been evolving since the ousting of Gaddafi in 2011. Grounded in the officially recognised policy of 'degaddafination', with much semblance to the infamous 'de-Ba'athification' in Iraq, the process of lustration in Libya has turned into a 'witch-hunt' (Sirte) with ethnic and racist shades (the Warshefana and Tawerghans), and with lamentable consequences for the whole region (the Touaregs).

The situation is further aggravated by the increasing amount of weaponry flowing through MENA countries, and the obvious presence of Al-Qaeda and other radical Islamist organisations, such as ISIS, drawn into the ongoing conflict. While the former Libyan revolutionaries seek to 'protect' their achievements by rooting out the opposition, the presumed core of the Arab Spring political transformation, democracy, grows less attainable by the day. With supposed civil liberties now degraded into militias-ruled chaos, it seems that Libya is on the way to 'Somalisation', rather than democracy.

MAKING A FAILED STATE: SEPARATISM IN LIBYA

It is now official: Libya is among the failed MENA states, on the same list as Iraq, Syria and Yemen. According to Paul Salem, the Middle East Institute's Vice President for Policy and Research, these are the countries 'with no longer any effective central authority over the expanse of national territory', similar 'conditions of low national unity', and bleak perspective of continuous 'deep crisis'. In the case of Libya, a clear failed state marker and a key cause of this condition is separatism, virtually piercing the new state's vitals.

Early separatist tendencies surfaced in the provinces of Cyrenaica (East) and Fezzan (South); in the two years after the 2011 uprising, these two regions consecutively proclaimed autonomy from Tripolitania (West), where the then official government was residing. Now that the 'official' authorities have been exiled to Tobruk, a city in eastern Libya, and the 'unofficial' ones have occupied their place in Tripoli, this geographical-oriented division may be no longer relevant.

The further split in central power remains an issue. The internationally recognised Libyan prime minister, Abdullah al-Thani, is considering resigning with 'at least five candidates secretly competing to succeed [him] … each claiming to be the most popular among the parliament's members' (Mahmoud, 2015).

At a more local level, the city-states with varying degrees of independence, like Derna and Misrata, with a plethora of rival militias whose radical extremist and racist agenda is threatening neighbours from places like Tawergha, are yet another destabilising factor.

Finally, the ongoing large-scale feud between Khalifa Haftar's Operation Dignity forces, linked to the Tobruk parliament, and the Islamist militias of Libya Dawn associated with the unrecognised authorities in Tripoli, is involving increasing numbers of participants (*see* Trew, 2014).

As has been pointed out previously, the country's population is surviving under considerable stress and pressure resulting from this all-out fight for power; thus, the ethnically and culturally diverse Libyan society also tends to split along tribal, ideological and political lines, to name the few.

On the one hand, it is a fact that the feuding militias organise according to tribal identity and ideology; while the other hand, for the civilian people who are forced to protect themselves and their families, the identity of the tribe is now more likely to come before national identity as Libyans. Hence, the resulting challenge to state building is the lack of political and social unity; the insecurity and conflicting identities rooted in the dependence on a tribe, and political convictions, seriously impede the national reconciliation process and create the conditions for the country's fragmentation.

To estimate the nature and effect of separatism in Libya, and reveal the driving forces behind it, it is useful to address the case of Ibrahim Jadhran, a self-proclaimed federalist leader in the eastern Libyan province of Cyrenaica. In order to make federalism a law, this former rebel commander, initially responsible for guarding export oil terminals in Eastern Libya, shut down four of them, imposing a blockade. The standoff lasted for almost a year, from August 2013 to July 2014, at which point an agreement was reached and acting Libyan prime minister Abdullah al-Thani officially announced the lifting of the blockade. However, during the standoff, a dangerous precedent was created: in mid-March 2014 the rebel forces under Jadhran's command attempted to export oil independently. Because the Libyan army and security forces proved unable to deal with the situation, US intervention was necessary to stop the loaded rogue tanker and return the crude under the control of the government in Tripoli (Caryl, 2014). The crisis was especially discrediting for the then prime minister, Ali Zeidan, who was forced to flee the country. Economically, the blockade cost Libya billions of dollars; because of the shut-down, oil production was brought below the 2011 level, which negatively affected the country's GDP in 2013 (Khan & Mezran, 2014).

Even though the issue is considered resolved – for the time being, at least – some forces have taken Jadhran's actions as exemplary. The tactics seem to have gained popularity throughout Libya: 'In the south-west, ethnic Tobu militias blockaded oil fields. Further north, Zintani and ethnic Amazigh brigades closed pipelines, and Amazigh forces twice closed the Melitah pipeline that exports gas to Europe' (Fox 2014). A more recent case with Libyan air force jets bombing a Greek oil tanker in the port of Derna, now occupied by ISIS, appears to be a reaction to an attempt by local Islamist powers to sell crude independently.

Oil is the lifeline of the Libyan economy, which is why the oil fields, production facilities, and the threat of disrupting trade in general, will be used as a means to press the 'weak' central government into the desired action. More importantly, the Jadhran case points at transformation in the understanding and appreciation of power, drifting away from the Arab Spring's initially most pronounced goal: a democratic Libya. The former rebel with impressive revolutionary credentials, officially trusted with the security of vital economic installations, is employing like-minded armed militias to pursue the political agenda of federalism in an open challenge to the government. Jadhran was obviously in control, even though he had not been elected democratically, and such a situation questions the very need for democratic procedures.

Eventually, the new scenario for coming to power in post-revolutionary Libya might totally exclude democratic institutions and processes, consolidating the 'failed state' condition of the country. The explosive mixture of multiple conflicting agendas pursued by a number of strong actors, such as militias, reinforced by a dangerous amount of arms, Islamist political and economic influence and blackmail, threatens the basis of the state, its integrity, and national unity. Against such a background, any sound and timely political initiative in Libya, including urgently needed political dialogue, is doomed from the start, by default becoming 'too little too late'. If, in the absence of the recognised authority of the centralised power, the dominance of militias and ideologically justified racism are finalised, the deeply divided Libyan society might find itself not just in 'deep crisis', but engaged in an eternal war of 'all against all'.

Democracy, the 'might-have-been' Libya and NATO's involvement

What is the actual status of democracy in Libya? As has already been emphasised, the transitional period that usually follows regime change in any country, and may indeed take years, does not necessarily turn into violent *interregnum* if new authorities have clearly defined goals and objectives, and can provide the conditions to give them life.

Obviously, 'you can Tweet a revolution, but you can't Tweet a transition' (Grand, 2014).

Ideologically, the new Libyan government failed to bring the population fully on side; neither the idea of unified resistance against the common enemy manifested in 'degad-dafination', nor the 'democracy' mantra helped to forge real national unity. Moreover, the democracy concept did not appear to transcend existing tribal and other conflicts now tearing society apart. Ironically, the Gaddafi-devised system of 'checks and balances', and national unity built around the core notion of 'Libyan' identity, so far proves to have no alternative. With the anchoring centralised power now gone, tribal identity linked to centuries-old feuds has overcome the 'citizen of a state' identity in the new society.

It is the new government's ideologically permissive policy, and its shaky stand on the issue of militias' disarmament, that initially caused a dramatic increase of the number of *thuwar* 'brigades'. The situation was perfectly described by Frederic Wehrey (2014), a senior associate in the Middle East Program at the Carnegie Endowment for International Peace:

> *Islamist brigades filled the security vacuum in Benghazi, prompting the weak transitional government … to put the militias on its payroll. …[T]hese subsidies swelled the ranks of the militias with new volunteers and spawned armed groups that had not participated in the uprising. … By a recent government count, there are roughly 165 000 registered 'revolutionaries', but only a fraction of these actually fought in the war.*

In this way, the government actually created the conditions for the current political situation, escalating the power crisis and deepening its own isolation. The current developments of the Arab Spring in Libya point in a direction very different from democracy. What was intended as the parliamentary battle of ideas, performed by various parties, was replaced by a fight for power among various factions, whose real interests are far from being even abstractly political. In other words, the authorities are now employing the militias, for money, to state their position in a very material way: 'Composed of ex-rebels who once fought Gadhafi, the brigades are heavily armed and allied with powerful political factions' (*Voice of America*, 2014).

Consequently, 'democracy' has come to be associated with loss of authority – a notion that relates to successive weak governments – first the National Transitional Council, then the General National Congress – which on many occasions proved unable to provide for their own people.

Under the *de facto* dictatorship of militias, a just, stable and secure state seems more elusive than ever, and thus Al-Qaeda and ISIS may emerge as strong ideological agenda-setters. Indeed, 'ISIS arose as the largest threat in the region's modern history, challenging political borders and order, and proposing political identities and governance paradigms' (*Democracy Digest*, 2014). The precedent has been created in Iraq; ISIS advances there demonstrate that democracy is not the only way to build a state, and people in all of the MENA countries, not only in Libya, are likely to be frustrated by the shocking difference between democratic expectations and what has evolved in reality.

Worse still, for Libyans, the well-defined 'Islamist Winter' outlook may appear to be making far more sense than the vague aspirations and narratives of the Arab Spring, especially since Sharia is now the officially recognised source of legislation in Libya. Groping for an alternative to chaos, some have come to support the radicalism (as in Derna), while others think that Libya needs a 'new fair dictator' (Sharqieh, 2014).

Naturally, when people are mere hostages to armed groups, deprived of the opportunity to shape the political and social agenda of their own country, it is no longer a question of choice between 'direct' democracy, outlined in the *Green Book*, and 'representative' democracy supposedly introduced by the Arab Spring). Ironically, the *Green Book* by far remains the most democratic document in Libyan political history; it is authentic, written by a native with natives in mind, and its network-centric system still appears to be relevant and well-suited for the unique tribal socio-political Libyan landscape. It presents Libyans with a balance between the identity of a 'citizen of a state' and that of a 'member of the tribe'. While the former is given priority, there is much respect and room for the latter.

Although the *Green Book* is written in a declarative-prescriptive and albeit idealistic manner, its points were not meant to be taken as axioms. Its main value now is that it reflects quite a lot about Libyan society, which is why this document may be especially useful for the new ruling elites, most of whom spent decades outside Libya. At the very least, it can present them with useful observations applicable in the search for solutions to the current crisis. As contradictory as it is, the *Green Book* is part of the historical background of the country; it is heritage not to be ignored, but rather addressed and built on.

Jamahiriya was Libya's first democratic experiment, and it failed not without the fault of the people: 'Inheriting a bland, non-participatory society, the [Gaddafi] regime devoted enormous time and resources after 1969 to creating units and institutions that would develop citizens aware of their role in the political system and actively participating in it' (St John, 2011).

Hence, if the government – and/or the Libyan people for that matter – were unable to fully grasp, implement and live by the outlined principles at that time, it is not immediately obvious that they will be able to direct the country's policy onto the right route now. The will to face the failure of 'direct' democracy and the 'State of the masses' project, which occurred many years before the 2011 uprising, and objectively reassess some of the *Green Book*'s points, especially those concerning the governmental system, could eventually produce a more viable set of democratic institutions in the new Libya.

It should also be noted that Egypt, the second North African country to experience the Arab Spring (after Tunisia), seems to have embraced its past and history. 'Nasser' was the battle cry of the second round of Tahrir Square protests, and the reference to this long-time ex-military leader, once aspiring for a united Arab world, was common during the 2014 election campaign, which ended in victory for former army general, Abdel Fattah el-Sisi.

Arguably, both during the uprising, and immediately after, Libya was not given a chance to revise its history or embark on urgent reforms. This may be considered one of the many tragic aspects of the infamous 'Libyan scenario'. The abrupt and violent regime change facilitated by NATO led to the destruction of the country's army and security forces, whose role is unquestionably vital in any political process. With state security virtually non-existent, no real parliamentary debate can commence; true democracy is incompatible with impunity, instability and hatred, and the defence and security forces are responsible for providing a solid basis for state building and decision making.

The Libyan Army suffered greatly during the uprising due to defections, and the need to contain the rebels' advances and resist NATO bombings. The split in the military was a reality, but it appears that the army *en masse* did not amalgamate with the opposition forces, even though they could have played the role of the 'revolutionary vanguard' of the people. Otherwise, it would have been impossible for the military to almost finish recapturing the cities occupied by rebels: the army units were stopped in the decisive battle of Ajdabiya (30 March 2011), the strategic gateway to Benghazi, the capital of the uprising. And a fractured army could not have resisted NATO air-strikes for so long, until the end of October 2011.

Further destruction of the Libyan military force, due to the purges commenced after the war was officially proclaimed over, cost the new Libyan authorities dearly. Currently, the government 'has no army with which to suppress [the Islamist-aligned militias] and is relying on its own militias'; the US-proposed plans to train Libyan security forces 'have collapsed due to the country's inability to pay for such training and develop the bureaucracy necessary to manage it. ...Fighting has only grown more intense ... raising questions about whether Libya is on the fast track to civil war – or already in one' (Mahanta, 2014).

In November 2014, alarming news came from the UK, where Libyan soldiers were involved in a British Army training programme as part of an agreement reached at the 2013 G8 Summit:

> Head of the army General Sir Nicholas Carter admitted the behaviour of Libyan soldiers ... was 'beyond the pale'. His remarks came after the Prime Minister demanded ... [to] explain the 'unacceptable' breakdown of discipline which saw hundreds of Libyan cadets sent home in disgrace amid allegations of rape, drunkenness, fighting and theft. ...the Government programme to train up Libya's army would be scrapped and all the trainees based in Britain deported. (McTague, 2014)

As the situation now calls for international attention, the old question arises as to whether NATO intervention was justified in the first place, and what political solution it offered? These are the issues that need to be carefully considered by the forces contemplating yet another military operation in Libya, possibly again on 'humanitarian grounds'. According to Kuperman (2013):

> United Nations and Amnesty International have documented that in all four Libyan cities initially consumed by civil conflict in mid-February 2011 – Benghazi, Al Bayda, Tripoli, and Misrata – violence was actually initiated by the protesters. The government responded to the rebels militarily but never intentionally targeted civilians or resorted to 'indiscriminate' force, as Western media claimed.

These conclusions are supported by findings of a number of other authors, including Forte (2012) and McKinney (2012).

Even if the initial goal was indeed to protect civilians, NATO failed in both its short- and long-term perspectives. The negative effects multiplied, which set the ground for yet another militarily 'failed state', probably worse than Iraq, Afghanistan, and Somalia. The way to dictatorship is now open, and once the struggle for power among the militias ends, it is very likely that a leader will appear, who, like the renegade general Khalifa Haftar, will attempt to restore the dignity of the country. His legitimacy will not be defined by democratic credentials, but by the people's view of him as the 'saviour of the nation'. As political theorist John Gray (2014) states:

> Political legitimacy is a slippery business; people don't want many things apart from prosperity, accountability and a low level of corruption. They also demand expression of their national myths, identities and enmities – and quite often attach more importance to this aspect of government than they do to democracy.

It is also hard to agree on whether the initial change to democracy can be delivered, especially if it the country's population is unanimously ready to accept and adopt the new political concept. Unlike Tunisia and Egypt, the toppling of the regime in Libya turned out to be worse than the dictatorship itself – at least in terms of the lives still being wasted.

However, the good news is that NATO will probably not intervene again, on the simple ground that it doesn't know who to bomb. 'Three years ago, with the rebels against Gaddafi, so it was – for NATO it was easier to know who to bomb … And now the common complaint is, well, who do we bomb? We have so many militias all fighting each other … that's the thing that's perplexing the international community' (Krever, 2014).

PERSPECTIVES AND OPINIONS

The future of Libya is almost impossible to predict. According to some analysts, Libya needs regional or broader foreign involvement, which might include another intervention. Others believe that it would only aggravate the situation.

The first viewpoint is grounded in the calls for international interference from Libyan officials. Mid-August 2014, Mahmoud Jibril, Libya's ambassador to Egypt, stated that Libya was 'unable to protect its institutions, its airports and oilfields'. At the beginning of September 2014, the country's ambassador to the UN, Ibrahim Dabbashi, asked the UN Security Council to disarm the warring factions (Elshinnawi, 2014).

Those against the intervention, such as the head of the UN support mission, Spanish diplomat Bernardino León, contend that '… more use of force will not help Libya get out of the current chaos, which would also impact countries in the region, in Europe and beyond' (Elshinnawi, 2014).

While the need for intervention may be well grounded by the grave security concerns of neighbouring and distant states alike, it may end hope for political settlement inside Libya. With intervention offering a short-term security solution, the process of vital decision-making by the Libyan government will be impeded. In the long term, this may lead to political catastrophe, including a complete erosion of local power institutions and a lasting 'failed-state' condition.

Two autonomous parliaments, existing simultaneously in Libya since September 2014, further deprive Libyan authorities of credibility, and point to an imminent partition. According to Michael O'Hanlon, a senior fellow at the Brooking Institution, Libya eventually might be divided: 'Realistically,' he said, 'it is possible that Libya would be partitioned in the future, or at least would be a confederation of some kind where you do have two ongoing parliaments' (Elshinnawi, 2014).

What is clear for now is that Libya lives by its own post-Arab Spring laws, which, at the very best, demonstrate half-hearted dabbling in democracy. Certainly, when the dust settles, and the relationships between people and power are re-formed from scratch, there eventually will be a new government. Ideally, accepted by all representatives of Libyan society, its authority will be firm and unchallenged, and probably come in some new indigenous political form. With the arrival of this new government, the reputation of the army as reliable guardians of security and state order will be restored.

The world is yet to see the real face of a viable Libyan authority as armed factions inside the country continue to consolidate the struggle for power. With the ISIS model readily available to them, and the borders glaringly porous, there is the real possibility that all political processes will come under grave threat of violent disruption.

NOTES

1. The term was, presumably, invented and introduced by Libyans on Twitter. *See* Mahfud (2012).
2. *Al-Akhbar English*, 4 May 2012.
3. *Middle East Eye*, 24 October 2014.
4. *Reuters*, 20 October 2014.
5. *The Economist*, 22 June 2013.

REFERENCES

Al Arabiya. 2013. 'Libya's southern Fezzan region declares autonomy', 26 September 2013. Available at http://english.alarabiya.net/en/News/middle-east/2013/09/26/-Libya-s-southern-Fezzan-province-declares-autonomy.html. Accessed 21 September 2014.

Al Jazeera. 2014. 'Libya's oil: A source of further tension?' 12 March 2014. Available at http://www.aljazeera.com/programmes/insidestory/2014/03/libya-oil-source-further-tension-2014312153859486187.html. Accessed 14 September 2014.

Al-Akhbar English. 2012. 'Libyan anti-Gaddafi law erodes free speech: Amnesty', 4 May 2012. Available at http://english.al-akhbar.com/node/6948. Accessed 14 September 2014.

Amnesty International. 2012. 'Libya: Militias threaten hopes for new Libya', 16 February 2012. Available at http://www.amnesty.org/en/library/asset/MDE19/002/2012/en/6b6a5b08-9874-4679-bc0f-c3d47bfd93a9/mde190022012en.html. Accessed 20 September 2014.

BBC. 2014. 'Libyan elections: Low turnout marks bid to end political crisis', 26 June 2014. Available at http://www.bbc.com/news/world-africa-28005801. Accessed 15 September 2014.

BBC. 2015. 'Greek oil tanker bomber in Libyan port of Derna', 5 January 2015. Available at http://www.bbc.com/news/world-africa-30681904. Accessed 8 January 2015.

Black, I. 2011. 'Bahrain protests will go nowhere while the US supports its government' in *The Guardian*, 16 April 2011. Available at http://www.theguardian.com/world/2011/apr/16/bahrain-protests-us-supports-government. Accessed 21 September 2014.

Bosalum, F. & Elumami, A. 2014. 'Protesters in Libya's Benghazi march against militias', *Reuters*, 1 August 2014. Available at http://www.reuters.com/article/2014/08/01/us-libya-security-idUSKBN0G155A20140801. Accessed 15 September 2014.

Caryl, C. 2014. 'SEALed and delivered in Libya' in *Foreign Policy*, 18 March 2014. Available at http://www.foreignpolicy.com/articles/2014/03/18/sealed_and_delivered_in_libya_0. Accessed 21 September 2014.

CNN. 2014 'ISIS comes to Libya', 18 November 2014. Available at http://edition.cnn.com/2014/11/18/world/isis-libya/. Accessed 7 January 2015.

Cook, D. 2011. 'The Arab Spring and the failed political legitimacy'. Institute for Advanced Studies in Culture, University of Virginia. Available at http://www.iasc-culture.org/THR/archives/Fall2011/Cook_lo.pdf. Accessed 1 August 2014.

Cunningham, E. 2014. 'Benghazi assassinations stun residents amid Libya's turmoil' in *The Washington Post*, 20 September 2014. Available at http://www.washingtonpost.com/world/benghazi-assassinations-stun-residents-amid-libyas-turmoil/2014/09/20/e9075bb0-9f9e-4441-999f-51c5feb188a5_story.html. Accessed 21 September 2014.

David, R. & Mzioudet, H. 2014. 'Personnel change or personal change? Rethinking Libya's political isolation law'. Brookings Doha Center, 17 March 2014. Available at http://www.brookings.edu/research/papers/2014/03/17-libya-lustration-david-mzioudet. Accessed 14 September 2014.

Democracy Digest. 2014. 'Triumph of liberal democracy far from assured', 26 September 2014. Available at http://demdigest.net/blog/triumph-liberal-democracy-far-assured/. Accessed 8 January 2015.

Democracy Digest. 2014 'Paradigms lost: Middle East's trends and drivers', 19 November 2014. Available at http://demdigest.net/blog/paradigms-lost-middle-easts-trends-drivers/. Accessed 7 January 2015.

Diab, K. 2011. 'The Arab Spring's bottom line' in *The Guardian*, 12 August 2011. Available at http://www.theguardian.com/commentisfree/2011/aug/12/arab-spring-bottom-line. Accessed 24 July 2014.

Dodge, T. 2012. 'Conclusion: The Middle East after the Arab Spring' in *After the Arab Spring: Power shift in the Middle East?* LSE Ideas Special Report, May 2012. Available at http://www.lse.ac.uk/ideas/publications/reports/pdf/sr011/final_lse_ideas__conclusionsthemiddleeastafterthearabspring_dodge.pdf. Accessed 25 July 2014.

Eljarh, M. 2014. 'In post-Qaddafi Libya, it's stay silent or die' in *Foreign Policy*, 24 September 2014. Available at http://foreignpolicy.com/2014/09/24/in-post-qaddafi-libya-its-stay-silent-or-die. Accessed 30 September 2014.

Elshinnawi, M. 2014. 'Libya's fate difficult to predict, analysts say' in *The Voice of America*, 6 September 2014. Available at http://allafrica.com/stories/201409060219.html?viewall=1. Accessed 8 September 2014.

Essam El-Din, G. 2014. 'Al-Sisi's Greetings to Egypt' in *Al-Ahram Weekly*, 3 April 2014. Available at http://weekly.ahram.org.eg/News/5866/17/Al-Sisi%E2%80%99s-%E2%80%98Greetings-to-Egypt%E2%80%99--.aspx. Accessed 22 September 2014.

European Commission. 2011. 'The EU's response to the Arab Spring', Press releases database, 16 December 2011. Available at http://europa.eu/rapid/press-release_MEMO-11-918_en.htm. Accessed 24 July 2014.

Forte, M.C. 2012. *Slouching Toward Sirte: NATO's war on Libya and Africa*. Quebec: Baraka.

Fox, S. 2014. 'Why Libya's lifeblood needs a transfusion' in *Middle East Eye*, 2 July 2014. Available at http://www.middleeasteye.net/news/why-libya-s-lifeblood-needs-transfusion-1479753240. Accessed 21 September 2014.

Grand, S.R. 2014. 'Keeping alive the spirit of Tahrir' in *Brookings*, 11 June 2014. Available at http://www.brookings.edu/blogs/up-front/posts/2014/06/11-democratic-change-arab-world-tahrir-square-grand. Accessed 8 January 2015.

Keating, J. 2011. 'Who first used the term Arab Spring?' in *Foreign Policy*, 4 November 2011. Available at http://blog.foreignpolicy.com/posts/2011/11/04/who_first_used_the_term_arab_spring. Accessed 24 July 2014.

Khan, M. & Mezran, K. 2014. 'Time is running out for the Libyan economy' in *Atlantic Council*, 7 July 2014. Available at *http://www.atlanticcouncil.org/blogs/menasource/time-is-running-out-for-the-libyan-economy*. Accessed 21 September 2014.

Krever, M. 2014. 'A mosaic of militias wreak havoc in Libya', *CNN*, 23 July 2014. Available at *http://amanpour.blogs.cnn.com/2014/07/23/a-mosaic-of-militias-wreak-havoc-in-libya/*. Accessed 23 September 2014.

Kuperman, A.J. 2013. 'Lessons from Libya: How not to intervene', Policy Brief, Belfer Center for Science and International Affairs, Harvard Kennedy School, September 2013. Available at http://belfercenter.

ksg.harvard.edu/publication/23387/lessons_from_libya.html. Accessed 23 September 2014.

Mahanta, S. 2014. 'Don't look now but Libya is falling apart' in *Foreign Policy*, 21 August 2014. Available at http://blog.foreignpolicy.com/posts/2014/08/21/dont_look_now_but_libya_is_falling_apart. Accessed 23 September 2014.

Mahfud, G. 2012. 'Opinion: Is Libya Degaddafinated?' in *The Tripoli Post*, 6 February 2012. Available at http://www.tripolipost.com/articledetail.asp?c=5&i=7847. Accessed 20 September 2014.

Mahmoud, K. 2014. 'Al-Qaeda flags raised in Eastern Libya' in *Asharq al-Awsat*, 6 April 2014. Available at http://www.aawsat.net/2014/04/article55330898. Accessed 20 September 2014.

Mahmoud, K. 2015. 'Libya's PM considering resignation: minister' in *Asharq Al-Awsat*, 2 January 2015. Available at http://www.aawsat.net/2015/01/article55339994. Accessed 7 January 2015.

Mandraud, I. 2013. 'While change shakes the Arab world, inertia still reigns supreme in Morocco' in *The Guardian*, 1 January2013. Available at http://www.theguardian.com/world/2013/jan/01/morocco-turmoil-reform-arab-spring. Accessed 20 September 2014.

McConnell, D & Todd, B. 2011. 'Libyan leader's embrace of Sharia raises eyebrows', *CNN*, 26 October 2011. Available at http://edition.cnn.com/2011/10/26/world/africa/libya-sharia/. Accessed 26 July 2014.

McKinney, C. (ed.) 2012. *The Illegal War on Libya*. Atlanta: Clarity Press.

McTague, T. 2014. 'Libyan soldiers who were ordered home in disgrace after "unacceptable" breakdown of discipline at UK barracks now claim asylum' in *Daily Mail*, 24 November 2014. Available at http://www.dailymail.co.uk/news/article-2847818/Libyan-soldiers-ordered-home-disgrace-unacceptable-breakdown-discipline-UK-barracks-claim-ASYLUM.html. Accessed 8 January 2015.

Middle East Eye. 2014. 'Libyan army retakes Benghazi airport, city's largest militia base', 24 October 2014. Available at http://www.middleeasteye.net/news/benghazi-2086436118. Accessed 15 December 2014.

Middle East Monitor. 2014. 'Acting Libyan prime minister announces oil standoff is over', 5 July 2014. Available at https://www.middleeastmonitor.com/news/africa/12576-acting-libyan-prime-minister-announces-oil-standoff-is-over. Accessed 21 September 2014.

Phalnikar, S. 2011. 'Unlike Egyptian counterpart, Libyan army won't stabilize the country' in *Deutsche Welle*, 24 February 2011. Available at http://www.dw.de/unlike-egyptian-counterpart-libyan-army-wont-stabilize-country/a-14867583. Accessed 23 September 2014.

Reed, M.M. 2014. 'Federalism and Libya's oil' in *Foreign Policy*, 3 February 2014. Available at http://mideastafrica.foreignpolicy.com/posts/2014/02/03/federalism_and_libyas_oil. Accessed 21 September 2014.

Reuters. 2014. 'Libya's parliament allies with renegade general, struggling to assert authority', 20 October 2014. Available at http://uk.reuters.com/article/2014/10/20/uk-libya-security-idUKKCN0I91B420141020. Accessed 15 December 2014.

Schenker, D. 2012. 'Arab Spring or Islamist Winter?' in *World Affairs Journal*, January/February 2012.

Available at http://www.washington.institute.org/policy-analysis/view/arab-spring-or-islamist-winter. Accessed 26 July 2014.

Segell, G. 2013. 'The Arab Spring and civil-military relations: A preliminary assessment' in *Scientia Militaria, South African Journal of Military Studies*, 41:2.

Sharqieh, I. 2014. 'Beware Libya's "Fair Dictator"' in *The New York Times*, 23 June 2014. Available at http://www.nytimes.com/2014/06/24/opinion/beware-libyas-fair-dictator.html. Accessed 22 September 2014.

St John, R.B. 2011. *Libya: Continuity and Change*. New York: Routledge.

Stevenson, T. 2014. 'Dozens killed in Tripoli suburb under siege' in *Al-Monitor*, 14 September. Available at http://www.al-monitor.com/pulse/originals/2014/09/libya-tripoli-suburb-siege.html. Accessed 16 September 2014.

Stocker, V. 2014. 'Bloody tribal fighting at the gates of Tripoli' in *Deutsche Welle*, 5 February 2014. Available at http://www.dw.de/bloody-tribal-fighting-at-the-gates-of-tripoli/a-17410142. Accessed 21 September 2014.

The Associated Press. 2011. 'Moammar Gaddafi's forces adapt to airstrikes, pound Libyan rebels', 30 March 2011. Available at http://www.masslive.com/news/index.ssf/2011/03/moammar_gadhafi_forces_adapt.html. Accessed 23 September 2014.

The Economist. 2013. 'Libya's ghost town: When bygones aren't', 22 June 2013. Available at http://www.economist.com/news/middle-east-and-africa/21579853-people-two-rival-towns-seem-determined-hate-each-other-ever-when. Accessed 20 September 2014.

Thurston, A. 2011. 'Qaddafi's African mercenaries head home. Will they destabilize the Sahel?' in *The Christian Science Monitor*, 30 August 2011. Available at http://www.csmonitor.com/World/Africa/Africa-Monitor/2011/0830/Qaddafi-s-African-mercenaries-head-home.-Will-they-destabilize-the-Sahel. Accessed 20 September 2014.

Trew, B. 2014. 'A ground invasion of the capital is imminent' in *Foreign Policy*, 29 December 2014. Available at http://foreignpolicy.com/2014/12/29/a-ground-invasion-of-the-capital-is-imminent-libya-dawn-haftar-militias. Accessed 7 January 2015.

Urban, M. 2012. 'Post-revolution Sirte a breeding ground for unrest', BBC, 21 February 2012. Available at http://www.bbc.com/news/world-17116657. Accessed 16 September 2014.

Voice of America. 2014. 'Libyan parliament challenges militias, seeks UN aid', 13 August 2014. Available at http://www.voanews.com/content/reu-libya-parliament-challenges-militias-seeks-un-aid/2412220.html. Accessed 22 September 2014.

Wehrey, F. 2014. 'The Battle for Benghazi' in *The Atlantic*, 28 February 2014. Available at http://www.theatlantic.com/international/archive/2014/02/the-battle-for-benghazi/284102/. Accessed 22 September 2014.

World Bulletin. 2015. Pro-Haftar forces strike Libya's Misurata port', 3 January 2015. Available at http://www.worldbulletin.net/news/152151/pro-haftar-forces-strike-libyas-misurata-port. Accessed 4 January 2015.

Chapter 3

Civil-Military Relations in Benin:
Out of the barracks and back – now what?

by Simon Akindes

Together with Uganda and Nigeria, the Republic of Benin (Benin) holds the record for coups d'état in Africa between 1958 and 2010: six out of a total of 81 on the continent. However, contrary to Uganda and Nigeria, whose military continued to experience coups until 1986 and 1993 respectively, the last one in Benin occurred in 1972. On average, the military staged a successful coup every two years for the first 12 years of independence from France in August 1960, and none since. The purpose of this chapter is to critically examine civil-military relations from independence to December 2014, with a view to determining their characteristics, causes and evolution. For analytical purposes, the era under consideration is subdivided into three periods that, to a certain extent, were defined by important turning points in the way the military, as a core institution of the state, either interfered or did not in Beninese politics and its relationship with civilians. This convenient division does not imply that each period represents a tabula rasa of the previous one; rather, each inscribes itself within the historical long term of civil-military interactions in Benin.

The period 1960–1972, which I have termed the 'High Military Visibility' period, was characterised by frequent appearances of the army on the political stage. To examine this phenomenon, it is material to understand the genesis of the Beninese army from the defunct French-commanded *troupes coloniales*.

During the second period, 1972–1990, which I qualify as 'Marxist-Leninist Wandering', the military played an increased role in politics, loosely following the Marxist-Leninist view that the military should be at the service of the people, but under the leadership and guardianship of the People's Revolutionary Party of Benin (PRPB).

The period 1990–2014 is labelled 'Return to the Barracks'. A successful transition to liberal democracy occurred, and, since 1991, free and fair elections have been held regularly, every five years.

Three regime alternations have occurred through the ballot as electoral politics appear to have firmly taken root. Breaking away from previous patterns, a new type of relationship exists between the army and governmental branches – the legislative, the executive and the judiciary. The 1991 Constitution clearly delineates the nature and limits of military involvement in politics. It even prescribes a code of conduct for civilians in cases of military coups d'état. Until 2014, the rules have been observed. According to traditional and normative approaches to civil-military relations propounded by Huntington (1991), and observed in many countries around the world, the army must submit itself to the legislative, judiciary and executive powers of elected civilian officials.

This proposition has not worked in many sub-Saharan or Latin American countries for a long time, even though there are signs that the norm is turning into a reality in Benin. After turbulent years of direct military intrusion, a new order appears to have come about. Given the tumultuous cultural and political history of Benin, does the change really represent the birth of new civil-military relations? The larger challenge of the civil-military relationship in Benin, and in many countries in the process of consolidating their liberal electoral systems, remains the demilitarisation of society and the creation of new civil-military beginnings from the old. The last part of this chapter gauges demilitarisation in post-1991 Benin on the basis of the recommendations proposed at the 22–24 July 1998 conference on the Leadership Challenges of Demilitarization in Africa held in Arusha, Tanzania. Special emphasis is directed at institutional and historical/cultural factors that have shaped civil-military relations over time, and continue to shape it today.

UNDERSTANDING THE ORIGINS OF THE MILITARY

The recruitment of soldiers from the French colony of Dahomey started when Africans from French colonies all over the world were massively recruited to the *armée coloniale,* which served two main purposes. The first one was offensive: attacking innocent people, acquiring more territory and expanding the empire were the sport of the day in Europe, starting from the 16th century. African recruits in the *troupes coloniales,* with a reputation for raw brutality, participated very early in territorial expansion, with the French using troops from one part of a territory to bring to heel other areas. The second purpose was more defensive. Fighting off local rebellions, resisters and insurgencies, and protecting territory 'discovered', conquered and occupied by French explorers and navigators from other European countries, were the core of imperialist adventures. French kings oversaw both defensive and offensive missions, and actually allowed a degree of autonomy on the ground for the organisation of troops. As the operations of commercial organisations and the military became larger and more complex, a more centralised system became necessary.

On 7 July 1900, legislation was passed that placed both metropolitan and colonial armies under the command of the Minister of War. Later, on 1 October 1902, a new decree placed all West African troops in the territories of Senegal and French Sudan (parts of today's Niger, Burkina Faso and Mali) under the leadership of one commander in Saint-Louis, Senegal.

The colony of Dahomey, established after the military defeat of King Gbehanzin in 1898, had one battalion that was principally made up of northerners. The urgency of French participation in the Great War of 1914–18 accelerated the massive recruitment of colonial subjects to fight in distant places in Europe, Asia and other African countries. As Dean III (p. 480) points out:

> After the war began, then, over 500 000 indigenous soldiers were recruited from all of France's colonies. One reason that most of the recruiting took place after the opening months of war was that the indigenous colonial troops who were initially deployed suffered enormous casualties (over 60 percent were wounded or killed). Heavy losses of metropolitan soldiers also forced the military authorities in Paris to look for more cannon fodder to fill the gaps in general combat personnel.

African soldiers were used in the Napoleonic and Crimean wars in the 19th century. Military contingents from West Africa contributed a great deal to the final conquest of Central Africa. In much the same way, *Tirailleurs Sénégalais* helped France in the Rif War in Morocco in 1925, in Syria against the Druses, and in Vietnam to quell peasant uprisings. Because of the pressures of colonial wars across continents, the French administration devised new strategies to enrol more soldiers. Until 1910, recruitment into the army was on a voluntary basis. After 1912, however, 18 months of obligatory military service was introduced for men between the ages of 20 and 28. By 1918, the *Tirailleurs Sénégalais* roughly numbered 211 259. Africans also participated in most of the wars and military missions during the colonial period. During World War II, the l'Afrique Équatoriale Française (AEF) and l'Afrique Occidentale Francaise (AOF) armies aligned themselves respectively on the Free France and Vichy causes. Later on, from 1954 to 1961, 30 000 *tirailleurs* combatted against Algerians in their liberation struggle.

The army that became the national army of Dahomey was built on an ethos of distrust and mistrust, on policies and practices of exclusion and manipulation, and habits of mind that cultivated suspicion and lies. This praxis plagued the army for a long time. As an institution, the army was an instrument designed to meet the strategic and national imperatives of the metropolitan power – not the colonised. African soldiers were moulded in professional experiences that had the following characteristics:

- The armies did not defend the communities from which their soldiers originated and, worse, often turned against them.
- Armies operated in an undemocratic, non-transparent environment in which the French officers were only accountable to their superiors for their treatment of Africans. As a result, many abuses, physical and financial, were simply ignored or covered up, and African soldiers did not have any recourse.
- African soldiers operated under circumstances of duress, arbitrariness and racism.
- A culture of divide-and-rule prevailed, pitting various groups against each other and creating a pervasive atmosphere of mistrust among soldiers. Recruitment was designed to serve this goal.
- Military training was the exclusive responsibility of French officers. A rigid and authoritarian system allowed orders to flow from the top downwards.
- Promotion was limited to mid-level positions.

France attempted to make of veterans and ex-servicemen who returned home a buffer group between them and other social or professional groups. It was important to prevent them from rebelling against the colonial system as group. They were kept away from the indigénat system. A sizable number acquired French citizenship, similar to members of the elite. This status entitled them to the same rights and privileges as their French counterparts. As First (1970) points out: 'In the French colonies, the ex-servicemen were among the most loyal and cohesive supporters of the administration.' They had the right to vote. In Dahomey, by 1948, ex-servicemen and active soldiers represented 58% of the electorate, which amounted to 54 000. Their ability to vote – which was a privilege – is significant as it marked their introduction to politics in a context where there was no universal suffrage. In fact, when these ex-servicemen returned home after three years of military service, they felt superior to other Africans who had remained at home. The broad horizons they had acquired in the course of their many experiences affected their attitudes considerably. They could and indeed did help in the enlightenment and political mobilisation of people, but generally, as a privileged group, they had internalised a set of complexes, values and habits linked to their history and, to a certain degree, to traditional values of masculinity, manhood and use of force. Very few sectors could guarantee employment as good, as stable and as prestigious.

THE ARMY'S CREATION AND ROLE BEFORE INDEPENDENCE

At the time of independence, the leaders of newly created states, in agreement with France, established their national armies. A state needed its own army to defend its territory and sovereignty. The Westphalian state was the norm and African countries could not imagine not having armies because of their history and certainly because of the decolonisation process. African leaders believed it symbolised the sovereignty and legitimacy of the state, and guaranteed recognition and diplomatic representation within international organisations such as the United Nations (UN). They also believed that armies would promote national unity and be effective in the process of state and nation building.

French leaders were visionary enough to understand that an army would facilitate their control over colonies politically, and would make it easy to trade weapons and military equipment with them. Thus, on 24 April 1961, the governments of France, Dahomey, Niger and Côte d'Ivoire signed a defence accord, in which all parties agreed to ask the French Republic for help under specifically defined conditions. In Article 4, they essentially acquiesced to allow France to freely circulate within existing air space and territorial waters, and to freely use all military facilities, ports, airports, rivers, roads, railways and post offices. France also had the right to build any facility or install any communication and/or transmission equipment for security and to carry out its mission. The Regional Defense Council was the decision-making body, made up of an officer from each of the four country signatories to the agreement.

The creation of the Dahomey army followed that of other French-speaking countries. The colonial administration transferred troops to the authority of the new state, making sure that the army structurally, logistically, technically and strategically remained dependent on France, which controlled every decision-making progress. Predicting the path they would follow depended on three factors:

- their role as an instrument of repression and conquest at the service of France
- their relative absence in the struggle for the independence of the country

- the privileges granted by the colonial administration that other civil servants with equal qualifications did not have (officers belonged to the national elite).

As future events demonstrated, these factors, and others that appeared after independence, weighed heavily on the nature their relations with civilians and their role in politics.

HIGH MILITARY VISIBILITY PERIOD (1960–1972)

What puzzled academics and the common observer of African politics was the frequent intervention of the army in politics over such a short period. Many political theorists have attempted to explain these recurrences. The causes vary from personal ambition, competing elites and ethnic affiliation, to economic pressure. Most scholars believe, like Huntington, that their interference borders on an anomaly. It is assumed that the army, as a professional organisation, should be apolitical or politically neutral. In reality, the army – no matter its composition, and despite its monopoly of force and its right to use it – is an integral part of society, is subject to societal conflicts and, at best, can only be on the margins of political calculations and the struggle for power. The military, even from the trenches, performs a significant role in politics everywhere. All polities – democracy, dictatorship, totalitarianism, socialism, etc., and all their branches – believe that the military should be subordinate to civilian rule. This tension existed during the time of the Roman Empire; Cicero, a statesman and orator, who deplored the overthrow of the Republic and the assassination of Julius Caesar, expressed the principle of army subordination to civilians in these terms: *Cedant arma togae, concedat laurea laudi* (Let arms yield to the toga, the laurel defer to praise). Even in Rome, the principle was valid and applied only *intra muros*. In the provinces, civilian and military rule were one and the same. Later, in the period following the fall of the Roman Empire, the monarchs cumulated the functions of chiefs of armies and chiefs of states. In the 1800s, Louis XIV and Napoleon led their armies to the battlefield. Today, in Europe, the USA, Russia and China, the military may not be in power, but they weigh heavily in decision making, especially on international issues. In socialist countries, military personnel are highly politicised in the sense that they not only function exclusively in their military roles, but are also appointed to strictly political and administrative posts. In China, the military constituted the backbone of Mao's Cultural Revolution, but were bound by the Chinese Communist Party's decisions, at least nominally. Because of its unique position and strength, the military is one of the most delicate and sensitive institutions in any political system. Recent events in Egypt have clearly demonstrated that they can do or undo any government; they can even trick social movements. As First (1970) stated: 'The coup is taken as the index of civil-military relations, but military organisations can exert a strong influence on government policy without recourse to a coup.'

In Benin, the rank and file of the hierarchy exhibited the characteristics of the rest of society.

During the first decade of independence, the military did not have to perform any 'traditional' military role, such as defending the country. They were alerted to the conflict of Lété Island, between Niger and Bénin, but no war took place. In 2005, the dispute was resolved at the International Court of Justice.[1] Soldiers did not carry out any substantial public infrastructure work, although this doctrine was perfectly acceptable within the governmental milieu. Sometimes they helped the police and the gendarmerie in their law and order-maintaining functions, especially when there were uprisings or riots. Occasionally they participated in road construction, but, by and large, their involvement in civilian life as contributors to nation-building and development projects was minimal.

PRE-1972 MILITARY INTERVENTIONS AND THEIR SIGNIFICANCE

It is appropriate here to distinguish two distinct periods. 'Young veterans' as First (1970) depicted them, represented by General Soglo, were a typical example of the first generation of soldiers that dominated the period 1960–67. Soglo served in Indochina for five years, was decorated and appointed military adviser to the first president, Hubert Maga. Soglo believed that the army was a political body that should intervene to restore constitutional order when it was in danger, but that it should be kept away from partisan politics.[2]

The first intervention of the military occurred in October 1963, at the insistence of demonstrators. Events revolved around Christopher Bohiki, a representative in the National Assembly who was accused of participating in the murder of Le Parti du Renouveau Démocratique (PRD) supporter, Daniel Dossou. The Union of Dahomean Workers (UGTD) supported Ahomadégbé, who was still in jail, and impressed upon the military to take over. Although called the 'October Revolution', it was not, by any stretch of the imagination, a revolution; a mere demonstration does not qualify as a revolution. Soglo suspended the constitution and dissolved the government. The stated aim of this intervention was to establish a new civilian rule as the trade unions had demanded. A new constitution came into force and the Second Republic was born. The Apithy- Ahomadégbé Coalition governed until November 1965, when Soglo staged another coup to end the discord between the two leaders and their followers. The discord led to a constitutional stalemate. Tahirou Congacou, president of the National Assembly, became the president of a provisional government made up of technocrats. However, on 22 December, Soglo returned to preside over the country with the same government of technocrats. This was the consequence of a succession of political and social movements against the new civilian government. In fact, the three leaders – Apithy, Ahomadégbé and Maga – had formed new political parties to compete in the elections. Soglo's regime acted as fully fledged government for two years.

In December 1967, Major Maurice Kouandété, a military officer of the younger generation, overthrew Soglo's regime owing to a host of unpopular economic measures. Once again, trade unions organised demonstrations in coastal towns and their leaders were arrested. This coup revealed the intergenerational conflict of Le Comité Militaire de Vigilance, the military committee that took over. This marked the end of the intrusive role of the first generation of officers and the start of the younger generation's involvement.

The younger generation had received better education than their predecessors – they were trained in French military schools – but they did not undergo exactly the same experiences as their elders. They also fought in colonial wars in Indochina and Algeria, which might have impacted their *tirailleurs* attitude to politics. Lieutenant-Colonel Alley then became president, and a new constitution was written and approved in a referendum. Elections were organised in May 1968, at which the three 'historic' leaders – Ahomadégbé, Apithy and Maga – were barred from running. Voter turnout was low (26%) and the elections were annulled. Two months later, the military handed over power to Émile Derlin Zinsou, an experienced politician who had served in earlier governments as an ambassador or as a minister. Zinsou submitted his nomination to approval by referendum, and by so doing conferred some legitimacy to his rule. On 1 August 1968, the military returned to the barracks as they had promised. However, 16 months later, Lieutenant Kouandété overthrew Zinsou. He was then Chief of Staff and claimed on radio that the army, aware of its duties, '…took up once more their responsibilities and decided that Zinsou, president of the Republic, was dismissed. A new government will be formed within the shortest time and Dahomey will honour all its international obligations' (author's translation).

Ronen (1970:212) argued that this coup differed from previous ones because 'it was planned and executed without civilian input, without the support, and probably without the knowledge of any of the high-ranking Dahomean officers (i.e. it was probably "a one-man show")'. Previous military coups were staged in the aftermath of generalised public discontent and strikes that led to some form of non-governability. Popular reactions to an economic crisis, economic insecurity and dissatisfaction, as well as power struggles within the ruling elite, were the background of previous coups. While Decalo's assertions may be correct regarding the style of the coup, some of Zinsou's policies were unpopular and his rule had become increasingly authoritarian.

In December 1968 and January 1969, students demonstrated against new educational reforms. In May 1969, students resumed demonstrations that lasted two months. Civil servants protested against cuts in family allowances. The approval rate of the regime was certainly low. These conditions often constituted the backdrop to coups and could be depicted as their civilian input. However, personal rivalries in the army also played a role.

Three lieutenant-colonels (Paul- Émile de Souza, Kouandété and Benoît Sinzogan) formed a military directorate, which called on the three former presidents to vie for presidency in free elections. The return of the three exiled leaders revived regionalist allegiances and sentiments, and they won the majority of votes in their respective regions. Zinsou, the fourth candidate, did not enjoy wide support. The elections were annulled and a rotating-three-man-presidency was established in 1970. Regionalism and instability were then institutionalised, and the distribution of ministerial posts reflected regional allegiances and cleavages. Under the triumvirate, all regions had to be satisfied in all public-related matters. For example, economic projects were equally distributed – the central region for Ahomadégbé, South East for Apithy, and North for Maga – when cooperation agreements were signed in 1970 between France and Dahomey.

As a conclusion to this period, a few general patterns of direct military intervention in politics can be identified: First, officers intervened either on the insistence of civilian leaders, as in the first coup, or as a consequence of union strikes and student movements' economic and social policies. Most of the strikes preceding military takeover were pay-strikes or expressed the discontent of trade unions and administrative civil servants about the economy.

Second, given the nature of the army, low levels of literacy, and lack of professionalism in military and other major areas needed to govern – finance, administrative skills, economic and educational expertise, medical knowledge, etc. – prevented the military from ruling effectively; they had to rule with civilians. Contrary to widespread belief, the military, especially in Africa, are not equipped to rule by themselves and will form alliances with the ruling elites to further the interests of such coalitions. They could coalesce for different reasons, but the wellbeing and welfare of the people did not constitute the focus of their political actions. December 1965 to December 1967 represented the only time of tangible military rule, but it was unsuccessful.

Third, because of their own shortcomings, because of civilian pressure, or because of their understanding that politics is not their place, the military quickly oversaw the writing of new constitutions to return to civilian rule. Contrary to other African countries such as Togo, no military leader ever had the intention of being a life-president.

Fourth, the military carry the contradictions of society within their institution. In Benin, regional politics were prevalent and centred on Maga, Ahomadégbé and Apithy. The competition between them was often civil and reverberated in the army too, resulting in political fragmentation along regional lines. The officers who led the coups often originated from the larger ethnic groups. Regionalism and ethnicity have generally been identified as the major problems to be solved in Beninese and African politics. The easy use of ethnicity as an explanation for major conflicts in Africa is over-emphasised. To rule efficiently, the colonisers cultivated regionalism and ethnicity. In Benin, people from the South (East and West) regard themselves as more intelligent and more 'civilised' than those from the central and northern areas. This is actually the result of unequal 'exploitation' by the colonisers. The percentage of northerners in the army was higher than that of southerners when compared with the civil service, which created feelings of frustration among northerners.

How is regionalism and ethnicity assessed? One should examine regionalism and ethnicity in the light of their objective functions and roles in the social praxis. To be an active defender of one's ethnic group has been a vital agent for social mobility, depending on the party in power. This can be extrapolated to the political scene, where the parties constitute the expression of the rapport de force between ethnic groups and regions. This has favoured the emergence of the bureaucratic bourgeoisie and reinforced the position of the petty bourgeoisie. As Hazoume (1972) points out:

> The ideology of ethnicity serves as a springboard from which, through an energetic and decisive leap, the new-born bourgeoisie places itself on the trajectory of its political use...In African societies, ethnicity counts among the major ideological instruments of the ruling bourgeoisie. Consequently, through

all the discreet and insidious cultural and political means that the state apparatus and its propaganda machinery provides them with, they must encourage its maintenance and reinforce its presence.

This represents one of the dominant factors that beset turbulent Beninese politics. The question is whether the military have been capable of staying above politico-ethnic rivalries? Do the military reflect the same ethnic regional cleavages and competition found in the petty bourgeoisie, or is it a professional body mainly preoccupied with its military function?

MARXIST-LENINIST WANDERING (1972–1990)

The young officers who took over on 26 October 1972, unequivocally stated their will to stay in power.[3] Their goal was to improve a worsening economic situation, but this time with the aim of liberating the country from its imperialist stranglehold. As the president stated:

> *The basic characteristic and the primary cause of the backwardness of our country is foreign domination. The story of that domination is that of political oppression, economic exploitation, cultural alienation and the development of interethnic and interregional conflicts.*[4]

The military were not equipped to carry out such a complex and massive task, and therefore sought to enlist civilian support. In his first address to the nation, the very day of the coup, Kérékou assigned the army the task of bringing about a new era for the people. In the following months, the military tried to associate the pre-coup youth organisations La Ligue (The League) and United Democratic Youth (JUD), women's associations and trade unions. It urged all youth organisations to create a National United Front for the Revolution (FUD), but the attempt failed. Organised youth had contradicting views about how unity should be achieved and, more fundamentally, the direction of the revolution. JUD sought to maintain the independence of its regional revolutionary organisations, such as Rassemblement des Jeunes du Mono (RAJEMO), and recommended unity be achieved gradually, in an organic way, from bottom to top. They opposed the existence of a central dictatorial authority. To the contrary, La Ligue viewed JUD's approach as 'a bureaucratic process'[5] and proposed that unity should be achieved at national level; only then could region-affiliated bodies be set up. The military, in their eagerness to centralise, command

and control, disagreed with JUD, and La Ligue and its ideologues became the most faithful civilian partner of the military. JUD, and youth in general, became sceptical and indifferent to the new regime; they were politically active and committed, as Kérékou acknowledged in a public speech.[6] This ideological and tactical split was fundamental to the revolutionary process, and became the most significant moment in the new relationship between the military, youth and other sectors of the population.

As a corporate body, the military is not revolutionary in its essence. Kérékou proclaimed that its mission was 'to restore the authority of the state'. In an interview with Afrique-Asie in June 1973, the president pointed out:

> *...Our earliest desire is that the Dahomean revolution be authentic. It should not burden itself with copying foreign ideology. You see, we do not want communism or capitalism or socialism. We have our own Dahomean social and cultural system which is our own.[7]*

Despite the egalitarian disposition of the 26 October 1972 proclamation, Marxism-Leninism was not yet an ideology ready to be adopted.

PUBLIC ATTITUDES TO THE ARMY (1972–1974)

From October 1972 to October 1974, the government showed no manifest interest in modifying the military structure. However, it seized the opportunity of a failed coup to purge the army of 'suspects', who were later tried and sentenced to 20 years' imprisonment.[8] The main preoccupation of officers in power was to control the army, not to transform it. In his address to the military on 24 November 1972, Kérékou listed a number of tasks for the 'new' context. The government appointed some officers in state-owned enterprises to act as controllers; they were appointed commissioners. Others were appointed members of the Comité Militaire Révolutionnaire (CMR) or the Conseil National de la Révolution (CNR), created in September 1973. These extra-military functions attributed to the officers were intended to reduce the coup risk, but they also reinforced the fact that military officers were part of the ruling elite. The assumption was that officers from a united and strong army were in a position to bring integrity, accountability and control to corrupt state-owned enterprises, and core values of the military – hierarchy, rigor in the execution of orders, discipline, efficiency, unity, cohesion and esprit de corps – should transfer to civilian life and the civil service.

However, the army was not actually the repository of such principles and values. At that time, nepotism, clientelism and corruption characterised the whole of society, including the military. Many financial scandals and embezzlement cases involved army officers.

During the period 1972–74, in its attempt to accelerate the process of institutionalisation, the military government expanded its presence and started militarising many aspects of society. The search for legitimacy within the army and in society became an obsessional imperative as government was quickly losing the support of youth organisations that had spontaneously supported the coup.

REORIENTATION OF CIVIL-MILITARY RELATIONS AFTER 1974

30 November 1974 marked the beginning of another epoch in the evolution of civil-military relations and the role of the military in the development of Benin. On that day, the military regime, under the influence of radical officers and civilians belonging to La Ligue, announced the country would follow a socialist path of development based on the philosophy of Marxism-Leninism. A succession of actions and steps designed to transform the social system were introduced including reformation of the army to draw the police, the gendarmerie and government forestry officers into a new body: the People's Revolutionary Army. On 26 February 1976, in a speech delivered at a ceremony commemorating the training of the second cohort of army recruits, Kérékou outlined seven principles that were to govern the 'new' army, whose primary role was to defend the revolution and serve the peasantry, workers and lower classes of society:

1. End bureaucratic working methods.
2. Strict discipline, based of democratic centralism.
3. Primacy of political and patriotic education.
4. Every act must be on the side of the lower classes of society.
5. The army must be an efficient and productive agricultural unit.
6. The People's Armed Forces would be responsible for the creation and training of the people's militia for civilian defence and protection.
7. The People's Armed Forces would engage actively in political awareness, mobilisation campaigns and the revolutionary education of the people.[9]

These principles clearly indicated that the army was now overtly politicised and that, in turn, it would militarise society. In another landmark speech that same year, Kérékou further explained the role of *Forces Armées Populaires* (FAP), from which the following conclusions could be drawn. FAP must be:

- the most advanced political organisation in society
- the most economically efficient and productive unit
- the moderniser and diffuser of science and technology
- the organisation from which vanguard ideas are originated
- the best organised corps for the defence of the territory and for the revolution.

Thus, Beninese society witnessed more intense militarisation based on the unproven assumption that the military were exemplary and ethical enough to lead qualitative change. Officers were represented in all higher decision-making bodies: all ministers were military officers and formed the majority in the CNR. Out of 67 members, 32 were military, four para-military (three policeman and one ex-serviceman, thirty civilians). Moreover, they were appointed to state corporations and units of production for accountability purposes. The end result was a military bureaucracy. First (1970:433) points out that 'the army bureaucratic coalition, which is preoccupied with the decree rather than the debate, and the letter of the law rather than popular support for it, makes with a jolt to its narrow base of power in times of crisis'.

Although the military bureaucracy was an obstacle to the process of internal democratisation of the army, because it reinforced internal divisions between the rank and file and the hierarchy, it did, to a certain degree, satisfy the military elite. However, it did not facilitate base consultation.[10] Kérékou recognised the persistence of 'bourgeois' methods among the officers and the 'doyen' of the government, and the cadres heading the state corporations used traditional and conservative management styles.

STRUCTURAL INNOVATIONS AND CONTINUITY

In 1976, civil-military relations were unambiguously redefined: FAP was faithful to the party and had to carry out its orders and abide by its political ideology. This pattern prevailed in most communist and socialist countries at the time. If, as in Europe and the United States, the military are also at the disposal of the party in office, we must make the distinction between being neutral, apolitical and actively committed.[11]

The new civil-military relationship did not really alter the nature of the military and FAP did not become a revolutionary force for the following reasons:

- It was unable to transform into an army whose primary function was brutal repression.
- Its ability to protect remained limited.
- There was no new ethos, thus authoritarianism remained the norm.
- In general, it had little or no political education, apart from propaganda education.

Changing the name of the military remained a symbolic gesture that did not, of itself, guarantee the qualitative improvement of social relations within the army; nor did it better the latter's relationships with society as a whole. The mode of recruitment remained practically identical, and ethnic balance remained a priority. The government used this method as a strategy to fend off coups. Promotion became easier for officers with mid-level formal education, and the enrolment of women, who underwent the same training as men, was an innovation. Although most of the soldiers still originated from rural areas, town dwellers had adjusted their views about the military and no longer regarded it as a profession reserved for rural inhabitants or people with little education.[12] There was also marked revision of the view that becoming a soldier was more appropriate for northerners as they recognised that it guaranteed good pay and promotion.

New thinking also emphasised the transition from the notion of a professional army to that of a nation at arms. Military training became compulsory for every citizen who would be expected to defend the country if attacked. People underwent pre-military training before they entered the civil service or the private or semi-private sectors. However, the idea of compulsory military training for students originated from the reality that there was a shortage of teachers in high schools. The notion that the people have to be ready for any possibility at any time is a very noble goal in an environment where the risks are high. However, this was not the case in Benin.

A great deal of diversification took place in the field of training. France no longer had the privilege of training all Beninese officers. Some went through the military school of Ouidah[13] before travelling to Russia, Cuba, Algeria or Libya, while others were trained at the Nigerian Defence Academy in Kaduna. The number of French military officers serving in the technical assistance programme was also reduced. Such diversification was repeated with equipment, with special emphasis on cooperation with the Eastern Bloc countries of Russia and Czechoslovakia (now Czech Republic and Slovakia). Except for the minor changes discussed thus far, the tendency was to preserve the advantages that were institutionalised under colonial rule.

The military kept secret their salaries, but, after 1972, rumour had it that they had been inflated while other sectors of the petty bourgeoisie suffered from the cancellation of fringe benefits, housing and medical allowances. The lot of the peasantry did not improve. Irrespective of whether the military did or did not receive salary increases, their salaries were already far higher than those of civilians with the same qualifications.

ARMY POLITICS AND IDEOLOGY

The unambiguous introduction of politics into the FAP certainly represented a significant change, and the army became regarded as a fully-fledged, non-neutral political body. Politicisation does not trivially imply seizing power or backing one ethnic political group or regional association over another. In this context, it entails not only the indoctrination of the military in Marxist-Leninist ideology, but also the readiness of the army to protect the gains of the revolution. In other words, it indicates the defence of the measures and decisions taken by the government and the party. To control the army, one had to control the officers. The concept of the 'new' army included a desire to prevent further coups, but the ideological aspect of political control was crucial to avoid contestation and insubordination. In that regard, a few practical measures were taken.

Political (ideological) courses increased in barracks all over the country. Ideologues and teachers of Marxism-Leninism from the National Center for Revolutionary Education (CENER) organised and supervised the syllabi. While they did deliver lectures, discussions were led by individuals or groups comprising the most learned soldiers.

Revolutionary Committees of the Garrison (CRGs)[14] were created in every barrack. They comprised soldiers with acknowledged moral integrity and hard-working ethics. They had to:

- identify and denounce all acts of sabotage and counter-revolutionary manoeuvres to the competent authorities
- inform workers about production targets, important decisions, decrees of the party and its national politburo, and those of the GMR
- guarantee security and be vigilant so that the unit of production ran smoothly and productive output increased
- make sure soldiers were assiduous and punctual

- actively counter all forms of sabotage and any attempt to harm agricultural productivity and, consequently, the unit of production.

In this era of Marxist-Leninist wandering, a new security institution was created: the people's militia. This was as a special para-military corps comprising volunteer militants who received casual military training and mobilised for economic production. Although their main function was civilian security, they could be summoned for state security duties. The unarmed people's militia was under the firm leadership of the party and it was supposed to be the advocate of the people. However, like many other institutions that were set up, they abused the little power they had and established clientelist or patrimonial links with the regime. After the Conférence Nationale des Forces Vives de la Nation (the National Conference) in 1990, they withered away.

THE ARMY AND THE NATIONAL CONFERENCE

In the late 1980s, Benin experienced a severe economic crisis and the government was unable to pay civil servants' salaries for many months in a row. The regime had lost all credibility and was on the brink of collapse as a result of protests organised by trade unions and students. The Communist Party of Dahomey, close to an Albanian brand of communism, had been the longest active organised group in opposition to Kérékou. In rural areas, they led civil disobedience actions such as boycotting tax collections, and coordinated resistance in alliance with student movements. The government, under intense pressure, convened a National Conference on 19 February 1990. Participants included the ruling party, Beninese diaspora representatives, religious leaders, former presidents, government representatives, traditional rulers, farmers, the military and other members of the urban political élite. Members of the diplomatic corps and officials from international financial institutions (IFIs) also attended. The conference opened with Kérékou's address vowing to carry out the International Monetary Fund (IMF) programme that his government had agreed to follow, and urging practicality and problem solving for the sake of the nation.

The risk of the military thwarting the process and instituting a coup was still a possibility in participants' minds, but the stakes were too high and there would be no support for such a move. It must be noted that Kérékou had resigned from the military in 1987 and that, in 1988, there had been two failed coup attempts. Kérékou accepted the decisions of the National Conference on the condition that he and many of his collaborators receive immunity from any type of future prosecution.

RETURN TO THE BARRACKS (1990–2014)

The National Conference laid out very early the role the army would play under the new constitution. They would be neutral, apolitical and go back to the barracks to protect the state and civilians. Articles 62 to 68 of the Constitution, which was passed in a referendum in 1990, clearly define the role of the armed forces, which had been reconstituted into the separate bodies it had comprised prior to the formation of the FAP. The president is the commander-in-chief and appoints the members of the High Defence Council.

It is a crime to attempt a coup. Article 66 of the Constitution is very explicit in the behaviour expected of citizens in the event of a coup:

> In case of a coup d'état, or a putsch, of aggression by mercenaries or of any action by force whatsoever, any member of a constitutional agency shall have the right and the duty to make an appeal by any means in order to re-establish the constitutional legitimacy, including recourse to existing agreements of military or defence co-operation. In these circumstances for any Beninese to disobey and organise himself to put a check to the illegitimate authority shall constitute the most sacred of rights and the most imperative of duties.

This means that legitimate bodies have the right to disobey and can even request the intervention of foreign forces if such agreements exist. This is a novelty, although it can be abused and may lead to chaos in cases of partisanship among legitimate groups.

In addition, Article 19 of the Constitution stipulates:

> Any individual or any agent of the state who shall be found responsible for an act of torture or of maltreatment or of cruel, inhumane or degrading treatment in the exercise of, or at the time of the exercise of his duties, whether of his own initiative or whether under instruction, shall be punished in accordance with the law. Any individual or any agent of the state shall be absolved of the duty of obedience when the order received shall constitute a serious and manifest infringement with respect to human rights and public liberties.

This poses a dilemma for the military, where questioning an order can occur only after it has been executed. Since 1990, the armed forces have retreated to the barracks and a number of reforms have guaranteed their praetorian behaviour. Morency-Laflamme (2012) identifies a number of measures taken to democratise the armed forces since the transition to liberal democracy. He posits that the USA, France and other Western European countries trained more and more officers and that, in the process, their support for the institution has somehow stabilised. He believes that the infusion of foreign funding and the participation of the military in, for example, peace-keeping operations have given the military an avenue for success and made them proud of their new roles. Although this may be true, it is not a sustainable solution if the economy of the country does not improve to the point of keeping the elite and other sectors of the population satisfied. Morency-Laflamme adds that, because of their training, officers now believe more strongly that the army should stay away from politics and be under the command of civilian institutions. However, the reality is more complex as officers in Benin and many other former French colonies where the army staged a coup – Burkina Faso, Mali, Central African Republic, Congo and Niger – were trained in France and other Western academies. Surprisingly, the countries where no coups occurred were pro-French or pro-West, or had a French military base. Although Morency-Laflamme recognised that many attempts at overthrowing Kérékou took place before 1991, he also affirmed that Kérékou's government had put in place a number of successful coup-preventing mechanisms. First, he could not use ethnicity as a political tool in the army as he originated from a small ethnic group himself. Second, a quota-based recruitment system assured that no ethnic group dominated the army, especially the officer corps. This active fragmentation system of balancing the armed forces ethnically contributed to its stabilisation by neutralising potential groups of coup makers and preventing the emergence of strong and powerful factions.

Since 1990, there have been occasions of high risk of military intervention. However, due to a battery of circumstances internal to the army, societal factors and an active opposition and civil society, this has not occurred.

As President Yayi Boni, elected for a second term in 2011, must pass on the baton, persistent rumours abound that his clan will try to hold on to power. Civil society is already demonstrating through mass actions, the intellectuals are agitating, and the press and other media are mobilising – all palpable signs of an active democracy. Nevertheless, the military remain an unknown. The society believes that, in the event of increased authoritarianism by the current government and manipulation of the constitution to hold on to power, the army would be the sole arbiter to attempt to restore constitutional order.

The simple fact that the army could come back into power is certainly unsettling. This would be an indication that institutions are weak, that it can still garner support from civilians, and that they themselves do not believe in the supremacy of civilian rule. The scenario would also indicate that a lot of effort needs to be made in terms of the military's relationship with society.

In the 1998 'Leadership Challenges of Demilitarization in Africa' conference held in Arusha, Tanzania, participants identified several areas vital for healthy civil-military relations. They proposed a holistic approach to demilitarisation: building consensus on demilitarisation; redefining the role of the military, especially in societies emerging from colonialism and civil war; improving civil-military relations; strengthening civilian policing through appropriate doctrine, education; capacity building; community involvement and accountability.

It was suggested that an institutional format be established to offset the cohesive power of the military with the mobilised power of civil society. In the case of Benin, the size of the armed forces (about 9 450 in 2011–12)[15] is relatively small in comparison with the size of the population: 10.32 million. Only 1% of the budget is allocated to military expenditure.[16] In addition, civil society has a long tradition of keeping tabs on the military that will not be easy to completely offset in favour of the military. When Kérékou was in power, he could not rely entirely on the army; neither could he rely on a strong ethnic following although Northerners associated with him. Such conditions created checks on power. The government's effort to rule with the military in every sector of society and the economy failed for a couple of reasons: the military were not structurally and mentally prepared to be challenged in the civilian world; and civilians did not quite understand that the military, as an organised group with specific habits that had been thrust into politics early in the history of the country, needed time and education to change.

After 25 years of liberal democracy, the relationship is better. However, the lack of economic progress and meaningful growth in many sectors of society, and the emergence of the Chinese, Singaporean and South Korean models, militate massively for the seductive power of a strong, centralised developmental state that pays little or no attention to civil liberties provided a certain form of economic development is taking place.

It has been recommended that the military's desire for prestige be constructively addressed in order to incorporate it into the democratic mainstream. As a professional body, the military must have professional ambitions: to establish an efficient corps, exemplary discipline, research and leadership in science and technology either on its own or in partnership with research institutions, brilliance in war and other security issues. This has not happened thus far, so the question arises as to whether the military articulate their ambitions in those terms or if they are simply another section of the elite or the ruling class that rely on clientelism and patrimonial relations for their advancement within an extraverted, aid-dependent and rent-oriented economy?

Balancing the ethnic, tribal and regional composition of the military represents necessary conditions for quality civil-military relations. To a certain degree, this balance was achieved by Kérékou and continued under subsequent governments. However, it should be enshrined through legislation and its monitoring must rest with parliament.

The question of the role of the army and its relationship with society lies at the core of civil-military relations in Africa in general. In Benin, a country that is not threatened by its neighbours, that is not afflicted by a civil war or internal conflicts linked with religion, resources, exacerbated identity, autochthony or citizenship issues like other African countries, what is and what should be the role of the army? In a country that is still agrarian, where the land is underutilised in terms of production, where housing, health facilities and schools are lacking in both number and quality, what should the army be doing? What skills should they be cultivating, and should there be across-the-board military discipline and obedience where every individual creatively contributes to the progress of society? Should the army simply make sure they keep in power an enlightened or visionary dictator? Or should they intervene to make sure that someone else is installed to power for the benefit of society? Answers to these crucial questions will diverge, but the traditional role of the army as it emerged from the Westphalian model and as it developed with the bellicose and war-mongering culture of European states, has not proved inefficient thus far. No easy civil-military relations will prevail until Benin starts answering such questions. It will not be enough to have the military subordinate itself to civilians.

This chapter has examined the role of the military in politics by focusing on three main periods. During the first (1960–1972), the military consistently intervened in politics by staging coups. Then, from 1972 to 1990, the country moved to a period where there was a clear attempt to merge the military and the civilian, but both had to subordinate to the centralised authority of the Marxist-Leninist party. Finally came the current period (1990–2014), already almost as long as the first two periods combined, where the military have retreated to their barracks, are playing a more Huntington-modelled role, but are not more prestigious than they were before, are still ridden with corruption, and, as a body, are still not trusted by the population. The issue of trust between the military and civilians will lie at the crux of any new civil-military relations, if there is ever going to be one.

NOTES

1. In January 1965, the presidents of Niger and Dahomey (now the Republic of Benin) met about ownership of Leté island, located in the middle of the Niger river which constitutes a natural border between the two countries. Diori (Niger) and Ahomadégbé (Benin), after direct talks, decided that, until the final resolution of the dispute, the citizens living on the island should live together, and that local authorities would peacefully solve all their problems. The fact that it was a little island, with very little at stake, certainly facilitated the process. In 2002, the matter was submitted to the International Court of Justice for arbitration after they could not agree on who owned the island. On 12 July 2005, the court gave Niger jurisdiction over Leté and 16 out of 25 of the other islands.

2. He expressed this view at a party congress held in Cotonou in August 1963.

3. In his declaration of 26 October 1972, Kérékou affirmed that the army, until further notice, would exorcise the plenitude of state powers (author's translation).

4. Speech made on 30 November 1972 outlining the programme to be followed by the GMR.

5. Statement by Gratien Capo-Chichi now member of the Politburo in *Daho-Express,* 6 March 1973.

6. Speech made on 25 October 1974 on the occasion of the second anniversary of the Dahomean Revolution.

7. Quoted from Ronen (1975). Lieutenant Colonel Kérékou in an interview with Afrique Asie at the beginning of June 1973, as reported in the *Africa Research Bulletin,* June 1973.

9. See Ronen (1975), p. 232.

10. 1. *All ranks, including commissioned and non-commissioned officers, must end their bureaucratic working methods so that the upper ranks actually help the lower ranks and always take into account the soldier's opinion.*

   2. *Discipline must be an iron discipline but at the same time an enlightened discipline, and Marxist-Leninist discipline based on mutual trust and democratic centralism which requires the constant submission of the lower bodies to the higher bodies; it also requires the real participation of the lower bodies in the active life in the garrisons and the whole army in a spirit of frank loyal and sincere comradeship.*

   3. *The love for the people and its class interests must henceforth guide all the actions within the FAP (Forces Armées Populaires or People's Armed Forces). In that respect, any subversive scheming at any level, any action aiming at carrying out or that commissioned the carrying out of the orders irreconcilable with the interests of the people, its army and its revolution must be denounced and fought back as a reactionary, anti-national and counter-revolutionary act and therefore as an act of state treason and dealt with accordingly.*

4. *Political and patriotic education must judiciously complement the intensive tactical and technical training of our troops so that the defence of our fatherland, our people and its class interests may be pursued to the supreme sacrifice, for 'though power grows out of the barrel of the gun, it is desirable that the revolutionary political power must command that gun'.*

5. *The total education of the FAP on the side of the masses in the process of increasing national production in all domains must enter its active phase. Thus, particularly in the agricultural sector, the FAP must produce much and better to feed themselves, for sale and for making reserves. In the very agricultural domain, the FAP must also take active part in the production and set the best example in the fieldworks, in the use of modern techniques and harvest, and the maintenance of crops and the primary commercialization of the farm products.*

6. *Our People's Armed Forces must above all help the peoples create the people's militia for civilian defence and protection in order to develop and reinforce within the working masses the action of patriotic education, the spirit of militant and revolutionary discipline, the spirit of self-sacrifice in the correct fulfilment of the task of the defence of the fatherland which rests upon any worthy national army. The FAP must also take active part in the campaigns of sensitisation, demystification, mobilisation and revolutionary education of the people in order to learn positively from the practical school of the civilian revolutionary forces.*

10. It creates a situation whereby the higher ranks engaged in purely political activities are nowhere to be found to tackle day-to-day problems within the barracks, especially where the scope of the initiative of the lower ranks is considered insubordinate or undisciplined.

11. Neutrality and apoliticalism are similar concepts. They are practically unviable since the army occupies a determinate position in production and reproduction. With the army being itself a state instrument, it is not surprising that the class interests of the army coincide with those of the state managers. The army simply plays a sided or partial role. Apoliticism or neutrality are myths meant to keep the army quiet, and ipso facto to maintain the status quo.

12. Town-dwellers, particularly Fon, who were recruited mostly among the officers and had come to believe as a result of French policy in recruiting personnel from allegedly 'militaristic' ethnic groups of the North that the military profession was not meant for them, have started reconsidering their views.

13. It has now become compulsory to undergo pre-military service at home before going abroad, which was not the case before.

14. CRG is the counterpart of the CDR in civilian life. CDR (Comité pour la defense de la Révolution) has a number of precise tasks, which are the same as those of the CGR.

15. See http://www.tradingeconomics.com/benin/armed-forces-personnel-total-wb-data.html.

16. See http://data.worldbank.org/indicator/MS.MIL.XPND.GD.ZS.

REFERENCES

Allen, C. 1992. 'Goodbye to all that: The short and sad story of Socialism in Benin' in *The Journal of Communist Studies,* Vol. 8, pp. 63-81.

Amin, S. 1973. *Neo-colonialism in West Africa.* London, Penguin.

Amin, S. & Cohen, R. (eds). 1977. *Classes and Class Struggle in Africa.* Lagos: Afrografika.

Bachmann, O. 2014. 'Civil-military relations in francophone Africa and the consequences of a mistaken analysis' in *Small Wars & Insurgencies,* Vol. 25(3), pp. 607 -627.

Bako-Arifari, N. 2001. *'La corruption au port de Cotonou: Douaniers et intermédiaires',* in *Politique Africaine,* Vol. 83, pp. 38–58.

Banégas, R. 1997. *'Retour sur une transition modèle: Les dynamiques du dedans et du dehors de la démocratisation béninoise'* in Daloz, J-P. & Ouantin, P. (eds). 1997. *Transitions démocratiques africaines.* Paris: Karthala.

Banégas, R. 2003. *La démocratie à pas de caméléon: Transition et imaginaires politiques au Bénin.* Paris: Karthala.

Banégas, R. 2014. 'Briefing Benin: Challenges for democracy' in *African Affairs,* Vol. 113/452, pp. 449–459. DOI: 10.1093/afraf/adu043.

Baron, T. 2013. 'The soldier and the State in the Congo crisis: The unprofessional legacy of the National Congolese Army' in *African Security,* Vol. 6, pp. 97–132, DOI: 10.1080/19392206.2013.788407.

Bebler, A. 1975. *Military rule in Africa Dahomey, Ghana, Sierra Leone and Mali.* New York, Praeger.

Bettelheim, C. 1976. *Economic calculations and forms of property.* London: RKP.

Bierschenk, T. 2008. 'The every-day functioning of an African public service: Informalization, privatization and corruption in Benin's legal system' in *Journal of Legal Pluralism and Unofficial Law,* Vol. 57.

Bierschenk, T. 2009. 'Democratization without development: Benin 1989–2009' in *International Journal of Politics, Culture and Society,* Vol. 22, pp. 337–357. DOI 10.1007/s10767-009-9065-9.

Bierschenk, T. & Olivier de Sardan, J-P. 2003. 'Powers in the village: Rural Benin between democratisation and decentralisation' in *Africa,* Vol. 73(2), pp. 145–173.

Blackburn, R. 1978. *Revolution and Class Struggle: A reader in Marxist politics.* London Harvester.

Camara, M.S. 2000. 'From military politization to militarization of power in Guinea-Conakry' in *Journal of Political and Military Sociology,* Vol. 28, pp. 311-326.

Cervenka, E. 1977. *The Unfinished Quest for Unity.* London: Africa Books.

Clark, J.F. 1991. 'Political Liberalization and Military Intervention in African States Since 1991'. American Political Association paper.

Conteh-Morgan, E. (1994). 'The military and human rights in a post-Cold War Africa' in *Armed Forces & Society,* Vol. 21(1), pp. 69-87.

Dean, III, W. T. (2014). The French colonial army and the Great War. *The Historian, Phi Alpha Theta.* 479-517.

Decalo, S. 1976. *Military Rule in Africa: Study in military style (Dahomey, Togo, Congo, Uganda)*. New Haven: Yale University Press.

Deroo, É. & Champeaux, A. 2013. 'Panorama des troupes coloniales françaises dans les deux guerres mondiales' in *Revue historique des armées*. Vol. 271, pp. 72-88. Available at http://rha.revues.org/7736. Accessed 15 March 2015.

Desjardins, P. 1977. *Les rebelles d'aujord'hui*. Paris: Presses de la cite.

Dickovick, T.J. 2008. 'Legacies of Leftism: Ideology, ethnicity and democracy in Benin, Ghana and Mali' in *Third World Quarterly*, Vol. 29(6), pp. 1119–1137.

Duhn, J. (ed.) 1978.*West African States: Failure and promise*. London, Cambridge University Press.

Duverger, M. 1977. *The Idea of Politics*. London: Methuen.

Engels, J.N., Stroh, A. & Wantchékon, L. (eds). 2008. *Le fonctionnement des partis politiques au Bénin*. Cotonou: Friedrich-Ebert-Stiftung & Editions COPEF.

First, R. 1970. *The Barrel of a Gun*. London: Penguin.

'Foreign interventions and the course of democratization in Benin and Niger' (preliminary version). Presented at the 45th Annual ISA Convention, Montréal, 17-20 March 2004.

Hazoume, G.L. 1972. *Idéologies tribalistes et nation en Afrique: le cas dahomeen*. Paris: Presence Africaine.

Heilbrunn, J.R. 1993. 'Social origins of national conferences in Benin and Togo' in *Journal of Modern African Studies*, Vol. 31(2), pp. 277–299.

Houngnikpo, M. 2010. *Guarding the Guardians: Civil-military relations and democratic governance in Africa*. Aldershot: Ashgate.

Huntington, S.P. 1991. *The Third Wave. Democratization in the late twentieth century*. Norman: University of Oklahoma Press.

Igué, J.O., & Soulé, B.G. 1992. *L'État-entrepôt au Bénin. Commerce informel ou solution à la crise?* Paris: Karthala.

Kieh, G.K. & Agbese, P.O. (eds). 2005. *The Military and Politics in Africa: From engagement to democratic and constitutional control*. Burlington, VT: Ashgate.

'Leadership Challenges of Demilitarization in Africa [The]'. 1998. Summary of the conference report. Arusha, Tanzania, 22-24 July 1998.

Lenin, V.I. 1952. *State and Revolution*. New York: International Publishers.

Lenin, V.I. 1969. *A Great Beginning in Selected Works*, Vol. II. Moscow: Foreign Languages Publishing House.

Magnusson, B. & Clark, J.F. 2005. 'Understanding democratic survival and Democratic failure in Africa: Insights from divergent democratic experiments in Benin and Congo (Brazzaville)' in *Comparative Studies in Society and History*, Vol. 47(3), pp. 552-582. Available at http://www.jstor.org/stable/3879391. Accessed 9 March 2015.

Martin, M.L. (2006) 'Soldiers and governments in postpraetorian Africa: Cases in the francophone area' in Caforio, G. (ed.). 2006. *Handbook of the Sociology of the Military.* New York, Springer.

Martin, M.L. 1985. 'The rise and "thermidoranisation" of radical praetorianism in Benin' in *Journal of Communist Studies,* Vol. 1(3–4), pp. 58–81.

Matlosa, K. 2014. 'Pan-Africanism, the African Peer Review Mechanism and the African Charter on Democracy, Elections and Governance: What does the future hold?' in South African Institute of International Affairs: *African Perspectives, Global Insights.* Occasional Paper No. 190.

Melotti, U. 1977. *Marx and the Third World.* London: MacMillan Press.

Morency-Laflamme, J. 2012. 'The armed forces as a political player: Democratization processes in Benin and Togo'. Paper presented to the 44th Annual Conference of the Northeastern Political Science Association. Boston: NPSA.

N'krumah, K. 1973. *Class Struggle in Africa.* London: Panaf Books.

Onwumechili, C. 1998. *African Democratization and Military Coups.* Westport, Conn.: Praeger.

Randall, V. & Lars, S. 2002. 'Political parties and democratic consolidation in Africa' in *Democratization,* Vol. 9(3), pp. 30–52.

Ronen, D. 1975. *Dahomey. Between tradition and modernity.* Ithaca, NY: Cornell University Press.

Schiff, R.L. 2009. *The Military and Domestic Politics: A concordance theory of civil-military relations.* New York, NY: Routledge. Reviewed by: Donald S. Inbody, Texas State University, San Marcos, TX, USA. DOI: 10.1177/0095327X10379722.

Seldon, D. (ed.) 1978. *Relations of Production: Marxist approaches to economic anthropology.* London, Frank Cass.

Shivji, I. 1976. *Class Struggle in Tanzania.* London: Heinemann.

Staniland, M. 1973. 'The three-party system in Dahomey' in *Journal of African History,* Vol. 14, pp. 291–312/491–504.

Suret-Canale, J. 1968. *L'ère coloniale (1900-1945).* Paris: Editions Sociales.

Sweezy P.M. & Bettelheim, C. 1970. *Lettres sur quelques problemes actuels du socialisme.* Paris: Mospero.

Vittin, T.E. 1991. 'Benin: du système Ké-ékou au renouveau démocratique' in Médard, J-F. (ed.), *Etats d'Afrique noire: formation, mécanismes et crise.* Paris: Karthala: Paris. pp. 93–115.

Welch, C.K. Jr. (ed.) 1970. Soldier and State in Africa. Evanston: Northern University Press.

Wlodzimierz, B. 1975. Socialist Ownership and Political System. London, RKP.

Chapter 4

Post-Liberation Relapse and Aborted Social Contract? Isaias Afwerki and Eritrea (1991–2015)

by Kealeboga J. Maphunye

From the 1950s onwards, when many African countries achieved independence, possibly the biggest question on African leaders' and their people's minds was what kind of political or governance system was most suitable for their ethnically, religiously and culturally diverse societies? Which system would ensure post-independence development, success and sustainability? Some countries embarked upon wars of liberation, but soon thereafter were confronting post-liberation failure characterised by bleakness and far more complex realities than their earlier systems – a story identical to Eritrea's situation.

Cohen (1997) states in his article on civil-military relations that one of the problems of governance is the 'growing divide between civil society and those who wear uniforms'. Perhaps this comes very close to describing the situation in Eritrea, a small country located in the Horn of Africa. Its neighbours include Sudan to west, Ethiopia to the south, Djibouti to the southeast and, to the west, the Red Sea. According to Bairu (2007), an observer stated that '… in 1961, the Eritrean nationalists resorted to the strategy of armed struggle in order to achieve national independence … [which] led to an extreme form of self-reliance that, in its turn [sic], led to the militarisation of Eritrean society'.

Before independence in 1991, Eritrea was briefly occupied by neighbouring Ethiopia and fought a bitter armed struggle led by the Eritrean Liberation Front (ELF) and the Eritrean People's Liberation Front (EPLF). Subsequently, 'Eritrea became the 53rd African Nation in 1993, following a UN-sponsored referendum on independence' (Weldemariam, 2014:4). Since independence, it has been ruled by the ELF. According to observers, '… in 1994, the EPLF conducted its first post-liberation congress and reconstituted itself as the only party of the new state, calling itself the People's Front for Democracy and Justice (PFDJ)' (Woldemikael, 2013: vi), currently led by President Isaias Afwerki. Ironically, Eritrea was not so long ago among a group of African states that were expected to perform better than others in the continent. As Woldemikael (2013:vii, citing Oloka-Onyango, 2004) notes: 'In the early 1990s, Isaias Afwerki, Yoweri Museveni of Uganda, Paul Kagame of Rwanda, and

Meles Zenawi of Ethiopia were dubbed the new generation of African leaders, leaders of this African renaissance.' Clearly expectations were very high, especially from some outside the continent:

> *Foreign journalists and Eritrean scholars wrote that Eritrea was different from the rest of Africa; they believed that the newly independent Eritrea could become a showcase for African development and recovery. The new sovereign nation-state of Eritrea was expected to generate economic opportunities and provide a stable political culture for its people. (Woldemikael, 2013: vi).*

Barely two decades later (1993-2015), none of these expectations seems to have been fulfilled. If anything, some expectations were betrayed because Eritrea is considered to be in a worse state than other African countries.

STATEMENT OF THE PROBLEM

From the 1960s onwards, African countries that gained their political independence through guerrilla and armed struggles became the envy of nationals of the countries that were still under white minority or colonial regimes, notably Mozambique, Rhodesia (Zimbabwe), South West Africa (Namibia) and South Africa. Despite post-liberation politics, these countries undertook what may be described as successful post-independence transitions towards democratic politics characterised by political pluralism, competitive elections that are generally acceptable in terms of international standards and best practice, and conferment of legitimacy to elected public representatives through the ballot based on the rule of law, constitutionalism, and basic rights and freedoms enshrined in national constitutions. Yet, from a promising post-liberation democratic experiment, Eritrea followed the same route but soon deteriorated to become one of Africa's examples of despotism, authoritarianism, militarism and one-party dictatorship, defying traditional civil-military relations (CMR) theories. CMR describes the relationship between civil society and the military organisation or organisations established to protect it. More narrowly, it describes the relationship between the civil authority of a given society and its military authority. This explanation might not neatly describe the situation in Eritrea, as there is not much that one can refer to as 'civil authority' in the strictest sense; it is a militarised polity underpinned by its indefinite national service or military conscription policy. Further, the country seems to be a case of an aborted democratic transition, or an attempt at democratic transition gone wrong. However, its situation also bears the hallmarks of a failed state and an unsuccessful nation-building project, which puzzles scholars, proponents and opponents of Africa's democratisation efforts.

BACKGROUND AND OVERVIEW

During colonial times, Eritrea and Ethiopia were occupied briefly by Italy (Weldemariam, 2014). After colonial occupation, Eritrea was amalgamated with Ethiopia to become part of the Federal Republic of Ethiopia. This union became a trigger point for the subsequent war of liberation against Ethiopia that was fought by several guerrilla forces, including the Eritrean Liberation Movement (ELM), from which ELF was later born. Owing to disagreements of tactics and strategy (as has happened elsewhere in the continent – notably in South Africa and Zimbabwe, where rival or splinter groups emerged), EPLF was formed by former members of ELF and other opposition forces who subsequently clashed with ELF in a bitter civil war that perhaps became a precursor to the country's present post-liberation independence woes (Weldemariam, 2014).

To maintain party cohesion, unity and forestall external opposition and internal dissent, EPLF became a hardened leftist organisation that allegedly admired some of the strategies of Mao Zedong's China. The EPLF won its war with Ethiopia, and like other liberation movements in Africa – the African National Congress (ANC) in South Africa, the Zimbabwe African National Union–Patriotic Front (ZANU-PF) in Zimbabwe, the South West Africa People's Organisation (SWAPO) in Namibia and the Mozambique Liberation Front (Frelimo) in Mozambique – it also came to power on a higher note as a 'people's liberator' (Weldemariam, 2014). It was expected to build a new Eritrean society based on democratic principles and respect for the rule of law; basic human rights such as freedom of expression and freedom of association; and to ensure tolerance of political and religious diversity, given the complex nature of Eritrean society. Of course, given its struggle history and the EPLF's inclination towards Marxist and Maoist governance practices, many in the liberation fraternity elsewhere in Africa and globally would have welcomed the emergence of a Marxist, socialist Eritrea, which would ostensibly address the contradictions and threats of global capitalism in the Horn of Africa.

However, once firmly in power, the EPLF became authoritarian and slowly created a regime that suppressed virtually all the human rights and freedoms that were to be informed by the country's new constitution, resulting in its suspension.[1] From then on the country inevitably flouted such instruments as the African Charter on Democracy, Elections and Governance, African Charter on Human and People's Rights, Universal Declaration of Human Rights (UDHR), and the African Union's (AU) Principles and Guidelines Governing Democratic Elections, among others. This drastic but clearly undemocratic situation, which was followed by the indefinite suspension of national elections, resulted in Eritrea being increasingly described as a 'failed state' (Bairu, 2007; Weldemariam, 2014). Such a state generally experiences crises of governance in the sense that the major arms of government and social control, such as the judiciary, legislature and executive experiences either collapse or fail to operate optimally. In fact, some suggest that the country is a totalitarian dictatorship. It is clear that, in order to understand the complex situations confronting such countries as Eritrea, one needs to go beyond the usual simplistic theories and studies of some civil-military relations that '… tend to concentrate on solving or preventing the *coup d'état*, something that is a dangerous but, arguably, occasional problem of civil-military relations in most states' (Bland, 1999 8). Dorman (cited by Weldemariam, 2014: 11) notes:

> It is difficult to capture how deeply the ethos of the liberation struggle and the EPLF appears to have penetrated Eritrean society – the streets of the capital Asmara are masked by the struggle, not just in renamed streets and official art and sculpture, but also in the names of shops and businesses.

This largely reveals the extent to which the party's pervasive presence in Eritrea might be a hegemonic force that understandably dominates society and impedes any attempts to reform the system or introduce democratic political reforms.

APPROACH, METHODOLOGY AND ASSUMPTIONS

The approach adopted in this chapter is that state formation and state viability are critical indicators of current and future democratisation, and, therefore, deserve attention. Based on a review of the extant literature, theoretical postulation on democratisation, state and nation-building, civil-military relations and post-liberation democratic transitions in Africa, this chapter examines Eritrea's attempts (and failure) at democratic transition. The chapter is based on the author's analysis of transitions to democracy elsewhere on the continent, especially those countries that have followed a similar armed-struggle-to-liberation route such as Eritrea.

One of the assumptions of this chapter is that states can enhance or impede democratisation, development and the rights and responsibilities of citizens according to the nature of statehood. This largely depends on the actions of authoritarian party leaders, whose despotic tendencies lead to the suppression of democratic elections in an attempt to avoid being replaced through the ballot. It is also assumed that Eritrea falls within the category of a few African states that suffered immensely after their liberation from colonial or foreign occupation; basically a story of state formation and democratic transition gone wrong. Such states cannot be among the examples of good governance, democracy and successful democratic transition since they simply do not measure up to this description.

THEORETICAL FRAMEWORK

Eritrea is a *de facto* one-party state and could have also been a *de jure* one-party state were it not for the suspension of its post-independence constitution. A careful analysis of Eritrea's politico-military rule suggests that much can be learnt from the classic works of American civil-military relations – Samuel Huntington's The Soldier and the State and Morris Janowitz's *The Professional Soldier* (Nielsen, 2005: 63) – which mark earlier attempts to conceptualise the role of the military in politics, control of the military by a civilian authority, and the usually problematic relations between civilian authorities and the military in many polities. Without claiming comprehensive coverage of the literature on civil-military relations, a review of much of this literature reveals a consistent focus on questions of control (of the military by civilians), organisation, effectiveness and professionalism (see Huntington, 1957; Janowitz, 1960; Clausewitz, 1976; Posen, 1984; and Dech, 1999 in Nielsen, 2005: 63-68; and Cohen, 1997). Some suggest that such relations are paradoxical, but indicate a comprehensive attempt to theorise the relationship (Feaver, 1996; Bland, 1999; Nielsen, 2005). However, one observer suggests that there is very little theorising on these issues (Bland, 1999: 7). Another proposes that '... the civil-military challenge is to reconcile a military strong enough to do anything the civilians ask them to with a military subordinate enough to do only what civilians authorise them to do' (Feaver, 1996: 149). Looking at the situation in Eritrea, neither of these two scenarios seems to apply because the country does not have a civilian government that 'controls' a military that is strong enough to do the civilians' bidding; nor does Eritrea have a military that is subordinate enough to do anything authorised by a civilian government. In fact, some say that '... there are no civilian authorities who are capable of exercising political control in Eritrea' (Bairu, 2007: 4). This is probably because of the argument that the military actually rules the roost, given the EPLF's intricate web of control of virtually all aspects of Eritrean civilian life (Feaver, 1996; Bairu, 2007; Weldemariam, 2014).

To some extent, the pervasive environment of fear that prevails in Eritrea can be understood in the context of the civil-military problematique, which, as Feaver (1996: 150) argues, '… is a simple paradox: because we fear others we create an institution of violence to protect us, but then we fear the very institution we created for protection'. Here, this refers to the creation of the military machine, but in terms of Eritrea's situation one may also extend this argument to the creation of a party that, ostensibly, protects civilians against foreign 'aggression', but which, in turn, terrorises civilians as it apparently fears democratisation of the country could result in the toppling of the regime. Extending this logic of militarisation, Bairu (2007: 2) argues that '… from 1997 onwards, it can be safely asserted that Eritrea was transformed into a guerrilla state – run by a guerrilla army. Henceforth, the Eritrean people referred to Mr Issayas [Isaias Afwerki] as the "Dictator"'. Generally, such a description is contrary to expectations of political leaders who are seen as liberators after mounting protracted struggle against an oppressive regime.

Theoretical postulation using theories of democracy, authoritarianism, tyranny and autocracy can assist in contextualising the pertinent issues facing the Eritrean national question. For instance, Eritrea can be perceived as a democratic transition gone wrong in the sense that extant literature outlines a case wherein Eritrean nationals actively participated and fought for political independence, but subsequently relinquished or loosened their checks and balances on their liberators (see Poole, 2013; Woldemichael, 2013; Weldemariam, 2014). For all intents and purposes, this seems to be a case in which African political elites at the helm of a liberation movement cum political party suddenly change course and metamorphose into an authoritarian and autocratic regime shortly after achieving political independence. Subsequently, this regime denied citizens basic human rights and suppressed liberal democratic freedoms on the pretext that the country or state faced an immediate external threat, especially from neighbouring Ethiopia (Weldemariam, 2014).

Overall, however, Eritrea is increasingly classified as an authoritarian state, and terms such as despotism, autocracy, and undemocratic rule are found in literature on the country's political situation (ICG, 2010; Weldemariam, 2014). All these types of rule may be seen as variables that explain the country's unsuccessful transition.

ISAIAS AFWERKI'S EPLF AND ERITREA'S POST-INDEPENDENCE POLITICS

Shortly after Eritrea's independence, Afwerki became the country's president and, since 1973, has been the chairman of the PFDJ. Literature on Eritrea's post-independence politics suggests that his protracted term of rule became increasingly authoritarian, despite initial signs of democratisation (Bairu, 2007; Weldemariam, 2014). Close analysis of Afwerki's rule suggests that Eritrean politics were characterised by personality politics based on his autocratic leadership style. Scholars state that '... whatever is said or done by Issayas is not questioned at all, irrespective of whether one agrees or disagrees' (Weldemariam, 2014: 18), which they associate with despotism and what they see as a personality cult in Eritrea.

> Intoxicated by the achievement of national independence, the Eritrean people gave a Blanc [sic] Check to Mr Issayas to do with Eritrea as he willed. Having secured the unquestioning adulation of the masses, Mr Issayas went about, unhindered, building a one man, one party, state. Mr Issayas' militarised nationalism was fast upstaging civilian values; the next step taken by the leader of the EPLF was to cultivate the cult of personality. From the moment Mr Issayas captured power, he launched a campaign of adducing to himself, the myth of the ultimate hero of the Eritrean Revolution. This militaristic ideological form, combined with the cult of the personality that accompanied it, prepared the way for one of the most violent dictatorships in the history of our [Horn of Africa] region. Bairu (2007:2)

Afwerki's leadership style entailed appointing EPLF loyalists, but he valued loyalty, patriotism and obedience above all other values. It is argued that the leader's '... dictatorship and absolute obedience by the subordinates became the culture of EPLF and continued as a culture of the regime in Asmara ... Those who fail to show absolute obedience and [show] less loyalty to the leaders face immediate isolation' (Weldemariam, 2014: 18). The main advantage of such a leadership style is that it gives the leader extensive power, influence and ability to control party members or citizens using fear as a tool of the trade. Furthermore, this kind of leadership style and political culture can enable a leader to easily manipulate party members and supporters by spreading patronage in the party and society, and simply entrench an authoritarian or despotic personality. The main disadvantage, however, is that it easily alienates politically conscious citizens and party members, which can result in a regime losing popularity and resorting to even more authoritarian measures to stay in power. Thus, it is argued that:

In 1994, at the 3rd Congress of the Eritrean People's Liberation Front (EPLF), Mr Issayas was able to remove the historical leadership of that organisation from his government, and to replace them by a group of cadres who were absolutely dependent on him. To make matters clear, he substituted the EPLF by an organisation of his making – baptised the People's Front for Democracy and Justice (PFDJ). He legitimised the new power structure by putting up a brand new parliament (composed of his military and civilian supporters) (Bairu, 2007: 2).

One observer alludes that this political culture is related to a unique political movement in the country and explains this phenomenon as follows:

The EPLF leaders including Issayas were the creation of the movement, one from which members could not escape or leave. People who are members of the Front are highly controlled. The Front was always based on absolute domination over the individual members in the name of centralism, who has not time for privacy and free movement (Weldemariam, 2014: 10, citing Poole, 1979).

This indicates how the rooted personality cult and leadership style of Afwerki has ensured the survival of his regime in Eritrea, and the entrenchment of his power and influence over the country's armed forces, partly through the hegemonic role of the only legal party. It is argued that '… since coming to power in 1991, EPLF/PFDJ has not allowed any organised political opposition to emerge within Eritrea,' (Weldemariam, 2014: 15). Furthermore, reference to 'highly controlled' party members reminds us of the political cultures of the former Stalinist Soviet Union and other Eastern Bloc countries, and the contemporary Democratic People's Republic of Korea (North Korea), which subjects its citizens to social control and heavy censorship. Such social control is almost always masked under the need for democratic centralism, which in principle is despotic as dissenting views are not tolerated and citizens dare not criticise the party and its leaders.

Referring to civil-military relations in Latin America, Diamond (1997: 35) argues that '… the armed forces must be removed from control over economic institutions (including banks, corporations and mass media) and surveillance or control over any aspects of domestic politics'. However, if the military permeates virtually every facet of Eritrean life, this clearly suggests that civil-military relations in this country are characterised by despotism and authoritarianism, given the fact that those who have attempted to oppose the regime have been ruthlessly suppressed. Thus, some have even dared to say that Eritrea is a failed terrorist state, which should be denied international legitimacy (Bairu, 2007: 3).

ERITREA'S POLITICS IN PERSPECTIVE

Eritrea's post-independence politics are characterised by a strong dose of military rule, which itself is subject to the despotism and authoritarian leadership style of one man: Afwerki. One of the key factors that might explain the persistence of this scenario is that the role of the military predominates the country's politics and, as one scholar states, the 'defence force is not a non-partisan national institution; it is the muscle of the PFDJ and the President, guarding the authoritarian regime with its exclusive policy that disunites Eritrea and Eritreans' (Weldemariam, 2014: 16). In such a state, one cannot speak about politics in the traditional sense of a ruling party that competes for and comes to power through elections, and allows democratic rights and inputs by civil society organisations.[2]

Although the country achieved its independence in the early 1990s, when the winds of change were blowing across Africa, Eritrea apparently took a detour away from democratisation and towards authoritarian rule. It quickly became a de facto one-party state that suppressed human rights and undermined democratic rule. Despite Eritrea being a multicultural and multi-religious country, religious persecution is said to be rife, with scholars pointing to the most cited case of the persecution of Jehovah's Witnesses (Weldemariam, 2014: 14).

In terms of international relations, the EPLF continued to behave as if it was still a liberation movement and quickly pursued an aggressive 'fight first, talk later' foreign policy, which resulted in the country being entangled in military hostilities with its neighbours, most notably Ethiopia.

To this effect, the usual questions of civil-military relations - How exactly is the military controlled by civil authorities? What policies and structures lead to civilian control? And what kind of civil-military relations best serve the interests of democracies over the long term? – might not apply in Eritrea's case.

IMPLICATIONS FOR PEACE-BUILDING AND CIVIL-MILITARY RELATIONS

The Eritrea case study suggests that the country's current political situation is severely affected by the state of civil-military relations, which effected its abortive transition to democracy. Adversarial or tense civil-military relations largely inform Eritrea's political culture and polity. Such relations essentially refer to the ability of a civilian authority government to control the military within its jurisdiction and for the military to operate efficiently within the confines of civilian political oversight. In Africa, such relations are known to have been conflictual and adversarial, resulting in military coups d'état. Traditionally, these have occurred mostly in West and North Africa, although Lesotho has recently veered from the regional norm in the Southern African Development Community (SADC) sub-region. Adversarial civil-military relations are generally seen as an aberration because, whenever the military becomes highly politicised or partisan (such as happened in Lesotho in 1998 and 2014–15), such a situation is assumed to be abnormal and unsustainable politically as members of the armed forces are not expected to run governments and never stand for election in their own right. In the case of Eritrea, civil-military relations are clearly adversarial owing to the country's national service programme, which coerces all able-bodied citizens to enlist in the military indefinitely. In turn, such relations tend to be characterised by tension between the regime and citizens, owing to the latter's dissatisfaction about the government's imposition of undemocratic forms of governance, including permanent military conscription.

It is only when such transformation is undertaken that Eritrea can possibly hope to attract the multitude of its citizens in the diaspora who are keen to see the end of authoritarian rule in their country so that democratisation and real nation-building can begin. Furthermore, such a country cannot hope to bring about development unless it is at peace with itself and its neighbours, which means that the current adversarial foreign policy of continual confrontations or tensions with the likes of Sudan, Ethiopia, Djibouti and Yemen will also need to change.

RECOMMENDATIONS FOR ERITREA'S DEMOCRATISATION

Among the recommendations on the Eritrean situation is the fact that the country cannot be forever seen as one of the region's rogue states, in line with the situation in Somalia. It therefore needs to demilitarise the country's politics by immediately halting permanent conscription or indefinite national service. This will also require the opening up of political space for democratic political participation, democratic freedoms and human rights, and restoration of the country's tarnished image. For a small country that is seemingly insulated from the rest of the Horn of Africa region, and the world in general, this might not be easy. It will require fundamental transformation of the country from despotic one-man, one-party rule to multi-party democracy based on the AU's continental instruments and global agreements on the rights of citizens to democratic free and fair and internationally accepted elections, which can bring about a change of government if the electorate so desires.

CONCLUSION

Eritrea's story is that of a country clearly dominated by the rule of one political party, at the helm of which is a leader who seems to be terrified of the possibility of change of power or simply wants to stay in power forever. The country is associated with despotic, authoritarian, and even totalitarian regimes worldwide, owing to the autocratic leadership style of the incumbent president and the pervasive power and influence of the EPLF/PFDJ – the only party deemed legal in the country.

This chapter has argued that the Eritrean situation is an African example of a failed state. By this we mean a state whose transition to democracy, rule of law and constitutionalism, regular democratic, free and fair and credible elections, and basic democratic rights and freedoms are severely compromised or absent. Such rights and freedoms include religious freedom, freedom of association and free political expression, political pluralism and competition, where the possibility exists that an incumbent can be replaced by the opposition through the ballot. This is not the case in Eritrea. This leads us to agree with an observer who argues that 'the situation in Asmara indicates that without demilitarisation of the society, proper institutionalisation of the state, democratisation, ensure human right [sic], inclusive policy, etc., the possibility of nation-building is highly remote' (Weldemariam, 2014: 13). Eritrea requires a new leadership ethos that is radically different from current practices in which one political party dominates the political landscape, suppresses basic human rights and democratic freedoms, and flouts virtually all the continent's pertinent instruments such as the African Charter on Democracy, Elections and Governance, which, among others, urges AU member states to work towards the democratisation of their societies.

An attempt was made to explain the Eritrean dilemma using a civil-military relations lens. This examined the extent to which civilian authorities control the military, the effectiveness and efficiency of the military, and how it relates to civilian political authorities. The pervasive role of the military in Eritrean society seems to suggest the relevance of civil-military relations in explaining the situation. However, the country's indefinite national conscription, ostensibly aimed at thwarting potential external threats, is intricately interwoven into its domestic politics and used to buttress the leader's and party's power. Thus, this situation seems to defy the basic logic or assumptions of civil-military relations as propounded by Huntington (1957) and Janowitz (1960). Thus, the situation was also analysed in terms of post-independence and post-liberation democratisation, suggesting that Eritrea's circumstance is that of an aborted transition to democracy which occurred soon after the country's independence. Contrary to continental and international expectations, this independence was soon characterised by despotism, authoritarianism, and state repression, following a personality cult and entrenched (one)-party hegemonic control of society. For it to return to the fold of free African nations on a democratic path, Eritrea will require fundamental socio-economic, political and other changes that will restore its dignity and tarnished image – starting with internationally acceptable elections, an end to despotism, and the restoration of its suspended constitution. Whether and how far such fundamental changes will minimise the growing divide between citizens and those in military uniform is difficult to ascertain, given the enormous damage done to ordinary citizens through Eritrea's forced conscription policy. However, this might go a long way towards arresting the country's post-liberation relapse and revival of its (damaged) social contract.

NOTES

1. It is further argued that 'Eritrea has no constitution, rules [sic] of law, opposition parties and private media. It is the private property of the President. He publicly declared that Eritreans are not ready for democracy' (Weldemariam, 2014: 17).

2. An observer argues that Eritrean societies exist only in the diaspora (Bairu, 2007: 5).

REFERENCES

Bairu, H.T. 2007. 'The Security Situation in Eritrea: Its Implications for the Region and Its Challenges to Security Sector Reform' available at http://111.gsdrc.org/go/display&type=document&id=4880. Accessed 11 June 2015.

Bereketeab, R. 2000. 'Eritrea: The making of a nation' available at http://uu.diva-portal.org/smash/record.jsf?dswid=9820=diva/. Accessed 16 April 2015.

Bland, D.L. 1999. 'A unified theory of civil-military relations; in *Armed Forces & Society*, 26: 1, pp.7-26.

Cliffe, L. 1999. 'Complex Political Emergencies and the State: Failure and the fate of the State' in *Third World Quarterly*, 20:1, pp.27-50.

Cohen, E.A. 1997. 'Civil-military relations' in *Orbis*, 41: 2, pp.177-186.

Conell, D. 2007. 'Strategies for Change: Women and politics in Eritrea and South Africa' in *Review of African Political Economy*, 26: 76, pp.189-206.

Constitution (Eritrea). 2015. Available at http://www.europaworld.com/entry/er.dir2. Accessed 16 April 2015.

Diamond, L. 1997. 'Consolidating Democracy in the Americas', Annals, AAPSS, 550, pp.12-41.

Dorman, S.R. 2007. 'Post-Liberation Politics in Africa: Examining the political legacy of struggle' in *Third World Quarterly*, 27: 6, pp.1085-1101.

Ellingson, L. 1977. 'The emergence of political parties in Eritrea, 1941-1950' in *Journal of African History*, 18: 2.

Eritrea Country Profile. 2015. Available at http://bbc.com/news/world-africa-13349078. Accessed 9 April 2015.

Europa World: Eritrea 2015. Available from: http://www.europaworld.com/entry/er. Accessed 11 April 2015.

Institute for Security Studies (ISS). 2008. 'Ethiopia and Eritrea in Turmoil: Implications for peace and security in a troubled region', ISS Situation Report.

International Crisis Group (ICG). 2008. 'Beyond the fragile peace between Ethiopia and Eritrea: Averting new war' in *Africa Report* No. 141, 17 June 2008.

International Crisis Group (ICG). 2010. 'Eritrea: the siege state' in *Africa Report* No. 163, 21 September 2010.

Iyob, R. 1997. 'The Eritrean Experiment: A cautious pragmatism?' in *Journal of Modern African Studies*, 35: 4, pp.647-673.

Matlosa, K., Khadiagala, G. & Shale, V. 2010. (Eds.), *When Elephants Fight: Preventing and resolving election-related conflicts in Africa*. Johannesburg: EISA.

Nielsen, S.C. 2005. 'Civil-Military Relations Theory and military effectiveness' in *Public Administration and Management*, 10: 2, pp. 61-84.

PFDJ National Charter, Adopted by the 3rd Congress of the EPLF/PFDJ, Naqfa, February 10-16, 1994, Available at http://ecss-online.com/data/pdfs/PFDJ-national-charter.pdf. Retrieved on 1 June 2015.

Poole, A. 2013. 'Ransoms, Remittances, and Refugees: The gatekeeper state in Eritrea' in *Africa Today*, 60: 2, Special Issue: Postliberation Eritrea, pp. 67-82.

Shale, V.R. 2004. *Ethnic Conflict in the Horn of Africa*. EISA Occasional paper No. 19, April 2004, Johannesburg: Electoral Institute for Sustainable Democracy in Africa.

Tronvoll, K. & Mekonnen, D.R. 2014. The African Garrison State: Human rights and political development in Eritrea. Woodbridge: James Currey.

Weldemariam, M.A. 2014. 'Nation Building Process in Eritrea: Challenges and opportunities', Master of Arts in Managing Peace and Security in Africa, Addis Ababa: Addis Ababa University.

Wikipedia, 2015. 'Civil-military relations' available at *http://www.en.wikipedia.org/wiki/* Accessed 17 June 2015.

Wiseman, J.A. 1995. *Democracy and Political Change in Sub-Saharan Africa*, London: Routledge.

Chapter 5

Democratisation in Kenya: The ambiguity of foreign military assistance

by Henrik Laugesen

In the scramble for successful democratic transition in Africa, it is increasingly argued that the military in well-established democracies are vital institutions for changing autocracies into democracies. One of the latest voices, retired United States Navy Admiral Dennis Blair (2013), a former director of National Intelligence, argues that influencing dictatorships through military interaction like foreign military assistance (FMA) is a powerful tool in changing autocracies. Military-to-military relations between democracies and autocracies are viewed as important catalysts in the democratic transition. Neglect the 'guys with the guns' and a peaceful transition towards democracy is impeded. As Blair (2013) states:

> During education and training courses, through rewards and sanctions, and in professional and personal discussions, the military forces of democratic countries can convey by both example and persuasion the advantage that the armed forces of democracies enjoy, and encourage their peers to support democratic transition in their countries.

In continuation of this argumentation, the Danish Ministry of Defence's website states: 'The overall purpose for the Danish Defence being in Africa is to support a democratic development.'[1] This indicates the clear ambition of a democratic effect resulting from military cooperation. This chapter will investigate the alleged positive correlation between the role of the military and democratisation, and argue that FMA can only peripherally target socioeconomic insufficiencies and, therefore, that the effect of FMA on democratisation is ambiguous, if existing at all. In the process of democratic transition, where old power structures and traditional cultural patterns are increasingly challenged by new ways of thinking, the African military often finds itself fixed in the traditional 'colonial role', as a tool to keep power in the hands of the rulers and not as a catalyst for democracy. As we shall see, FMA rarely changes that.

Approaching any civil-military relation (CMR) analytically usually starts from one of two classic perspectives. The first, often referred to as the 'Problematique'[2], is represented by

Huntington and Janowitz[3] as the most predominant voices in the debate on CMR since the 1960s. The bottom line of this debate is the degree of civilian meddling in military affairs, or, as Huntington puts it, the 'division of labour'. Whereas Huntington argues for military autonomy (i.e. a minimum of civil meddling in military affairs) as the best approach to political neutrality and voluntary subordination of the military, Janowitz points out the unavoidable politicisation of the military and the need for accommodating the military profession in accordance with an ever-changing world.

The second perspective, 'modernization', takes quite an opposite approach. Instead of focusing on how society gains voluntary subordination of the military, it observes how the military acts as a catalyst for development. In the mid- and late 1960s, Andrew Andreski assessed the impact of military organisations on social structures by introducing the concept of the Military Participation Ratio (MPR): the proportion of the general population in military service. The idea was to view the military as the 'school of the nation'; training and education, and the structural and organisational merits applied by the military would eventually lead to economic growth.

However, neither of these approaches seems to be useful as analytical framework. Both tend to view the military as an isolated and homogeneous institution controlled by society, which makes very little allowance for the socioeconomic dynamics that always affect government institutions. As pointed out by Jarstad and Sisk (2008:251): 'The analysis or context-specific assessment of war-to-democracy transition is needed for a theoretical understanding of a particular context.' In other words, no institution, including the military, can be viewed as an isolated and homogeneous institution completely unaffected by the context in which it exists. Accordingly, my analytical approach will be context-based and my argument on the effect of FMA will be in three parts. First, with reference to data from the Freedom House index and my fieldwork, I will argue that Kenya's democratic identity suffers from a lack of inclusiveness. The contemporary socioeconomic context strongly affects the ability to embrace all Kenyans in the democratic process, leaving it operating in an unbalanced democratic environment. Second, the armed forces are the recipient of FMA and the professional military position of the armed forces in the Kenyan context is pivotal for understanding its utilisation. I will argue that the Kenyan Defence Force's (KDF's) present professional military position does not enable it to act as a catalyst for democratic transition. Moreover, the analysis seems to suggest that the professional military position and the supposedly embedded FMA ability to support democracy are also hampered by socioeconomic conditions. Kenyan rulers have sacrificed long-term institutionalisation and professionalism of the military for short-term political survival. However, just because any traceable democratic effect of FMA appears to be missing, does not mean that it is impossible to create. Third, I will evaluate the utility of selected FMA programmes in order to demonstrate that even the most ambitious FMA can only peripherally target socioeconomic insufficiencies and that its effect on democratisation is therefore ambiguous, if existing at all.

THE KENYA CASE

Kenya appears to be unique in that it is a recipient of a substantial amount of FMA[4] and is progressing with democratic transition.[5] This is important because, without one of the two variables, the effect of FMA cannot be established. Furthermore, if the positive effects of FMA were not traceable in this relatively stable democratic transition in Kenya, it would be difficult to imagine FMA having an effect anywhere else. Metaphorically speaking, if the crop cannot grow in the most fertile ground, where can it grow? The number of countries in democratic transition in Africa is increasing, and those countries in transition are becoming more democratic. In recent years, African democracy appears to have flourished and elections have become commonplace[6], accentuating Ghana in west, South Africa in the south and Kenya in the east. Kenya has uncoiled the idea of democracy to an unprecedented level, although great challenges still lie ahead.[7] Three milestones are worth noticing: the introduction of the multiparty system from 1992, the passing of the new constitution in 2010, and the initiation of a process of devolution as a consequence of the election in 2013.

Since 1996, the Kenya's Armed Forces have received extensive military training and financial support which have enabled it to enlarge its military capacity considerably. Kenya is one of the top five global recipients of US State Department security assistance (Blanchard, 2013:16-17). Kenya is an active partner with the US in military-to-military programmes such as International Military Education and Training (IMET) and Africa Contingency Operations Training and Assistance (ACOTA). Further, Kenya is hosting the East African Standby Force Coordination Mechanism (EASFCOM) and has, with support from the UK, trained one (out of three) Rapid Deployment Capabilities (RDC) units that fulfilled an essential role in establishing the EASF reaction force. The combination of East Africa and Kenya, therefore, is a unique case for testing the extent, if any at all, to which there is a connection between advancing democratisation and the substantial amount of FMA given to the country.

DEMOCRACY IN KENYA

The democratic ambition of Kenya was set out in the constitution approved by the people in 2010. The constitution reflects universal democratic values such as human rights, equality, freedom, social justice and rule of law. As always, the idea of measuring democracy is a controversial matter and, without some sort of common acceptance of what democracy is, it becomes meaningless. However, the characteristic of the Kenyan constitution makes possible a departure from a theoretical understanding of democracy as suggested by Dahl (1973): When countries are in a process of democratisation, meaning moving forward from one position of democracy towards another, there seems to be primarily two ways for that particular country to choose. In the process of democratisation, the road towards full democracy can either begin with increasing liberalisation and later expand to include larger parts of the population, or it can take its starting point as including the whole of the population and slowly increasing the extent of liberal rights. But how does is one approach distinguished from the other? Among the literature on the subject, there are ambitious attempts to measure the level of democracy – for example, by institutions such as Freedom House[8] and the Economic Intelligence Unit.[9] Even though these indices are usually criticised for being too superficial and leaving out important analytical and technical details (Munck, 2009), to a large extent problems of causal inference have overshadowed the equally important problems of conceptualisation and measurement, which represent some of the few possible ways to understand the democratic transition. In the 2010 constitution, Kenyans put forward their latest democratic ambition and, by using Freedom House concepts of measurement, one can begin to identify how far they have progressed in their democratic transition.

Freedom in the World, Freedom House

The Freedom in the World Index is the most used comparative assessment. Freedom House (FH) has collected data since 1973, which offers high sensitivity on democratic fluctuation over time. The index can produce both the 'track record' and a high number of respondents needed for a valid assessment. In Figure 1, selected data is presented from Freedom in the

World reports published between 1996 and 2012.[10] The criteria for selecting the presented values were 'substantial change in the FH rating' to uncover as much 'democratic fluctuation' as possible. An interesting feature related to this index is that 'electoral processes' are attached to the measurement of participation (or 'political rights' as it is called by FH). By mixing participation during election with participation between elections, the index provides a strong and comprehensive indicator for participation. The biggest leap forward along the axis of participation occurred between 1998 and 2002, when multiparty democracy was introduced, and represented the ending of the Moi period and the consequent shift in rating from 'not free' to 'partly free'. Between 2003 and 2012, however, we find a major drawback in participation (political rights), likely inflicted by post-election violence in 2007.

Figure 1: Selected measurements from Freedom House (FH) between 1996 and 2012

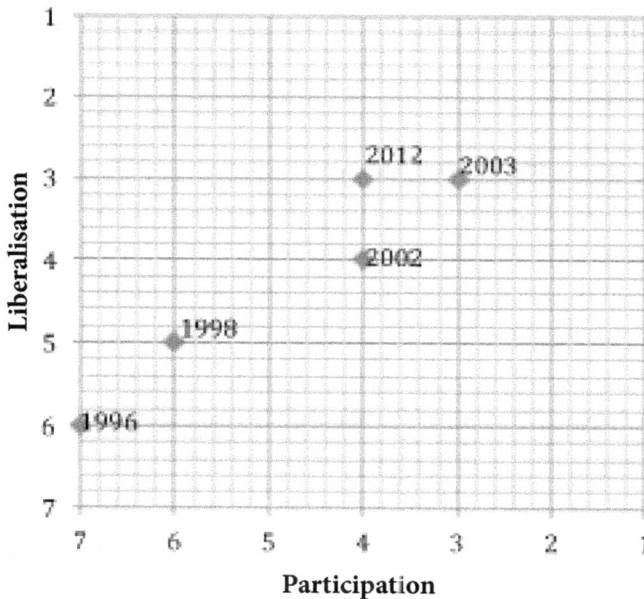

Despite the relatively strong and comprehensive indicator on participation in the FH surveys, the surprising conclusion is an unbalanced democratic development profile – unbalanced in the sense that democratic development seems to be stronger on the axis of liberalisation and weaker on the axis of participation. In other words, Kenya's democratic identity is characterised by an increasing exclusion trend.

Exclusiveness in Kenya

The trend of exclusiveness suggested in the FH analysis has been supported and, to a certain degree, consolidated in my research. According to the majority of respondents, corruption and ethnicity are salient points because of their dissemination, recognition and impact.

Local and national politicians engage in misconduct within the financial and administrative arenas. Corruption among civil servants is well known (Kenya Law Society, 2013), and the consequences of uneven distribution of land and national financial support reduces political participation. Irrespective of which ethnic background the respondent comes from, or what level of education the respondent has, very little, if any, trust is placed in politicians when it comes to the handling of official funds. This seems to be a very clear and unambiguous statement from respondents, but why? During an interview in January 2013, among other things, the send-off package[11] introduced by the Kenyan parliament in which parliamentarians had awarded themselves life-long diplomatic status, a state funeral, and other privileges were discussed. The respondent[12] stated: 'I think you have to look at our political system as an extractive system so people are getting in to get out ... to what they can benefit for personal gain.'

This statement indicates a corrupt political system where the primary goal for a politician is personal gain instead of serving the people of Kenya. We can recognise this kind of system from many places around the world, but it does not necessarily involve corruption. Another respondent addressed corruption more directly: 'Because corruption issues in Kenya that is still a big problem. Just to give you an example of the utilisation of the Constituency Development Funds[13], it is a lot of money and most of those constituencies and most of those MPs failed the test of implementation so ... some of them tried opportunities of ... making underground deals engaging in corrupt acts, looting the money ...'.

In general, the interviews lined up a profile of government institutions involved in corruption. This trend is coherent with several other surveys and reports: In 2012, Transparency International rated Kenya number 137 out of 176 countries involved in the survey.[14] Also in 2012, the Kenyan Police were ranked the four most corrupt institution in East Africa – not a very flattering position for Kenya. Unfortunately, it appears that corruption has been a widespread phenomenon for many years. According to a report from the Truth, Justice and Reconciliation Commission released in May 2013, there is a long history of grand corruption[15] in Kenya that has deprived the people of Kenya of millions of Shillings – money that was meant to be spent on securing their constitutional rights and ability to participate in democratic procedures. The report mentions four serious cases: the Ken Ren Scandal 1971, the Goldenberg Scandal 1991, the Charter House Scandal 2004, and the Anglo-Leasing Scandal 2004.

A 2013 report from the African Centre for Open Governance (AfriCOG) directs a fierce critique of the administration of the Arid Lands Resource Management Project (ALRMP). The project was set up to mitigate the effects of drought and poverty in arid and semi-arid areas, especially in north-east Kenya, an area already burdened by severe poverty-related problems. For Tana River alone, the suspected fraud amounted to 44% of the total amount pledged to the area. Allegedly, the money was used to pay fictive expenditures and thereby funnelled into the wrong pockets.

The presence of corruption is a fact in Kenya and, judging from available reports and surveys, occurs on an extensive scale. In a democratic context, participation is much more than having the opportunity to place your vote every fourth year. According to the Kenyan constitution, it is also about equality and inclusiveness, the ability to fully participate in the democratic system and enjoy the constitutional rights. The United Nations Office on Drugs and Crime (UNODC) describes corruption as a complex social, political and economic phenomenon that affects all societies all over the world.[16] It argues that corruption undermines democratic institutions, slows economic development and contributes to government instability. Corruption works against democratic transition and participation, and violates the very fundamental ambition stated in Kenya's constitution.

Ethnic patronage –where political or economic power is used for select ethnic groupings – has been recognised since liberation in 1963, and creates a high level of disapproval and exclusion from the democratic process (Haugerud, 1995). Since the time of Jomo Kenyatta, ethnicity has been a contested political tool (Orvis, 2001), and judging from the voting patterns of the March 2013 election, ethnicity still has a significant presence in Kenyan politics (Lynch, 2013). There is a deep mistrust of politicians' ability to not compromising any public or official interest in favour of personal interest. It appears that, irrespective of ethnic, social or educational background, the idea of a politician who works for the country and not for him- or herself is an illusion. One respondent offers what looks like the beginning of an explanation:

> *They [referring to children whose parents were involved in politics] were left with this big shoe and it's a curse. It's a curse … I don't know whether it's a curse or they like or they don't … but … you feel … the society or the community feels*

like you just have to step in there or you have an arrogant attitude because your
father was this you were cut to lead people ... I think [this] is a phenomena that
we are seeing in the whole of Africa. Kabila [tribe] and Kabila [tribe] ... you
know that kind of a thing and now we have Uhuru Kenyatta.[17]

At least two questions arise from this statement. First, why is the community expecting
a certain family name to rule, and, second, what is the 'Kabila phenomenon'? It appears to
be part of a survival strategy, building on an interdependent relationship between a leader
and his community. The same respondent explains it in terms of spending many years living in a Nairobi slum:

It's where the politics started ... When I look back in the slums the person who
would become a politician is the first person who owned a shop in that area or
the first person who owned a [car] ... whenever somebody gets sick they would
take them to the hospital ... it doesn't matter whether you pay him to take
you there but he's afforded the opportunity to show that he has something that
others don't have. And because they feel like ... oh he has done us a favour or
something ... so it is up to you ... or because if you feel as a shopkeeper you owe
him because you haven't paid something ... whenever there is an opportunity
you flatter him and you tell him 'Why don't you stand here?' ... we will give you
this opportunity.[18]

Judging from the respondent's statement, interdependency is based on the shopkeeper
providing services for the community in return for the support of the community. Sub-
stituting the shopkeeper with Uhuru Kenyatta, as suggested by the respondent, we find a
family that successfully has provided services for a particular community in return for its
support for many years. The survival strategy is clear: by keeping your 'big man' in power,
your chances of survival increase.

What is the Kabila phenomenon? *Kabila* means 'tribe' in Swahili. Here, the respondent is very likely referring to ethnic preferences in Kenya. Seeing ethnicity in the light of
the survival strategy is only logical, and the ethnic-based community is seen as a way of
strengthening the survival strategy – choosing a leader from their own ethnic grouping.
However, in democratic transition, it is vital that Kenyan loyalty is placed with the government (legal-rational) and not with the community (patrimonial). Apparently, though, this
is not the case. Given that fact that almost half of the Kenyan population announces loyalty
to their ethnic community before anything else gives rise to concern, at least from a demo-

cratic point of view. The feeling of being excluded in the democratic process is a personal one as well as a collective one, and works directly against the idea of participation presented in the Kenyan constitution. On a personal level it weakens personal trust and encourages individuals to seek protection outside the state institutions. On a community level it feeds the idea of the client as the only viable survival strategy and raises hope for a patron to reach power by a shortcut.

Conclusion

Combining quantitative and qualitative investigation reveals a trend of democratic exclusiveness. Thus, the argument of exclusiveness has to be considered a reliable contribution in understanding Kenya's democratic identity and the challenges of contemporary democratic transition. Establishing an argument on Kenya's democratic identity also lays open reflections of the socioeconomic context in which democracy in Kenya exists, which is heavily influenced by corruption and ethnic dynamics. Not only does this context affect democracy as an institution, but also the military's ability to develop military professionalism and support democratic transition.

THE PROFESSIONAL MILITARY POSITION

Kenya's present military position does not enable its defence force to act as a catalyst for democratic transition. Moreover, the analysis presented below seems to suggest that the professional military position and the proposed embedded ability to support democracy is hampered by the same socioeconomic conditions of corruption and ethnic tension as presented previously.

Professionalism

The armed forces in Africa must be 'professionalised'. According to Howe (2001), who wrote about the US African Crisis Response Initiative (ACRI), the US FMA contribution to democracy was to professionalise the army. He emphasised that interoperability, the ability to operate with others through common doctrines and logistics, was paramount to African countries in gaining legitimacy as reliable partners on both regional and international levels. A serious attempt to professionalise the KDF was made by Kenya itself. Lieutenant General Daudi Tonje could very well be described as the 'moderniser' in the sense that he challenged the KDF's colonial heritage in least in three areas. First, Tonje directed the military's attention towards external threats by organising the army leadership into a dual structure with an Eastern Command and a Western Command. Each command would train and equip for the purpose of defending Kenya against outside threats (Somalia and Uganda). Second, he introduced 'reading and writing' for soldiers, a phenomenon known from modernisation theory, to raise the perception of the army as the 'school of nations'. Third, he reformed the system for advancing in the ranks. Instead of advancement based on corruption or ethnicity, it should be based on professional qualification. In addition, a position could not be held for longer than four years.[19] Tonje's attempt to professionalise was sensational in the history of the armed forces in Kenya. The effect, however, was transient and eventually ousted by socioeconomic factors.

As early as 1960, American sociologist William J. Goode was one of the few people who had undertaken extensive research on professionalism, especially within the organisation of the health care system, which in many ways is comparable to military organisations. The hierarchical approach to leadership in particular is salient. Goode (1960) operated in two dimensions when defining the idea of a profession. The first dimension was described as 'a prolonged specialised training in a body of abstract knowledge' and the second dimension 'a collective or service orientation'. The first dimension is best explained by focusing on the meritocratic structure in a profession. To what extent does the profession determine its own standards of education and training? How strongly does the professional representative affiliate to this? To what extent is evaluation and control an internal matter? The higher a profession rates within this meritocratic structure, the more professional it becomes. The second dimension is best described by the degree of collectivity or service orientation towards the society. Goode does not use much paper defining this particular dimension, but he does highlight that 'social acceptance' from the society is a mandatory part of rising from an occupation to a profession. Without social acceptance and public acknowledgement, a profession cannot reach the level of 'self policing' required for a very high degree of professionalism. Today we recognise this in medical institutions, fire departments and in some countries' police and military. This dimension of social acceptance in professionalism can, to some extent, be seen as the gateway and most likely opportunity for the military to have a democratic impact on society. The process of developing a profession therefore begins with a strong meritocratic structure, followed by an increasing level of service orientation, and ending with social acceptance and public acknowledgement.

Through the author's own work, the theoretical approach initiated by Goode has been developed and refined. On the meritocratic dimension, however, the author takes a similar stance to Goode, focusing on identification and affiliation to the military profession, education and training, and evaluation and control. The author also includes variables such as integrity, political control and legal rights during service (which Goode does not specifically mention), which serve as important indictors for the social acceptance and public acknowledgement a profession must develop to reach the highest degree of professionalism. Generally speaking, the higher the rating within these two dimensions the more professional an organisation can claim to be.

The military in Kenya have not yet reached the level of social acceptance and public acknowledgement (democratic interdependence[20]) required of a profession. Consequently, the idea that the military operates as a catalyst for democracy seems to be purely theoretical. The reason, as we shall see, is not surprisingly found in the socioeconomic context of corruption and ethnicity. As indicated by this survey[21], meritocratic structure is slightly stronger than service orientation. In responding to the topic of integrity, everyone who participated in the survey agreed that acting with integrity influenced the military's ability to operate professionally. This indicates that integrity most likely has a directly proportional relationship with professionalism.

Figure 2: Survey result (ACOTA) Nairobi, January 2014

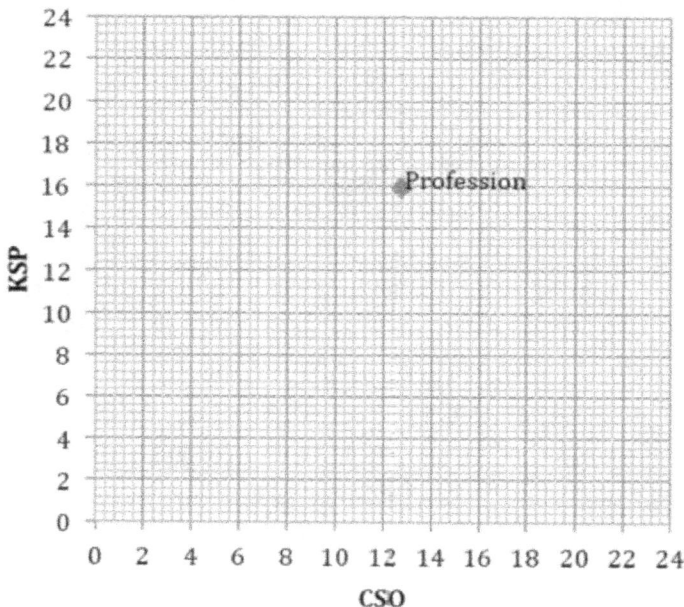

Interestingly, when it comes to implementing integrity in military practice, things looks slightly different. More than half (65%) inferred that there is room for improvement, but a worrying 22% disagreed. This means that 87% either partly practice or choose to ignore the idea of integrity in the line of duty. Professional integrity involves making personal choices based on moral and ethical considerations of what is right or wrong, and unfortunately it appears that from the very first day young men and women engage with the military in Kenya, their sense of right and wrong is challenged. One male respondent went to a KDF recruitment camp in Kakamega for three years in a row, but was never recruited because he could not pay a bribe. During the final medical check the doctor examine the recruits for fallen arches (flat feet). Writing the amount of money you are willing to pay on the soles of your feet is considered a discrete way of communicating with recruitment board officials. Unfortunately, this does not appear to be an isolated case. A KDF Ethics and Anti-Corruption Committee press statement dated 16 August 2012 acknowledges credible information about a similar case in Borabu where KSh40 000 was paid for facilitating the recruitment of a candidate. However, this seems to be only the first step in crossing the fine line between right and wrong. Other articles and reports[22] indicate that in-service corruption, from conducting military operations on the ground to administrative functions at ministerial level, is very much present. The *Hiiraan Online*, an independent newspaper offering coverage on news in Somalia, alleges that Kenyan forces stationed in Somalia are involved in corruption. After Operation Linda Nchi (October 2011), the KDF, in cooperation with forces from the African Union Mission in Somalia (AMISOM), took control of the Port of Kismayo. It was anticipated that, with their control, smuggling would be reduced, but, according to Hiiraan Online, the facts on the ground suggested otherwise. Sugar imports into Somalia are mainly financed by the export of charcoal[23] to the Middle East, and when KDF took over Kismayo, it disregarded a UN request to uphold the ban of the export of millions of tons of charcoal through the port. Consequently, the importation of sugar and, hence, its smuggling to Kenya has continued with the alleged knowledge of and benefit to the KDF. This picture is, to a large extent, supported by the Transparency International Defence and Security Programme (TI-DSP). According to its last survey, only moderate transparency has been achieved during military operations since 2011. Military intelligence units are officially assigned to address corruption risk, which is a procedure with significant shortcomings. Furthermore, TI-DSP suggests that the military might receive facilitation payments when the army is digging boreholes in arid and semi-arid areas (people may be inclined to bribe officers to get services at the borehole). So, the deviation between knowing and doing among respondents may very well express their knowledge of how corruption is violating their professional integrity. Corruption, however, is not the only variable challenging the soldier when making a personal professional choice of what is right or wrong. Ethnicity has had a great impact on why the military has not yet fully reached the social acceptance and public acknowledgement required of a profession. Currently it is a constitutional requirement that the composition of the command of defence forces reflects regional and ethnic diversity, but this is not reflected throughout the military organisation. The Pan African need for the military's loyalty to the personal ruler gave rise to corruption and to ethnicisation of the military, and Kenya is no exception (Howe, 2001). The idea that ethnicity matters in a military unit originates from the recruitment procedures of the colonial army. To some extent it was believed that some African communities had 'martial qualities' and they became the natural choice of a soldier (Parsons, 2003). Since the days of independence, different rulers then have reflected their particular ethnic preference in the composition and organisation of military and paramilitary units. A good example is the reorganisation by Moi following the 1982 coup attempt. Moi was a Kalenjin, and he dramatically increased the demographic footprint of the army to avoid it turning against him. Senior officers are often promoted without having completed basic training courses; 'cronyism, tribalism or ethnicity may be considered instead.'[24]

Conclusion

There is no evidence to suggest that the military is capable of acting as a catalyst for democracy. Moreover, the analysis suggests that the professional military position and the proposed embedded ability to support democracy is hampered by the socioeconomic conditions of corruption and ethnic tension. Since liberation, Kenyan rulers have sacrificed the long-term institutionalisation and professionalisation of the military for short-term political survival. Civil control of the armed forces has been obtained through military corruption and ethnic selection, and any given government in office has never broached this topic. Despite the fact that FMA was given to Kenya, the idea that the military has been operating as a catalyst for democracy appears to be purely theoretical; it has not produced any traceable effect on the process of democratisation. Findings thus far support the general argument that the effect of FMA on democratisation is ambiguous, if it exists at all. Although a theoretical connection is possibly, FMA interventions left the need for social acceptance and public acknowledgement unattended.

FOREIGN MILITARY ASSISTANCE IN KENYA

Even the most extensive FMA programmes have only peripherally targeted socioeconomic insufficiencies, with disputable results. Investigations into the idea of FMA have to begin by taking a closer look at the content of FMA.[25] There is no universal definition of FMA, therefore it needs to be understood as everything from providing financial budget support to engaging in more ambitious political partnerships involving strategic defence planning and military education. In order to evaluate the theoretical utility of FMA programmes in promoting social acceptance and public acknowledgement, it is necessary to categorise the different FMA programmes according to the variables presented by Goode: knowledge-based meritocratic structures and value-based service-oriented structures. It is the author's suggestion that all types of FMA programmes to some degree contain both variables (as represented in Figure 3), although very few enjoy their full effect. Using the matrix, it is possible to identify what kind of FMA programme will best support the military as an important catalyst in the democratic transition.

Figure 3.

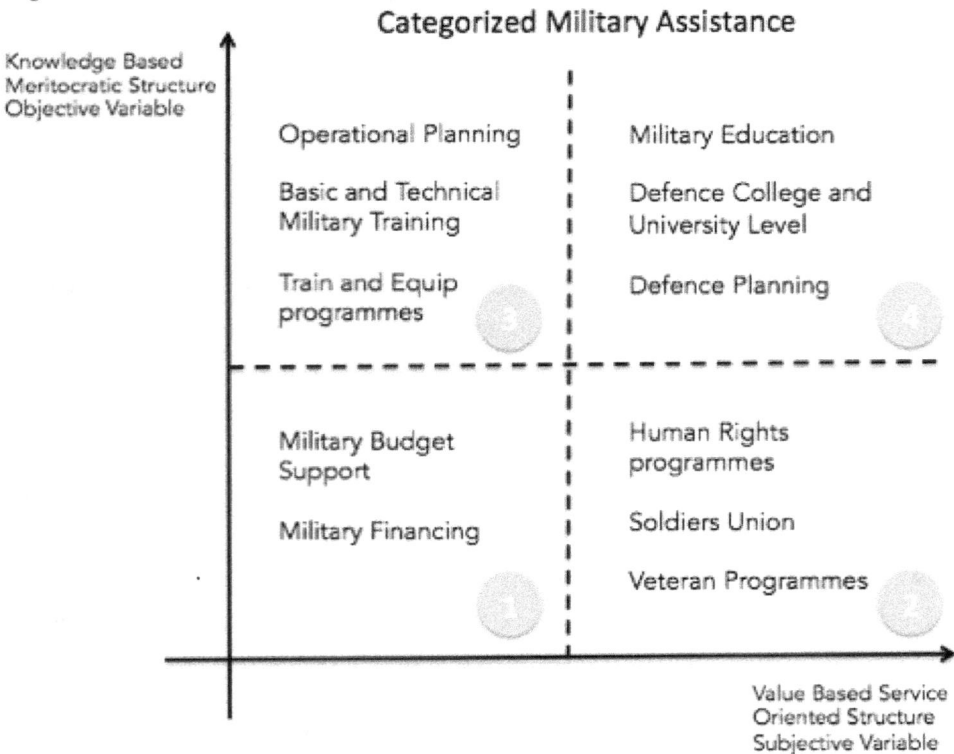

Categorized Military Assistance

Knowledge Based
Meritocratic Structure
Objective Variable

Operational Planning

Basic and Technical
Military Training

Train and Equip
programmes

Military Education

Defence College and
University Level

Defence Planning

Military Budget
Support

Military Financing

Human Rights
programmes

Soldiers Union

Veteran Programmes

Value Based Service
Oriented Structure
Subjective Variable

According to the categorised military assistance matrix presented in Figure 3, increasing social acceptance and public acknowledgement is best supported by squares 2 and 4, since these programmes, at least from a theoretical point of view, are estimated to have the highest value-based service-oriented content. The obvious conclusion is that, if military-to-military relations are meant to support the military in being important catalysts in the democratic transition, the bulk of the programmes executed must origin from squares 2 an 4, or at least contain various elements from these squares. To get closer to an answer about whether this is the case in Kenya, every significant programme and donor ambition has to be examined.

FMA in Kenya

Security assistance from donor countries to Kenya has developed steadily over the last 25 years. The so-called 'war on terror' has been a catalyst in boosting military relation with East Africa, in particular Kenya. Kenya ranks among the top US foreign aid recipients in the world, receiving significant development, humanitarian, and security assistance (Blanchard, 2013). According to Human Rights Watch (2012), significant donors to Kenya's security forces include the US, the UK, Japan, Denmark, Sweden, France, the Netherlands, and the UNODC.

The US and Kenya have had an enduring diplomatic partnership since Kenya's independence from the UK in December 1963.[26] The general US assistance strategy is guided by four strategic objectives: strengthen democratic institutions; spur economic growth, trade and investment; advance peace and security; and promote opportunity and development.

The USA's engagement in Kenya is extensive in both financial support and programme diversity. Specific data on the Kenyan defence budget is hard to obtain, but the author's estimate based on available statistics[27] and interviews in Nairobi is that the USA–Kenya relation alone constitutes just over half of all FMA in Kenya. The USA–Kenya relation is thus considered an ample and suitable example for generalisation.

Kenya is among the largest recipients of US security assistance in Africa.[28] Since around 2000, US military assistance to Kenya has focused on improving the country's capability to control its land and sea borders, and to counter terrorism. Kenya also purchases military equipment through the US Foreign Military Sales (FMS) programme, including fighter aircraft, helicopters and air force computer systems. According to a report from the Congressional Research Service,[29] foreign assistance to Kenya has reached almost USD1 billion annually in recent years.[30] The US State Department requested USD568 million in 2014 to sustain ten main security programmes currently running in Kenya. Five of these programmes address security issues, but only two – FMF and IMET – involve KDF and, thus, have a potentially positive effect on increasing social acceptance and public acknowledgement. Furthermore, these two programs constitute two extremes in the author's categorisation of FMA.

FMA programme analysis

On the State Department website, the FMF programme is described as follows:

> *FMF is a critical foreign policy tool for promoting US interests around the world by ensuring that coalition partners and friendly foreign governments are equipped and trained to work toward common security goals and share burdens in joint missions. In that regard, FMF is vital to supporting US coalition partners in the war on terrorism.*

The State Department continues:

> *By increasing demand for US systems, FMF also contributes to a strong US defense industrial base, an important element of US national defense strategy that reduces cost for Department of Defense acquisitions and secures more jobs for American workers.*

Since 2010, approximately USD5 million has been spend on purchasing equipment and funding training in Kenya. In relation to the ambition stated in the assistance strategy and the four strategic objectives presented earlier,[31] it is relatively easy to establish that this programme has the biggest impact on economic growth, trade and investment, even though the budget is relatively small. Thus, the programme presumably has the lowest impact on KDF ability to support democratic transition. Although one of the objectives of this programme is to maintain support for democratically elected governments that share values similar to the US in terms of democracy, human rights and regional stability, it does not change the impression dramatically. On the contrary, according to Transparency International UK, among others, it is more likely that funding military procurements in Kenya will slow down democratic transition. Transparency in the Kenyan National Defence budget is low and actuates corruption. The defence procurement cycle, from assessment of needs, through contract implementation and sign-off, all the way to asset disposal, is not transparent to the public.[32] Usually issues of national security are invoked to restrict public access. In some cases, such as procurement of classified equipment, this may be necessary, but, according to Transparency International, never to the extent present in Kenya. Lack of transparency in military procurement leaves room for corruption, including the establishment of sham companies and oversized tenders. Such a scam was revealed in 2006, involving the construction of Nexus (military communication centre) when USD37 million was directed to a Dutch Company, bypassing the Department of Defence's tender committee.[33] If social acceptance and public acknowledgement of a profession is the ambition, this FMA programme clearly does not address relevant issues. As Figure 3 shows, this and other financial support programmes are categorised in square 1, which has the lowest impact on knowledge-based meritocratic structures and value-based service-oriented structures. Presented in the context of exclusiveness, and given the current professional military position, FMF will most likely do more harm than good in the democratic transition.

On the US State Department website the IMET programme is described as follows:

> The International Military Education and Training (IMET) program is an instrument of US national security and foreign policy and a key component of US security assistance that provides training and education on a grant basis to students from allied and friendly nations. In addition to improving defense capabilities, IMET facilitates the development of important professional and personal relationships, which have proven to provide US access and influence in a critical sector of society that often plays a pivotal role in supporting, or transitioning to, democratic governments. IMET's traditional purpose of promoting more professional militaries around the world through training has taken on greater importance as an effective means to strengthen military alliances and the international coalition against terrorism.

The IMET programme provides funding to train foreign military and civilian leaders at approximately 150 institutions in the USA. During the administrations of both George W. Bush and Barack Obama, the programme experienced a dramatic increase in funding to a budget of more than USD102 million for the 2013 financial year. In 2012, participating partners reached the level of 47 African countries involved in this programme. Since 2010, approximately USD4 million has been spend on IMET training and education in Kenya. Furthermore, as pointed out by the State Department, IMET has had a positive effect on participants and recipient countries beyond actual training, which plays an important role in the IMET programme. From the beginning, this programme appears to have had promising potential to move the KDF further along the axis of social acceptance and public acknowledgement. The programme as it is presented today is generally twofold. It offers scholarships to students in the field of technical training (e.g. technical and operational training for officers on equipment) and professional military education (e.g. in specific military issues like leadership or pilot training). Examples of E-IMET courses include its Advanced Management Program Course (AMP), Civil Military Operations, Democratic Sustainment, Civil Affairs, Law of War, and Military Accounting.[34] The E-IMET programme has the potential to embed the alleged democratising effect, but, even with a fairly high degree of social acceptance and public acknowledgement potential, there is no guarantee that exposure to Western values and the professionalism of the US military will automatically have an effect. Mali's Amadou Touré, who overthrew the country's democratically elected president in a coup in 2012, received military training in the US (through the IMET programme) on multiple occasions.

The effect of FMA appears to be ambiguous, and a report compiled by the US Government Accountability Office (GAO) in October 2011 confirms such. The report points out two main problems with IMET. First, GAO suggests that the agencies providing training should take steps to emphasise general human rights. In reviewing 29 country plans for countries ranked 'not free' by Freedom House, only eight cited human rights-related topics as objectives. From the perspective of increasing social acceptance and public acknowledgement, a level of understanding of human rights is essential to counter ethnic grouping inside the unit organisation. Moving soldiers' understanding of rights from an ethnic point of view to human point of view is required to create social acceptance and public acknowledgement. Second, GOA points out that programme monitoring and evaluation ability is severely limited due to the lack of a performance plans stating measurable programme objectives, and incomplete information about students after graduation. If the intention is to push KDF along the axis of social acceptance and public acknowledgement by teaching civil-military operations, democratic sustainment, civil affairs, law of war and military accounting, this demands that programme monitoring and evaluation be put in place. The IMET programme is one of the best and most ambitious attempts to educate African officers that has been seen so far. However, judging from the GOA report, there are serious doubts about the extent to which the effectiveness of the programmes can be raised. As the matrix shows, this and other educational programmes are categorised in square 4, which, at least from a theoretical point of view, should have the highest impact on knowledge-based meritocratic structures and value-based service-oriented structures. However, in practice, the effect of IMET is ambiguous and it supports the argument that FMA can only peripherally target socioeconomic insufficiencies. Thus, the effect of FMA on democratisation is therefore ambiguous, if it exists at all.

Conclusion

Contemplating the various examples of FMA highlights some interesting perspectives: What really is the effect of this type of programme and what can we realistically expect of FMA when the socioeconomic context is so 'infected', as in the Kenyan case? Could Blair be right when he argues that influencing dictatorships through military interaction is a powerful tool in changing autocracies, and military-to-military relations between democracies and autocracies are viewed as important catalysts in the democratic transition? The analysis shows that military financing most likely has the opposite effect and that not everyone who joins the IMET programme is receptive to the influence of American values.

CONCLUSION

In this chapter it has been argued that FMA can only peripherally target socioeconomic insufficiencies and that the effect of FMA on democratisation is therefore ambiguous, if it exists at all.

First, the democratic identity of Kenya is unbalanced. In Kenya's contemporary socioeconomic context, liberalisation precedes inclusiveness, therefore the argument over exclusiveness must be considered a valid contribution in understanding Kenya's democratic identity. By establishing the argument on Kenya's democratic identity, the author exposes reflections of the socioeconomic context in which democracy in Kenya exists – one heavily influenced by corruption and ethnic dynamics.

Second, the KDF's professional military position is strongly challenged and the military in Kenya has not yet reached the level of social acceptance and public acknowledgement ascribed to a profession. Consequently, no evidence has been found that the military is capable of acting as a catalyst for democracy. Moreover, the analysis suggests that the professional military position and the proposed embedded ability to support democracy is hampered by the socioeconomic conditions of corruption and ethnic tension.

Third, the evaluation of various examples of FMA suggests that military financing does not address corruption. Most likely, FMF has the opposite effect, and not everyone who joins the IMET programme is receptive to the influence of American values.

Thus, the final conclusion is that FMA can only peripherally target socioeconomic insufficiencies and the effect of FMA on democratisation is therefore ambiguous, if, in fact, it exists at all.

NOTES

1. See http://www.fmn.dk/videnom/Pages/Langsigtetstabilitetgennemkapacitetsopbygning.aspx.

2. The 'Problematique' refers to the dilemma between military and civil institutions. The state needs the military to protect it from outside threats, but how does the state protect itself from the military? See Feaver (1996: 149).

3. Huntington (1957) and Janowitz (1960) are the most predominant works on this matter.

4. Kenya ranks among the top US foreign aid recipients in the world, receiving significant development, humanitarian and security assistance.

5. International Crises Group: 'Despite various shortcomings and allegations of irregularities, Kenyans averted a repeat of the 2007-2008 post-election violence.' National Democratic institute: 'Despite some flaws in the electoral process, domestic and international election observers characterised the polls as mostly credible.' National Endowment for Democracy: 'After teetering on the brink of civil war in the aftermath of post-election violence in 2007, Kenya achieved significant reforms which helped to promote a peaceful electoral process in 2013 that contributed to a strengthening of its democracy.'

6. According to *The Democracy Index*, compiled by the Economist Intelligence Unit, the average democracy rating for sub-Saharan countries is slowly increasing.

7. International Crises Group: 'However, the conflict drivers that triggered the 2007 bloodshed, including a culture of impunity, land grievances, corruption, ethnic tensions, weak institutions and regional and socio-economic inequality, have yet to be addressed adequately.'

8. *See* http://www.freedomhouse.org/.

9. *See* http://www.eiu.com/Default.aspx.

10. *See* http://www.freedomhouse.org/report/freedom-world/2013/kenya.

11. *See* http://www.vanguardngr.com/2013/01/difference-between-a-politician-and-a-statesman/.

12. For security reasons, the name of the respondent is not disclosed.

13. The mission of the CDF is to provide leadership and policy direction on the optimal utilisation of

devolved funds for equitable development and poverty reduction at the community level. *See* http://www.cdf.go.ke.

14. *See* http://www.transparency.org/country#KEN.

15. The report differs between grand corruption and petty corruption. *See Report of the Truth, Justice and Reconciliation Commission*, May 2013, 2B: 344.

16. *See* http://www.unodc.org/unodc/en/corruption/index.html?ref=menuside.

17. For security reasons, the name of the respondent is not disclosed.

18. For security reasons, the name of the respondent is not disclosed.

19. *See* http://www.timeshighereducation.co.uk/news/soldiers-need-degree-for-promotion/153544. article.

20. Democratic interdependence is understood as the armed forces submission to civil control and the public's need for protection handled in a democratic framework.

21. The survey was conducted among 23 students during staff training (ACOTA) 2013. Further research is necessary and an application has been sent to the KDF regarding this issue.

22. *See* http://www.hiiraan.com/news4/2013/Dec/52290/kenya_how_illicit_trade_in_guns_sugar_thrives_along_porous_border.aspx.

23. According to 2013 figures, charcoal valued between USD35 million and USD50 million is exported from Kismayo annually.

24. *See* http://government.defenceindex.org/results/countries/kenya.

25. Military assistance only as a military (donor) to military (recipient) relation.

26. *See* http://www.state.gov/r/pa/ei/bgn/2962.htm.

27. *See* SIPRI Military Expenditures at http://www.sipri.org/research/armaments/milex/milex_database.

28. *See* Blanchard (2013).

29. Ibid.

30. USD200 million to AMISOM, USD200 million to USAID and USD568 million to security.

31. The four objectives are: strengthen democratic institutions; spur economic growth, trade and investment; advance peace and security; and promote opportunity and development.

32. Transparency International UK, International Defence and Security Programme. Government Defence Anti Corruption Index Kenya, p. 20.

33 *East African Standard*, 10 February 2006, p. 4.

34. *See* http://www.allgov.com/departments/department-of-defense/international-military-education-training-imet?agencyid=7378.

REFERENCES

AfriCOG. 2013. *Kenya's Drought Cash Cow: Lessons from the forensic audit of the World Bank Arid Lands Resource Management Project*. Nairobi: AfriCOG.

Blair, D.C.2013. *Military Engagement, Influencing Armed Forces Worldwide to Support Democratic Transition Vol. 1: Overview and action plan*. Washington DC: Brookings Institution Press.

Blanchard, L. 2013. *US-Kenya Relations: Current Political and Security Issues*. Congressional Research Service. Available at https://www.fas.org/sgp/crs/row/R42967.pdf.

Dahl, R.A. 1973. *Polyarchy: Participation and opposition*. New Haven CT: Yale University Press.

Feaver, P.D. 1996. *Armed Forces and Society*. Winter 1996: p. 149.

Goode, W.J. 1960. 'Encroachment, Charlatanism and the Emerging Profession: Psychology, Sociology and Medicine' in *American Sociological Review*, 25:6, pp. 902–914.

Haugerud, A. 1995. The Culture of Politics in Modern Kenya. Cambridge: Cambridge University Press.

Howe, H.M. 2001. *Ambiguous Order: Military forces in African States*. Boulder London: Lynne Rienner Publishers.

Human Rights Watch. 2012. *Criminal Reprisals: Kenyan Police and Military Abuses against Ethnic Somalis*. Human Rights Watch, Kenya.

Huntington, S.P. 1957. *The Soldier and the State*. Cambridge MA: Harvard University Press.

Janowitz, M. 1960. *The Professional Soldier*. Illinois: Free Press.

Jarstad, A.K. & Sisk, T.D. 2008. *From War to Democracy: Dilemmas of peacebuilding*. New York: Cambridge University Press.

Kenya Law Socety. 2013. Realizing Integrity Law, Walking the Talk: A consolidated analytical account of adversely mentioned persons as contained in publicly available reports. Nairobi: Kenya Law Society.

Lynch, G. 2013. 'The vast majority of Kikuyu and Kalenjin voted for the Jubilee Alliance, and the majority of Luo voted for CORD'. Available at *http://blog.oup.com/2013/04/kenya-ethnic-politics-2013-election/*.

Munck, G.L. 2009. *Measuring Democracy: A bridge between scholarship and politics*. Baltimore: The John Hopkins University Press.

Orvis, S. 2001. 'Moral ethnicity and political tribalism in Kenya's virtual democracy' in *Journal of Asian and African Studies*, 36:1, pp. 17–38.

Parsons, T.H. 2003. *The 1964 Army Mutinies and the Making of Modern East Africa*. Westport CT: Praeger Publishers.

Transparency International UK (London). Government Defence Anti-Corruption Index Kenya.

US Government Accountability Office (GAO). 2011. 'International Military Education and Training: Agencies Should Emphasize Human Rights Training and Improve Evaluations. Available at *http://www.gao.gov/products/GAO-12-123*.

Chapter 6

Challenges of Relationships and Social Identities: The paradox of the consequences of Kenya's military intervention in Somalia

by Irene Limo and Williams Muna

INTRODUCTION

This introduction aims to appraise the context and circumstances under which one of the most volatile militant groups in East Africa, Al Shabaab, was formed, and offers readers a comprehensive background to its dynamics and development. It also provides information on the Somali community under which Al Shabaab formed and continues to thrive. This prelude is significant in shaping and understanding civil-military relations (CMR) and Kenya's involvement in the Somali conflict. It also brings into play international role players and the consequences of their interventions.

Somalia is located in the Horn of Africa, to the north-east of Kenya. While the country is notably poor by world rankings, the Somali people, argued to be largely homogenous, share a long history of culture and language. However, Ahmed and Green (1999) regard this homogenous classification as fallacious. They interpret it as a reductionist trap; evidence of the ignorance of the complexity of Somalia's geopolitical reality. For this reason, they strongly oppose the classical argument that classifies all Somali people as belonging to one ethnic group, speaking the same language, and sharing a common culture and tradition. Ahmed and Green also contend that Somali society has always been divided into nomadic pastoralists in the north and agro pastoralists with distinctively different cultural, linguistic and social structures in the south. Although Somalia can be regarded as one state among independent states, it has largely been characterised by economic hardship, civil wars and terrorist occupation.

In the days when Somalia had a central government, little was known of these Islamic militants; the Somali people enjoyed one culture and one religion. However, after a political vacuum was created following the fall of the central government in 1991, a favorable breeding ground for Islamic militant groups was established. One of the groups that thrived in this vacuum was Al Shabaab, which was founded and began fighting the Somali government in 2006. Its main aim at the time was to establish an Islamic state, ruled under Sharia law. Trying to achieve this aim through the strategies adopted by Al Shabaab, which included war and terror attacks, has caused Somalia and the region to lose many lives and a lot of money.

Initially, fighting by the group was concentrated within Somalia's borders, and thereafter spread its threats and attacks to other countries in the Horn of Africa, recruiting members both locally and internationally. Some were drawn from other African countries, the United States (US), Europe, and other Arabic-speaking countries. The group has communicated its interest in attacking the US and its allies, revealing a potential to execute these threats and thus presenting a real and imminent danger to international security. Based on the progression of attacks mounted by Al Shabaab, both within and beyond Somali borders, it is becoming apparent that this militant group has access to sophisticated and valuable assets to conduct fatal international terror strikes.

Kenya is considered an ally of the US and has, therefore, suffered several terror attacks staged by several terrorist groups, including Al Shabaab. These attacks are hurled against regions making significant contributions to the tourism sector, one of Kenya's largest revenue providers, with the aim of crumpling the industry.

Since 11 December 1963, Kenya and Somalia have established relatively good diplomatic relations. However, Al Shabaab, with its Somali origins, is considered a black spot in this relationship, considering the various attacks and related kidnappings of tourists and aid workers in Kenya by this group and its related associates. Further, Al Shabaab's prolonged cross-border invasions into Kenya offer proof of concerns of an ever-increasing instability and volatility in the East African region. In the latter part of 2011, Kenya, for the first time, launched a direct military intervention inside Somalia: Operation Linda Nchi.

The most immediate and stated factor that acted as a catalyst for Kenya's action was a series of kidnappings, attacks and the killing of foreign tourists on Kenya's coast by suspected Al Shabaab militias. The then minister for internal security motivated the rationale behind this attack as an attempt 'to protect its territorial integrity from foreign aggression' (Akolo, 2012). Al Shabaab has not only shown resilience in fighting Kenyan troops in Somalia after the military intervention, they have also aggressively turned against the Kenyan population.

Al Shabaab believes that Kenya should be punished both for the role it has played in Somalia since 2011, and for being used as an instrument by the West to destabilise Al Shabaab's functions and activities in Somalia. This punishment has manifested itself in incidences such as the terror attack at the Westgate shopping mall in Nairobi on International Peace Day, 21 September 2013, an event for which Al Shabaab leadership claimed responsibility. As Ombok and McGregor (2013) maintain, the raid was the deadliest attack that Kenya has suffered since the bombing of the US Embassy in 1998 which left 213 people dead. Ultimately, these terrorist attacks on Kenyan soil can only make Kenya's war on terror, especially against Al Shabaab, very complex and costly. The perceived prolonged military operation in Somalia, coupled with the high cost of maintaining troops there, pushed the Kenyan government to incorporate its battalion under the command of the African Union Mission in Somalia (AMISOM) in 2012.

Kenya's growing role in the maintenance of regional security, highlighted by the country's 2011 invasion of Somalia and the continued participation of 5 500 Kenyan troops in AMISOM, has had outcomes that can be considered contradicting. This chapter interrogates the contradicting outcomes of this military intervention in Somalia. It also interrogates the argued increased role of Kenya in the maintenance of regional security against its own state security and the security of its citizens, its economy and its territory, as well as the security of the citizens of Somalia and Somali refugees in Kenya. While Kenya's foreign policy and the decision to pursue Al Shabaab gains some popularity in the region and globally, there are other factors that may have been given little attention when the intervention was planned and executed. These factors, covered in this chapter, can be considered as political, socio-economic, security and regional alliances challenges that affects Kenya, Somalia and the region as a whole.

CONTEXTUALISING SOMALIA'S CRISIS AND KENYA'S MILITARY INTERVENTION

Kenya's military intervention in Somalia and its consequences to civilians is linked to the history of the conflict in Somalia. This section forms a continuum of the understanding of the Somali crisis and blends it to the intervention and associated consequences.

Since 1991, following the ousting of then President Siad Barre, Somalia has been without a functional government. The Transitional Federal Government (TFG) of the Republic of Somalia is the most recent attempt to restore national institutions in Somalia, notwithstanding its vast challenges in governing the fragile state. The TFG was established in 2004 and is recognised internationally. At over two decades without a functional government, this makes Somalia the longest running case of complete state failure in post-colonial history. With the ousting of Barre in 1991, the Somali people entered an era of anarchy and brutality, equated only with the Hobbesian world; one with no laws or institutions, or protection of the most vulnerable from the most brutal. Violence erupted and halted economic production and food distribution, and resulted in a humanitarian crisis that cost the lives of tens of thousands.

Neighbouring countries, including Kenya, have also been affected by this violence, directly and indirectly, with refugees from Somalia looking for safety and food in these countries. The resultant Somali catastrophe caused alarm in the international community, forcing various states and international agencies to intervene. Interventions from many international forces thus far have all been propelled by various interests. Allegedly for Kenya, among the major interests are protecting national interests and securing regional stability.

These interests have also manifested themselves in border conflicts. The porous border between Kenya and Somalia has been fraught with instability for as long as the two countries have existed. Other interests reinforced by, for example, Kenya and Ethiopia, have added to the complexity in conceptualising Somali's border conflicts. In the 1960s, Kenya was involved in a cross-border conflict (the Shifta War) against Kenyans of Somali origin. This endeavour was supported by Somalia in its quest to reunite territories that were lost to both Kenya and Ethiopia. This intense conflict ended in 1967, with Kenya emerging victorious against the quest of the Somalis in the North Eastern province that borders Somalia (IPSTC, 2013). The years that followed saw Kenya retreat from political interference in the ongoing social economic affairs of Somalia. Then, in 2011, claiming protection of national interests, Kenya launched a military operation in Somalia.

Kenya and the international community recognise that countries emerging from conflict typically confront a wide range of urgent demands to build and sustain peace, yet they often face a critical shortage of capacity to meet priority needs quickly and effectively. Somalia has lived this reality. This, coupled with weak systems, provide loopholes that pose serious challenges to the development of the state. Extremist groups in a country like Somalia understand this too well and are taking full advantage, and turning it against the Kenya Defence Force (KDF) and other forces fighting Al Shabaab.

Figure 1: Political map of Somalia, 2013

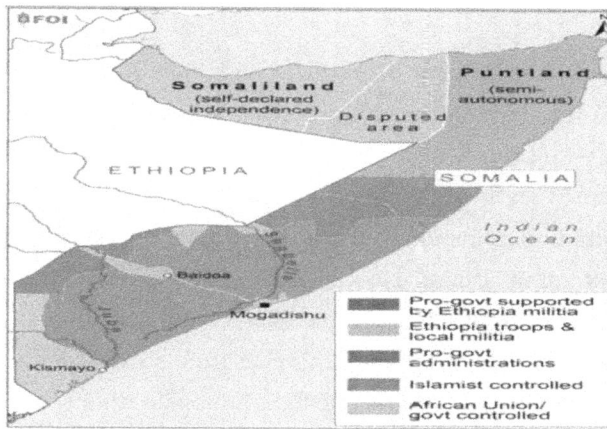

Source: Wiklund (2013)

IDEOLOGICAL TRAJECTORIES AND ITS STAMP IN REGIONAL SECURITY TERRAIN

Marangio (2012: 6) outlines that one of the central factors that links Somalia to the extant crisis is related to conflicting Islamic orders. He differentiates between the Sufi sect (mostly apolitical and strictly legitimised through blood ties within close groups, family and clans) and the Wahhabi group (supported by Saudi Arabia since the 1960s and aimed at diluting Soviet influence in Somalia). Wahhabism was more dynamic and politically opinionated, and easily immersed in political struggle after the Ogaden War with Ethiopia between 1977 and 1978. The struggle for Islamic identity later ensued between the Wahhabis (who considers themselves true believers and accuse the rest of apostasy) and the Sufis. Generally, those who maintain traditional practices have particularly heightened the insurgency in Somalia. This struggle had a strong ideological support base which has, over time, propelled out of control and found its way into religious extremism. The International Crisis Group (ICG) (2010) argues that Islam should be considered one of the central factors in defining Somalia's social, political and economic complexity. Regionally, and beyond Somalia, Islamic extremism has increased in Kenya and has influenced some aspects of Kenya's foreign policy when dealing with security issues relating to Somalia. Young men of Kenyan origin (mostly affected by high unemployment rates) have also been lured into joining extremist groups as a source of income or in protest against the government for perceived marginalisation.

THE RISE OF AL SHABAAB TERRORISTS, INTERVENTIONS AND CONSEQUENCES

According to Harnisch (2010), Al Shabaab is a name of Arabic origin, literally translated as 'the youth', and began to function as an autonomous group in 2007. Because the group is not a monolithic one, but very fluid, with contending cases of positions of leadership, ideology and strategy, there is no consensus on the exact time and manner of the emergence of Al Shabaab, nor on the details about its commanding structures. However, according to popular belief, it formed as an offshoot of the Islamic Courts Union (ICU) to drive Ethiopian troops away from Somalia. Ethiopian troops had occupied Somalia in 2006 to assist the UN-mandated TFG in destroying the ICU. Although Ethiopian troops succeeded in defeating the ICU, the military wing resisted and continued to fight Ethiopian troops.

Al Shabaab adopted the combat characteristics of a terrorist group, such as roadside bombing, suicide bombings, grenade attacks and assassinations. At the time of the Ethiopian invasion, Al Shabaab's warfare was limited within Somali borders. Over time, however, this group has expanded to include foreign recruits. As Shinn (2011) recalls, the ICU, from which Al Shabaab sprouted, had begun foreign recruitment in 2006, when young British Somalis were persuaded to fight in Mogadishu.

As Roque (2009) posits, although Al Shabaab's jihadist tactics were seen to have regional rather than global focus, the US government branded Al Shabaab a terrorist group in 2008, with an established link to Al-Qaeda. Similarly, Shinn argues that the impact of Al Shabaab's foreign networking has two dimensions: the strategy transfer, tactics and ideology that Al Shabaab leaders learnt during their interactions with the Taliban and Al-Qaeda terrorists; and the enrolment of foreign militants. Largely, this exposure continues to give relevance and dominance to Al Shabaab compared to the TFG. Al Shabaab continues to use extreme means and tactics through threats and attacks to achieve its objectives. This violence, coupled with drought, among other reasons, has forced many Somalis out of their country. African countries other than Somalia that host large Somali populations, such as Uganda, South Africa and Kenya, have been accused of providing safe havens for Al Shabaab terrorists.

Kenya's approach to terrorism has been noticeably ineffectual. Even after Uganda and Tanzania established stringent anti-terrorism laws following the 1998 Al-Qaeda bomb attacks on the Nairobi and Dar-es-Salaam US embassies, and the subsequent terrorist attack on the Paradise Hotel in Mombasa, Kenya took nearly ten years to establish a law on anti-terrorism; one that did not contain any significant strategic approach. This is worrying considering Kenya, compared to Uganda and Tanzania, has suffered the most from terrorist attacks. It is a known fact that Al-Qaeda has a long-standing, historic infrastructure in the Kenyan city of Mombasa, as well as in the outskirts of Nairobi, and, given recent collaborations, Al Shabaab can easily establish itself unnoticed. Following a series of kidnappings and terror attacks in the country, Kenya launched a military intervention in 2011 in Somalia, in pursuit of Al Shabaab.

Kenya remains the only country within the region that has launched a direct attack against Al Shabaab since the latter's warfare with Ethiopia. Furthermore, Kenya also remains the longest-serving sponsor of contracted peace negotiations for the stabilisation of Somalia, a process that culminated in the establishment of the TFG, a government that Al Shabaab does not endorse and fights against. Thus, Kenyan military intervention was reported to have the backing of the transitional government in Somalia, whose formation was mediated by Kenya. However, the intensity at which Kenya invaded Somalia is disproportional to the magnitude of attacks hurled against Al Shabaab militants.

Motives not spelt out in the public domain, but that may have ignited a reaction, included the creation of a secure trading[1] environment between Kenya and Somalia, and the protection of strategic developments in the Lamu district. Here, the construction of a deepwater port bordering Somalia will serve as the depot of a new oil conduit from Uganda and Southern Sudan to serve all of East Africa. This multi-billion dollar project is expected to include pipelines, railways, highways, an airport, and an oil refinery. According to Wicklund (2013), an improved secure environment may also boost Kenya's chances of selling oil and gas concessions in Lamu. It is also believed that Lamu contributes significantly to Kenya's foreign revenue with its coastal tourism industry (ICG, 2012). Throup (2012) notes that other possible motives that Kenya may have include gaining control and access of the lucrative port of Kismayo in southern Somalia; advancing the interests of Kenyan-Somali sub-clans in southern Somalia; and testing Kenya's well-resourced but underutilised army in battle. It is also believed that there are huge and unexploited oil reserves off the coast of Kismayo and southern Somalia, which Kenya seeks to control (ICG, 2012).

In order to resist Kenya's imposition, Martin (2013) argues that Al Shabaab has since revised its strategies. It has adopted a more radical course of action as it continues to be increasingly dominated by extreme jihadists. These young fighters have vowed to reclaim Mogadishu, Somalia's capital, as well as take back the port of Kismayo that was lost to

AMISOM, spearheaded by Kenyan troops. Eventually, they aim to establish Somalia as an Islamic state ruled under Sharia law (Martin, 2013). Al Shabaab have, since the intervention by Kenya, sought ways to retaliate this act, and has done so even on Kenyan soil. Richardson (2013) believes that the main reason Al Shabaab has turned aggressive on Kenya is that:

> The incursion by Kenyan troops helped liberate strategic areas in Somalia from Al Shabaab's control, including the port of Kismayo in October 2012. Kismayo was key to the group's ability to collect taxes to finance its activities and receive weapons and supplies. Income from Somali ports earned the group as much as $50 million a year, the UN Monitoring Group on Somalia said in 2011.

Surprisingly, a terrorist attack, such as what happened at Westgate Mall in Nairobi, was long foreseen, but Kenyan authorities seemingly did very little to avert it. On 7 January 2012, Chonghaile (2012) reported from the Foreign Office that terrorists were planning a massive attack in Nairobi, Kenya's capital. Reiterating the warning, a spokesperson said:

> We believe that terrorists may be in the final stages of planning attacks. Attacks could be indiscriminate and target Kenyan institutions as well as places where expatriates and foreign travelers gather, such as hotels, shopping centers and beaches.

Kenya's president, Uhuru Kenyatta, in a national address following the attack, vowed to remain resolute and more determined in pursuing the enemy. Kenyatta dismissed a demand by Al Shabaab that he pull Kenyan forces out of Somalia, saying he would not relent in a 'war on terror' (Miriri & Macharia, 2013). Since this commitment to pursue the enemy across borders may mean allocating more resources for security, greater pressure will be placed on the Kenyan economy, with the possibility of escalating the cost of living of Kenyan citizens. This cause that sought to protect national interests may have realised some impact, but not all of it is positive.

Barely a week after the terrorist attack on Westgate Mall, Ombati (2013) reported that men believed to be terrorists had, on 26 September, stormed a police station in Mandera Town near the border with Somalia leaving two police officers dead. They also injured three other police officers, destroyed at least 11 vehicles and burnt down a local District Officer (DO) office by throwing a rocket-propelled grenade before escaping at around 3 a.m. This succession of attacks in Kenya by groups linked to Al Shabaab militants remain complex, particularly due to large numbers of Somali refugees in Kenya who offer protection to these mercenaries. These incidences can only expose the evidence that Al Shabaab terrorists remain well connected and maintain links with their proxies beyond Somali borders. This reality is an alarming phenomenon that continues to threaten and jeopardise the peace and stability of the Horn of Africa region – a reality that may have been underestimated.

It is also clear that the presence of AMISOM troops in Somalia since 2007 in order to neutralise Sharia-inspired militia is insufficient. Although it is undeniable that Al Shabaab was weakened by withdrawing from the strategic port of Kismayo, it still remains a threat. As the spokesman for Al Shabaab threatened in October 2011, it was ready to retaliate if Kenya did not withdraw its military from Somalia. Ali Mohamud Rage was quoted as saying: 'We, the Mujahideen, say to the Kenyan government: Have you thought of the repercussions of the war against us? We are far more experienced in combat than you'.[2] Massive retaliation of a huge magnitude was also forecast by Menkhaus (2012), when he argued that there was an imminent threat against Kenya if it continued to retain its forces inside Somalia. He also argues that it was likely that Al Shabaab could appeal for local and international support by rallying Somalis and international allies against a foreign invasion, in the similar way Al Shabaab enjoyed overwhelming local support against Ethiopia's occupation of Somalia in 2007 and 2008.

CONTENTIONS OF SOMALI IDENTITY/RELATIONSHIPS AND REFUGEE STATUS IN KENYA

Ahmed (2014) contends that many Somalis opted to seek refuge in Kenya because of its neutrality over Somali affairs. Particularly in the 1990s, both Somalis of Kenyan origin and refugees from mainland Somalia succeeded in penetrating the Kenyan market, with huge stakes in real estate, transportation, oil and gas, imports, exports and wholesale business. The Somali-owned market in Eastleigh, Nairobi, is considered the largest in the region. The function of the Somali people, both locals and refugees, cannot therefore be underestimated.

In recent years however, the neutrality of Kenya on Somalia and people of Somali origin has dwindled. The Kenyan government is arguably being blamed for exacting enormous pressure against Kenyans of Somali decent and refugees from Somalia. According to Amnesty International, there is increasingly intensifying restrictive requirements for Somali people to apply as asylum seekers in Kenya, and indeed since 2012, the process is almost impossible. It is undeniable that security tensions in Kenya attributed to Al Shabaab have worsened the situation, even of genuine refuge seekers from Somalia. Noticeably, Kenya has remained reluctant to register new refugees from Somalia, and most of the offices responsible for conducting this exercise remain closed.

The manner in which Kenya, through its security factions, is handling people of Somali background (whether nationals or not) will painfully escalate towards defining a sore relationship between the two countries. The protracted conflict in Somalia has resulted to the displacement of millions of people seeking refuge in other countries, while the rest have remained internally displaced. It was reported by the UN High Commissioner for Refugees (UNHCR) (2012) that, by 2012, approximately 1 017 649 Somali were seeking refuge in neighbouring countries, particularly in Kenya, Djibouti, Eritrea, Ethiopia, Tanzania, Uganda and Yemen, while an estimated 1.4 million people were internally displaced in various regions of Somalia. In Kenya alone, the number of refugees almost tripled between 2006 and 2011, reaching 500 000. To date, Kenya hosts close to a million Somali refugees, a sensitive reality that continues to define the relationship between the two countries. The Kenyan government was heavily censured by international aid agencies when it showed reluctance to allow the free flow of refugees into the Dadaab camp following the drought. While the government may have explained its reasons, including the fear of overcrowding in refugee camps, there was little doubt that the main concern was the risk of Al Shabaab militants infiltrating and mingling with Somalis in refugee camps and in other towns in Kenya after finding their way out of the camps.

Today, Somali people are perceived with suspicion, particularly following the days when Al Shabaab instituted a series of attacks against Kenya. Since the Kenyan government has made it increasingly difficult for asylum seekers to register, many run the risk of being arrested for being in the country without formal documentation. Amnesty International (2014) discovered that, between March and May 2014, after the minister for internal security, Joseph Ole Lenku, ordered all refugees to confine themselves in designated refugee camps, 331 individuals were arraigned in court for contravening the directive. Some 64% of these were from Somalia. In as much as stringent laws are justified under counter-terrorism policies, the majority of these individuals are genuine refuge seekers under international law. While Kenya has legitimate security threats, gazetting encampment policies will only further isolate the Somali community and is likely to backfire and increase security threats against Kenya. Kenya feels it is bearing a disproportionately high burden of sheltering refugees fleeing conflict and drought.

POLITICAL GAINS AT THE EXPENSE OF SOCIAL AND ECONOMIC PROGRESS

In addition to the impact of Somali piracy on its image and economy, Kenya has cited other incidences of Somali-linked transnational crime. Considering recent trends, Kenya's most pressing concern is the real threat of terrorism linked to Al Shabaab. The Westgate Mall attack, launched in retaliation for Kenya's military presence on Somali soil, highlights Kenya's ongoing security challenges that both drive the country's increasingly outward-looking posture and threaten its bold plans for further economic and infrastructural development. Economic regional integration has served Kenya well, but a newly hawkish foreign policy that jeopardises domestic stability threatens to undermine one of Africa's foremost success stories. While Kenyan troops continue to march on Somali territory, it is worth remembering that Nairobi plays a far more important regional role, notably as a hub for trade and infrastructure.

By committing troops to Somalia, Kenya has continued to exert enormous pressure on its civilians who are the real funders of this invasion through taxation. This chapter aims at exposing and understanding the costs, and the consequences, of such an invasion. Even though Kenya does not publish its military budgetary allocations, it is estimated that Operation Linda Nchi (Swahili for 'protect the country') costs Kenyan taxpayers at least KSh210 million every month to maintain personnel alone, with a total expenditure of KSh236 billion budget deficit. These estimates were calculated on the assumption of a force of 1 000 soldiers at Ksh7 000 per day per soldier. However, there is probably a higher number of soldiers deployed in Somalia, with a correspondingly higher cost (ICG, 2012). The intervention meant to protect national interests has taken its toll on other aspects of the economy. Questions have been asked about whether Kenya should withdraw, but have been met with unsatisfactory answers.

Even after Kenyan troops were formally combined with the AMISOM force authorised by the UN Security Council, the KDF budgetary allocation accounted for the highest budgetary increment in the 2012/2013 budget, amounting to KSh70 billion (ICG, 2012). Huge spending on war continues to exact insurmountable pressure on Kenya's economy as funds that could have been allocated for other basic and urgent needs, such as development, food and health, are being diverted to war. If the intervention's cost is not contained, already high inflation will worsen, along with increased local discontent due to the high cost of living. Throup (2012) attests to the fact that Kenya's intervention in Somalia has increasingly become financially unsustainable, with estimates suggesting that it was costing USD180 million and claiming 50 lives per month. Even though there has been overwhelming patriotic enthusiasm from the general Kenyan public, massive economic hardship has been recorded in the North Eastern Province, along with the disruption of the tourism industry in the Lamu district.

According to Sipus (2011), it is common knowledge that payments flow to Somalis living in Eastleigh, a Nairobi suburb, and are later diverted to fund Al Shabaab's operations in Somalia. In addition, individuals linked to Al Shabaab-owned assets exercise direct control over some of the major businesses in Eastleigh, and many of the shops there sell videos of Al Shabaab's propaganda. In this way, Al Shabaab has been able to source revenue from Kenya to fund its operations. It is also believed that much of the money handled by Al Shabaab is transmitted through banks in Kenya. Therefore, the amount of information that Kenya's intelligence agency has on Al Shabaab is sufficient to establish the security hazard the group poses to Kenya. Seizure of these resources would hamper their operations severely and perhaps boost the existing military operation (ICG, 2012).

Borrowing from the American experience, the war on terror not only has financial impact, but also contributes to a significant loss of life, both military and civilian. For example, following the 11 September 2001 attacks in New York and Washington DC that left nearly 3 000 dead, including 19 terrorists, the US launched a retaliatory attack on Afghanistan, the hideout of Al-Qaeda leadership. Similarly, the US invaded Iraq because Saddam Hussein was allegedly storing and supplying his enemies with weapons of mass destruction that could have been used to attack the US and its allies. From 2001, when the US declared its 'war on terror', until April 2013, the lives of 5 281 servicemen and women have been lost. As at August 2013, the number of wounded was a staggering 671 846. The wars in Iraq and Afghanistan are projected to have cost the US up to UDS6 trillion, which is approximately 357 times greater than Kenya's 2013 national budget (Onyango-Obbo, 2013). Thus, as Kenya continues to commit itself to a direct offensive against Al Shabaab, it is going to be necessary to take into account the cost (fiscal and human) of such operation in the long run. In this case, Kenya will need to review its military strategies and engagements, and seek less expensive yet effective means of dismantling Al Shabaab operations.

While there may be lessons to learn from the American experience, Kenya continues to confront its own economic growth challenges. Kenya is making desperate attempts to persuade foreign tourists and investors that its famed sites are still safe, despite the travel warnings and bans issued by Western countries. These travel advisories are bound to have a dramatic impact on the country's multi-million dollar tourism industry. Patrol bases set up near the coastal border with Somalia are seen by analysts as an attempt by the Kenyan government to ensure it can contain Somali raids at the coast, one of the stated reasons for Kenya's invasion of Somalia. An intervention that sought to protect the national interests and citizens of the country has left many ordinary people exposed to a greater security risk in the form of terror attacks, as well as economic hardship, as the government tightens its tax regulations to support the economy and the continued presence of Kenyan troops in Somalia.

KDF: PROFESSIONALISM OR COLONIAL LEGACY BURDEN?

Decades after the end of colonisation, the intellectual debate over the positive and negative impacts of colonisation in Kenya is still very much alive. This is centered within Kenya's problematic decolonisation experience and the wider context of the Cold War ideological confrontation. The trajectory of development in Kenya continues to be determined by the conjuncture of precolonial, colonial and post-colonial socio-political and economic structures. This is the case in various spheres of life, including Kenya-British military relations, one of the enduring independence period legacies in Kenya. Long after independence, there are systems and structures in Kenya that have a colonial footprint. Some are beneficial, while others can be challenged, and the military is one of them. Even after formally relinquishing power, the inherited armed forces were still influenced by colonial powers and remained the most organised and powerful bodies in the newly independent countries. They could, and often did, intervene to force political change or assume power.

The civil wars that often closely followed independence threatened secession and played a role in forming African defence forces. Immediately after independence, most armies assumed the role of protecting the president, the elite, and then the populace. This was the case in Kenya and, for over two decades after independence, this was the common trend. With multiparty politics coming into play in 1991, the military role was put to test, but over time there has been progress in streamlining professionalism within the KDF.

However, the war against terror, like any other, requires preparations at all levels of command, weaponry, special tactics and rules of engagement, and a legal framework within which to act. Despite the unanimous denunciation of terrorism by all nations, most find it very difficult to meet these requirements. Kenya has found itself in this situation over and over again. The KDF learned several lessons following the conflict with the Somali irredentist fighters in the 1960s. At the time, the KDF did not have adequate knowledge about the people they were fighting and understood little about the enemy's habits, culture and traditions. This, coupled with inadequate information on the terrain and geography of the battlefield, choked professionalism, if there was any. Today, all the sophisticated equipment, trained personnel, personnel who have served in mission areas, and information technology, have made it easy to reclaim professionalism. But how professional KDF is has been challenged by several scholars and practitioners.

Until its October 2011 incursion into Somalia, the KDF had not engaged in battlefield combat with an enemy force, and some have argued that the force is inexperienced. Kenya has recently invested more in modern hardware as the KDF seeks to package itself as a professional army that is not only well-trained in modern warfare, but also boasts intellectual experts in various international peace and development fields. The KDF has also retained the confidence of the last three presidents who, in order to reform key areas of national security, have tended to appoint military personnel to posts that were initially held by civilians or police.

During the 1960s conflict with Somalia, a number of Somali-speaking officers and men defected from KDF to Somalia in support of the irredentist movement and ideology. Such cases have not been reported by KDF. The recruitments that have been undertaken by the armies have increased their background checks, but there have been no cases of candidates being rejected on the grounds of ethnicity, more so of Somali descent. AMISOM in Somalia have found it hard to incorporate the locals in their systems due to a lack of adequate information to clear someone for a position in the mission.

SECURITY AND REGIONAL ALLIANCES CHALLENGES IN THE WAKE OF ASYMMETRICAL THREATS

Minyandazi (2012) believes that the root cause of Somalia's conflict and social, political and economic instability is entrenched in inter-clan clashes and rivalry for power among contending warlords, in their quest to control certain strategic regions. These warlords receive support from neighbouring countries or other international actors, who may not necessarily have the objective of ending the crisis in Somalia. A sustainable solution to the conflict in Somalia is largely dependent on regional stability and the presence of well-established domestic security institutions, not only in Somalia but also in the regional countries. The major challenge of the regional states in East Africa is the achievement of political stability, a situation in which general elections are held without violence and negative tribal manipulation. This has been elusive for most states in the region, with violence being part and parcel of elections.

For political stability to be viable, state security machinery should be felt in all areas of the country, and the right to use force should remain the preserve of the central government. Unfortunately, the use of force is Al Shabaab's main approach in realising its objectives. Terrorist attacks occurring in Kenya since 2011, the year that Kenya launched Operation Linda Nchi against Al Shabaab militants in Somalia, are proof that Al-Qaeda has a strong presence in Kenya. It is critical to note that Al Shabaab has been more offensive against Kenya than any other country within the Horn of Africa.

The regional dimensions of the ongoing crisis in Somalia are of capital importance to understand the recent dynamics of the conflict. In different ways and degrees, most of neighboring countries are implicated: Ethiopia and Eritrea are the two major regional actors in the Somalia crisis, each having their own reasons. Kenya's reasons saw the country resort to military intervention in Somalia. Further, it was expected that the launch of the military operation would help firm up regional security and deter the threat of terror groups. The asymmetrical threats, with terrorism posing more problems, has called for a common regional approach to solving the problem. Collective security can be understood as a security arrangement – political, regional or global – in which each state in the system accepts that the security of one is the concern of all, and therefore commits to a collective response to threats to and breaches of peace.

However, the use of hard power by states, unless legitimised, is considered illegitimate, reprehensible and needing remediation of some kind. The use of force by states is controlled by both customary international law and by treaty law. UN Charter article 2(4) reads:

All members shall refrain in their international relations from the threat or use of force against the territorial integrity or political independence of any state, or in any other manner inconsistent with the purposes of the United Nations.

Even with this guidance from the UN, Kenya went ahead and launched a military operation in Somalia, arguing this act using the UN Charter, Chapter VII, article 51, which states that:

Nothing in the present Charter shall impair the inherent right of individual or collective self-defence if an armed attack occurs against a Member of the United

Nations, until the Security Council has taken measures necessary to maintain international peace and security. Measures taken by Members in the exercise of this right of self defence shall be immediately reported to the Security Council and shall not in any way affect the authority and responsibility of the Security Council under the present Charter to take at any time such action as it deems necessary in order to maintain or restore international peace and security.

Even though many regional, continental and international actors have intervened in Somalia since the state collapse in 1991, their conflicting interests and objectives have only worsened the crisis. For example, not only are East African countries grappling to take control of Somalia, but actors far beyond its borders are also showing interest. Hitherto, there is a falling out over a regional policy to stabilise Somalia and suppress Al Shabaab. Unless the rivalry between Ethiopia, Kenya and Uganda (and of course other international stakeholders like the African Union (AU) and the UN) is tackled, and a common stabilisation strategy developed, they may find themselves undermining one another's efforts and compound Somalia's political and security crisis.

The ICG (2012) argues that the military intervention of Kenyan troops, now under AMISOM, has made significant steps in renewing the interest of the international community to fight Al Shabaab, perceived as undesirable for international security. The initiative by Kenya to combat Al Shabaab on their home soil has revived the UN Security Council's Resolution on Somalia by deploying more troops, thus expanding AMISOM's presence in the country. Kenya has, therefore, united the international community towards fighting a common enemy, particularly in southern Somalia, on the Kenyan border. Despite all these decorations, the insecurity that is attributed to the very presence of Kenyan troops in Somalia has continued to rise.

In 1993, American and UN peacekeepers were humiliatingly defeated in a two-day bloody battle against Somali militias. Years later, Ethiopia tried too, and licked the same bitter wounds of defeat. This can be interpreted to mean that Kenya and AMISOM are up against an enemy that is proving hard to squash.

CMR IN CONFLICT SITUATIONS

Following Kenya's independence from British colonial rule in 1963, the country faced serious armed conflict with the Somali community in the Northern Frontier District, which was receiving support from the government of neighboring Somalia. Following these unrests, the Kenyan government contemplated introducing military forces in the Northern Frontier District to combat the envisioned protracted guerrilla campaign by the Somali irredentists. This led to the establishment of military posts in the towns of Mandera, Garissa and Wajir. However, the relationship of these forces and the local community for a long time was nothing to go by. This has changed over time, but security threats, including supporters and sympathisers of Al Shabaab, have made it hard for these forces to trust the local population. This lack of trust has since been addressed by having Somali personnel of Kenyan origin as part of the forces.

With the presence of the military establishments in the region, any counterattacks meant civilians would be caught in the middle of the conflict. Either caught in the crossfire or directly targeted by unscrupulous actors, each year millions of civilians suffer from physical violence or are denied access to essential services. Protecting civilians in conflict is not just a moral or legal imperative – it is a necessary component of and pragmatic step towards sustainable peace. However, in sub-Saharan Africa, CMR and a coordinated protection of civilians approach remains work in progress, with a long way to go. There are too many priorities that push CMR onto the secondary list, including poverty, conflict, development, and humanitarian crisis; the list goes on and on. With all these competing priorities and, as Kenya seeks to address serious security challenges like the asymmetrical threats, CMR should indeed have a space in all these efforts. Kenya has suffered several terror attacks that have prompted the government to be proactive on this front. However, past criticism of the previous government's aggressive counterterrorism approach has been highlighted. Particular concerns have been raised on how counterterrorism policies have been too tight on anyone of Somali descent. This has seen increasing complaints from the north eastern region where much of the populace is of Somali descent.

National security has experienced a paradigm shift and is no longer viewed through military lenses alone. It has expanded multi-dimensionally, incorporating civilian perspectives. While this is evidenced in the recent reforms in Kenya's security and defence sector, the impact of this approach has been considered relatively slow. The relationship between the citizens and the KDF in the North Eastern Province and other regions, like Nairobi, where a populace of Somali origin is found, is not considered good. The northern region is predominantly inhabited by ethnic Somalis, who often complain that they have been neglected by central government. This claim of neglect can be a strong source of rebellion.

With the rise of Islamic extremism, counterterrorism operations have joined the throngs of humanitarian operations operating from northern Kenya, but often servicing neighboring countries.

In its widest sense, the 'defence against challenges to a nation's vital security interests' in Kenya has been interpreted differently, with some of the consequences being termed human rights violations. The role and image of the military within a society should be explained to the citizenry as a basis for strengthening CMR. Kenya's increasing military and counterterrorism efforts in Somalia risk generating a political backlash and more attacks by Al Shabaab. History has shown time and again that military approaches do not solve, but rather exacerbate, the challenges Somalia has faced, with civilians always getting caught in between.

CONCLUSION AND RECOMMENDATIONS

The international actors' policies on security with respect to Somalia are currently framed by counterterrorism, with armed groups like Al Shabaab being considered a priority security concern. The question of whether Kenya should withdraw its troops from Somalia has been considered a premature discussion, while the Kenyan government continues to insist that it can only withdraw its troops once the objectives of the incursion have been achieved. Kenya is collaborating with the TFG in fighting Al Shabaab. At the same time, the TFG continues to grapple with attempts to establish institutions that will gradually address teething governance challenges. Increasingly, both local and international stakeholders continue to forge a way to tackle the crisis in Somalia, with the aim of establishing peace, stability and eventual reconciliation. This is not only going to be beneficial to the Somali population alone, but to all who reside within the Horn of Africa and the world at large.

The peace process in Somalia cannot ignore major armed groups that control almost 80% of the south of the country. Every possible way to restart a dialogue should be explored. Any attempt to solve the Somalia crisis should therefore be based on a realistic, not ideological, assessment of the situation. Further, a coordinated military, political and psychological campaign in the region is necessary to counter the insurgency with a balance of non-military approaches in resolving the conflict in Somalia. Kenya, Djibouti, Uganda and Sudan, at least through the Intergovernmental Authority on Development (IGAD) sponsored dialogue process, are playing a certain role. More of such processes should be considered. The focus on terrorism and counterterrorism is considered counterproductive. Non-military and non-security alternatives should be explored in order to address the root causes of the crisis.

Consequently, it is important to recognise the existence of critical regional dynamics of the conflict, and their contributions in solving or propagating the problem. On CMR, the final capability, and perhaps the most important for civilian protection, is the development of a specific protection of civilians doctrine and guidelines by member states at national level. These are crucial in preparing peacekeepers for the difficult task of protecting civilians in armed conflict. These capabilities will also increase the understanding of CMR in volatile conflict situations where the military deployed are the early peacebuilders.

NOTES

1. Kismayo port in Southern Somalia has become a large smuggling trade destination. Goods that arrive through this border are transported across transnational borders, including Kenya and Ethiopia. Goods such as sugar from Pakistan or Brazil find their way to Wajir, Mandera, Dadaab and Garisa, and the far towns and cities of Nairobi, Isiolo and Mombasa (ICG, 2012: 11).

2. *See* Euronews (2013).

REFERENCES

Akolo, J. 2012. 'Kenya vows to defend its territory', KBC News, 15 October 2012. Available at http://www.kbc.co.ke/news.asp?nid=72938. Accessed 13 July 2012.

Amnesty International. 2014. 'Somalis are scapegoats in Kenya's counter-terror crackdown'. 4 October 2014.

Branch, D. 2014. 'Why Kenya invaded Somalia' in *Foreign Affairs*, 6 September 2014. Available at http://www.foreignaffairs.com/articles/136670/daniel-branch/why-kenya-invaded-somalia.

Chonghaile, C.N. 2012. 'Kenya: warning of imminent terrorist attack' in *The Guardian*, 7 January 2012. Available at http://www.theguardian.com/world/2012/jan/07/kenya-imminent-terror-attacks-warning. Accessed 25 September 2013.

Euronews. 2013. 'Al Shabaab's war with Kenya: Terrorist group may have even surprised itself', 25 September 2013. Available at http://www.euronews.com/2013 / 09/25/behind-Al Shabaab-s-war-with-kenya-terrorist-group-may-have-even-surprised-/. Accessed 26 September 2013.

Harnisch, C. 2010. 'The terror threat from Somalia: The internationalization of Al Shabaab', American Enterprise Institute, 12 February 2010. Available at http://www.criticalthreats.org/sites/default/

files/pdf_upload/analysis/CTP_Terror_Threat_From_Somalia_Shabaab_Internationalization.pdf. Accessed 7 October 2013.

International Crisis Group (ICG). 2010. 'Somalia's Divided Islamists', Africa Briefing: 74, 18 May 2010. Available at http://www.crisisgro up.org/~/media/Files/africa/horn-ofafrica/somalia/B74%20 Somalias%20Divided%20Islamists.pdf.

International Crisis Group (ICG). 2012. 'The Kenyan military intervention in Somalia', Africa Report: 184, 15 February 2012.

International Peace Support Training Centre (IPSTC). 2013. 'Enhancing capacity for regional peace through peace operations training'. Issue Brief Series No. 4.

Ismail, A. & Green, R.H. 1999. 'The heritage of war and state collapse in Somalia and Somaliland: Local-level effects, external interventions and reconstruction' in Third World Quarterly, 20:1.

Lyman, P. & Morrison, S. 20014 'The terrorist threat in Africa' in Foreign Affairs, 83(2004).

Martin, P. 2013. 'Kenya attack shows extreme jihadists now in control of Al Shabaab'. Reuters, 23 September 2013. Available at http://www .theglobeandmail.co m/news/world/kenya-attack-shows-extreme-jihadis-now-in-control-of-al-shabaab/article144587 58/. Accessed 24 September 2013.

Menkhaus, K. 2012. 'After the Kenyan intervention in Somalia' in Enough, January 2012. Available at http:// www.enoughproject.org/files/MenkhausKenyaninterventionSomalia.pdf. Accessed 13 December 2013.

Miriri, D. & Macharia, J. 2013. 'Militants hold out as Kenya forces try to crush cross-border jihad'. Reuters, 23 September 2013. Available at http://www.re uters.com/article/2013/09 /23/us-kenya-attack-idUSBRE98K03V20130923. Accessed 24 September 2013.

Miyandazi, L. 2012. 'Kenya's military intervention in Somalia: An intricate process' in Accord, Issue 19, November 2012.

Ombati, C. 2013. 'Suspected terrorists kill two police officers in Mandera town' in Standard, 26 September 2013. Available at http://www.standardmedia.co.ke/?articleID=2000094 325&story_title=suspected-terrorists-kill-two-policemen-in-mandera. Accessed 26 September 2013.

Ombok, E. & McGregor, S. 2013. 'Kenya police begin assault to end mall siege after 68 die', Bloomberg, 23 September 2013. Available at http://www.bloomberg.com/news/2013-09-22/kenya-police-begin-assault-to-end-mall-seige-after-68-die.html. Accessed 23 September 2013.

Onyango-Obbo, C. 2013. 'In Westgate, Al Shabaab fought the wrong war, suffered the right defeat' in Nation, 25 September 2013. Available at http://www.nation.co.ke/oped/ Opinion/Al Shabaab-fought-the-wrong-war-suffered-the-right-defeat/-/440808/2006948/-/i1uo5v/-/index.html. Accessed 26 September 2013.

Richardson, P. 2013. 'Al Shabaab attack fulfills threat in Kenyan support for Somalia', Bloomberg, 22 September 2013. Available at http://www.bloomberg.com/news/2013-09-22/Al Shabaab-attack-fulfills-threat-in-kenyan-support-for-somalia.html. Accessed 23 September 2013.

Roque, P.C. 2009. 'Somalia: Understanding Al Shabaab', Institute of Security Studies Situation Report, 3 June 2009. Available at http://dspace.cigilibrary.org/jspui/bitstream /123456789 /31014/1/ SABAAB040609.pdf?1. Accessed 8 October 2013.

Shinn, D. 2011. 'Al Shabaab's foreign threat to Somalia'. Foreign Policy Research Institute. Available at http://www.fpri.org/articles/2012/08/al-shabaabs-foreign-threat-somaliaqz.

Sipus, M. 2011. 'Armed non-state actors: Support for Al Shabaab through the diaspora' in *Forced Migration Review*, 37(2011).

Throup, D. 2012. 'Kenya's intervention in Somalia', Center for Strategic and International Studies. 16 February 2012. Available at http://csis.org/publication/kenyas-intervention-somalia. Accessed 30 September 2013.

UN Charter Chapter VII: Action with respect to threats to the peace, breaches of the peace, and acts of aggression.

UN Civilian Capacities. 2011. 'Civilian capacity in the aftermath of conflict: Report of the Secretary-General', A/66/311–S/2011/527.

UN Security Council Resolution on Somalia (S/RES/2036), 22 February 2012. Available at http://www.u n.org/Docs/sc/unsc_ resolutions12.htm.

UNHCR. 2012. 'Refugees in the Horn of Africa: Somalia displaced crisis'. Available at http://data.unhcr. org/horn-of-africa/regional.php. Accessed 3 October 2014.

Wiklund, C.H. 2013. *The role of the African Union Mission in Somalia: AMISOM - peacekeeping success or peacekeeping in regress?* Stockholm: FOI Report 3687. Swedish Defence Research Agency.

Chapter 7

The Role of the Military in Politics in Africa's 'Phantom State': The Central African Republic, 1960–2014

by Martin Rupiya

> *The French, almost at will, install and eject CAR leaders. As a result, French soldiers are referred to as the 'Barracudas' on the impoverished streets of Bangui.*[1]

On 24 March 2013, Séléka rebels – or the 'alliance' in local Sango *lingua franca* – led by Michel Djotodia, comprising local militia and mercenaries from Chad, Sudan and the dreaded Janjaweed, unhappy about the lack of political will to implement changes based on the 2008 Gabon-Libreville Agreement invaded Bangui, ransacked the presidential palace and set forth a train of chaotic events in the capital and across the country.[2] The rebels raided the town, and looted and burnt down properties while torturing citizens and conducting public lynching, rape and other human rights violations. According to United Nations (UN) agencies, out of fear over one million people fled their homes into neighbouring Chad, while twice the number were reduced to seeking shelter in the forests as internally displaced people (Agger, 2014:4; Somerville, 2014).

The local standing army, *Forces armées centrafricaines* (FACA), offered no resistance, with cadres deserting posts and arms. President François Bozizé, accompanied by close family members and aides, fled to the nearby Democratic Republic of the Congo (DRC). Meanwhile, the former colonial power, France, with permanent military bases in Bangui, Camp Beal and Bouar, reacted to the Séléka triumph by increasing its deployed force from 350 to 600 troops for the purpose of protecting 1 000 French citizens.

These developments in the capital Bangui further confirmed the security vacuum that characterises the situation in the rest of the country where the Ugandan Lord's Resistance Army (LRA) continues to roam at will.

Djotodia's military success was yet another familiar route for taking power in the country, which had begun in January 1965 when Jean-Bédel Bokassa overthrew David Dacko's regime (Stapleton, 2013:216).

The impact of the invasion was immediate as the State and its institutions collapsed. FACA, dissolved itself, while the civil service became paralysed and dysfunctional. Public schools, the university and churches closed, as did several shops and the only service station, and were looted, leaving hospitals barely functioning with the only available medical services offered by international aid agencies such as the International Committee of the Red Cross (ICRC) and *Médecins Sans Frontières* (MSF).

Hitherto, in damning opinion pieces, several authors and organisations had cited the Central African State as a 'phantom state'. In 2007, the International Crisis Group (ICG) and Reuter's news agency produced reports citing that the crisis in the Central African Republic (CAR), a phantom state, represented something worse than a failed state. The same reports proceeded to apportion blame almost exclusively on the shoulders of the local political elite and other domestic players. In January 2014, the African Development Bank's *High-Level Panel on Fragile States Report* confirmed the status of Africa's phantom states, citing South Sudan and CAR as countries in crisis, requiring urgent, multifaceted and sustained intervention. As for its genesis, a former senior French official described the CAR as:

> ...the outcome of hazardous explorations, diplomatic agreements and the whims
> of colonial administrators – [resulting] in a caricature of a post-colonial state –
> which is a geographic expression rather than a nation. (Somerville, 2014).

Leaping to the defence of the phantom state criticism more recently, Hovil (2014) has challenged this glib reference, arguing instead that this is a manifestation of the misdiagnosis of highly complex and integrated factors at play. She argues, convincingly, that this 'reductionist analysis, most favoured by human rights groups, NGOs and the French Government, [that is] prone to finding easy scapegoats' leaves out other influential factors and players that should be included if we are to come up with appropriate policy interventions. However, we need to ask some fundamental questions: Is CAR a phantom state? And, if so, why?

In other words, where we find differing analyses and yet there is a significant number of citizens in Central Africa, either in exile or internally displaced, it is important to seek to discover the actual conflict drivers that guide and influence the reality of the political, socio-economic and security developments in CAR.

The purpose of this research is to critically examine the substantive factors that have influenced the role of the military in politics and its subsequent relationships with society in CAR since independence. A related objective is in line with the call-to-action issued by the African Development Bank's High-Level Panel on Fragile States to provide credible policy options for the reconstitution of a sustainable defence and security establishment for the new regime, beyond that of the interim authority of acting president Catherine Samba-Panza, for lasting, peaceful conditions in CAR. This has been the missing dividend during the last 54 years.

There are at least three important and related questions to be asked in order to answer the underlying perception of a phantom state created and maintained by CAR's political elites with the active assistance of foreign powers. First, what was the colonial objective of establishing CAR? Have these interests changed and, if so, how? Second, who benefits from the maintenance of a particularly weak, fragile and vulnerable state and its institutions in Bangui? To this end, why has FACA, as an institution, remained incapable of offering credible security to its citizens and the state, and maintaining the territorial integrity of the country? If we are able to answer these three integrated questions, what are the options going forward?

The objective of this chapter is to offer country-based clarity, focusing on Africa's complex civil-military relations and its political trajectory. It argues that CAR represents the greatest success of French-Africa Francophone policy implemented through the collusion of the metropolis working through local political and military elites. In Bangui this has been particularly successful, with an early and sustained French military presence in the two bases in the capital. In executing this policy, every time the local dominant player has sought to deviate and forge relationships with other foreign powers, the French intervene, as in Operation Barracuda (1979), Operations Almadin I and II (1996–97) and Operation Vimbezela (2012). The French-Africa policy established in 1946 has since been transformed, following the extensive devaluation of the French Franc and the Abidjan position taken on 12 January 1994, in which the French continued to pursue the same objective, but in a multilateral role enmeshed through sub-regional players and even UN peacekeeping (see Martin, 1998:102-105). To this end, the sub-regional interests of CAR's neighbours have coalesced with French interests in keeping Bangui weak. The interests of external players have also benefited from the geographic location of CAR, surrounded by five neighbouring countries, two of which – Chad and Sudan – have experienced protracted conflict since the 1960s, and more recently from the DRC, Darfur, South Sudan and even Uganda.

It may therefore be true that, until some of these conflicts are concluded, their ability to undermine CAR stability is likely to continue.

This chapter traces the evolution and role of the military in each of the five presidential eras since independence. It begins by examining the president David Dacko era (August 1960 to January 1965), followed by his successor, Colonel Jean-Bédel Bokassa after the first successful coup in January 1965. This eccentric dictator, who declared the country a monarchy, was later deposed through French intervention under Operation Barracuda in September 1979, after which Dacko was reinstated. In September 1981, Dacko was replaced by the twin leaderships of the Chief of Staff, General André-Dieudonné Kolingba and French Lieutenant Colonel Jean-Claude Mantion. In October 1993, Ange-Félix Patassé won a second-round election with 53.5% of the vote, which ended 12 years of military rule. Patassé ran the country for two terms, before being deposed by his Chief of Staff, General François Bozizé, in March 2003. However, Bozizé found himself isolated and run out of the state house and town on 27 March 2014 by his former consul in the town of Nyala in Darfur, Michel Dodjotia. The first Muslim president of CAR drew strong reaction from international and regional leaders, forcing him to hand over power to interim president Catharine-Samba Panza in January 2014. Panza's mandate is to prepare the country for free and fair elections in 2015 before stepping down as she is barred from contesting.

In the event that a new armed force is established, several key questions that relate to the history, purpose, role(s), function, affordability, and constitutional and legal frameworks for security, political governance and oversight have to be answered. For example: What has been the politico-military role of the security establishment since independence? Has this contributed to consolidating the state or the reverse? What national security factors have influenced military roles in the post-colonial era? Why has there been a security vacuum in the post-colonial era and how can this be addressed?

CAR'S POLITICAL, SOCIO-ECONOMIC AND SECURITY DYNAMICS IN PRE- AND POST-INDEPENDENCE ERAS

> *Decolonisation was a painful process for the French. The wartime leaders of the Free French ruled out independence (or even self-government) for the colonies, though they promoted a new vision of economic and social development through the Union française established in 1946. (Aldrich, n.d.)*

In 1958, faced with the imminent prospect of former Francophone states becoming independent during the cold war era, France quickly reached secret agreements with the emerging political leaders – also known as *le village franco-africain or la Francafrique* – aimed at retaining exclusive access, control and responsibility in the defence and security arena, succeeding to create the *Domaine Reserve or Chasse*. This enabled the French to exercise control of military affairs, permit French intervention as and when required, gave Paris the right to station troops permanently in the former colony, and ensure no pacts would be entered into with any foreign powers.

At the domestic level, pre-independence political events shaped the early trajectory of the internal force established on 13 August 1960. The initial drive was to create a federation of French Equatorial African countries or Afrique Équatoriale Française (AEF), comprising Chad, CAR and Mali. During the 1950s, Barthélemy Boganda, a catholic priest serving as a deputy in the French National Assembly was appointed the first president of the Grand Council. In parallel, Boganda created the Movement for the Social Evolution of Black Africa (MESAN). When the AEF failed to materialise, Boganda concentrated his efforts on his country carved out of two rivers – the Oubangui and the Chari – located between Chad and Congo-Brazzaville. In a referendum on self-governance held on 8 December 1958, MESAN won the poll by 97%. Soon afterwards, however, tragedy struck when, on 25 March 1959, Boganda died in an air crash. He was succeeded by his nephew, David Dacko, who, as the leader of MESAN, took the country into independence on 13 August 1960.

Dacko's new regime aimed at creating a one-party state and, in 1961, banned the emerging Movement for the Liberation of the Central African People (MLPC), confining its leaders to house arrest. This development effectively limited the political space opposing the sitting government. The following year, Dacko declared CAR a one-party state.

Suspicious of Bokassa, Dacko appeared to be convinced that the existing force represented a threat to his rule. As a result, the head of state proceeded to establish two units – a 120-man presidential guard and a 500-man gendarmerie, paramilitary police force, whose commanders reported directly to him – outside the control of the standing army. In 1964, Dacko, was re-elected president, running as the sole candidate. During this period, the French were responsible for providing government budget support, including the salaries of armed units.

THE FIRST COUP D'ÉTAT: ITS PROPONENTS, EVOLUTION AND IMPACT (1966–1979)

Despite Dacko's attempt at creating a deterrent and competing force, his fears were soon realised when, on New Year's Eve 1965, Bokassa staged the first successful, bloodless military coup in CAR.

The reign of Emperor Bokassa, who enjoyed support from France, emerged as one of the disastrous periods of CAR's post-colonial history. In rapid succession, the megalomaniac rule of Bokassa created international outrage and French embarrassment.

On seizing power, Bokassa suspended the constitution and, on 4 March 1972, declared himself president for life after promoting himself to General. This was soon followed by the dissolution of the National Assembly on 4 December 1976, and the renaming the country: Empire of Centrafricaine. In 1977, the increasingly eccentric Bokassa conducted one of the most lavish and extravagant coronations ever witnessed, costing over USD22 million, paid for by the French. This drew worldwide consternation and ridicule, and was something the French could not continue to be seen to be supporting.

Bokassa managed to turn FACA into a repressive machine, willing and able to torture, burn homes and plunder from citizens with impunity. In May 1978, both MESAN and FACA were compelled to recognise the Emperor as the sole political entity in the country.

When students took to the streets in January 1979 to protest government profligacy, Bokassa, now known as the 'Butcher of Bangui', ordered his army to suppress the riots, resulting in over 250 students being killed. This development reflected a force that was prepared to commit human rights abuses against is citizens.

In May 1979, reacting to Bokassa's eccentric behaviour, which had placed Paris in the dock of international public opinion, the French withdrew diplomatic, economic and security support. In response, Bokassa turned towards Libya's Colonel Muammar al-Gaddafi and China for support. This infuriated Paris as it violated one of the key provisions of the 1958 agreement. Given the track record of Francophone post-colonial control, Bokassa had committed political suicide and, soon after, the French embarked upon a 90-day plan to depose him. Operation Barracuda was carried out by French troops, which removed Bokassa from power in a bloodless coup d'état. FACA did not intervene. The invading force accompanied the former president, Dacko, who was then reinstated, while Bokassa fled and eventually sought refuge in France.

THE ERA OF KOLINGBA AND MANTION (1981–1993)

Dacko returned to power closely supervised by a French Secret Service officer, Lieutenant-Colonel Jean-Claude Mantion, who later became known as the unofficial 'pro-consul' and General André-Dieudonné Kolingba as the new Chief of Staff. On 1 September 1981, Dacko appeared exhausted and unwilling to continue in office, and was reported to have voluntarily ceded power to Kolingba and Mantion. In the new relationship, Zapata (2012) asserts that Kolingba left the running of the state to Mantion while he concentrated in deploying his ethnic group – the Yakoma – into government, parastatals and the armed forces. His record shows that the Kolingba reign until 1993 was the most divisive in the recruitment and composition of the civil service and the armed forces.

Kolingba suspended the constitution and established a military junta, the Military Committee for National Recovery (CRMN), which he chaired, to run the country and especially military affairs. Much later, in 1985, 'guided by Paris' Kolingba established a new civilian cabinet, and in 1986 created a new political party, the Rassemblement Démocratique Centrafricain (RDC), banning all other political parties. Thereafter, efforts towards expanding the political space stalled while attention focused on changing the composition of the army.

However, Kolingba's reign coincided with the global winds of change of the 1990s, events that soon confirmed that France would be unable to pursue an autonomous Francophone policy.

France's foreign policy adjustment resulted in the increased role of CAR's neighbouring states in its internal affairs, including the secondment of security and defence tasks. While this policy evolved, attention towards reforming African political elite behaviour continued, albeit with French military presence still on the ground. In this, France was joined by the group of countries known as GIBAFOR, comprising France, USA, Germany, Japan, the European Union, the World Bank and the UN, during the 1990s. Through their intervention and pressure, Kolingba was forced to hold elections in October 1992, but refused to accept the results. Further unrelenting pressure led to the establishment of the Commission for the Provisional National Political Council (CNPPR) and the first electoral commission on which representatives of all political parties would be represented. This followed close on the unbanning of political parties in the country. Ultimately, in 1993, the first civilian political leader, Ange-Félix Patassé of the MLPC – the party banned by Dacko in 1961 – gained 53% of the poll.

MULTIPARTY DEMOCRACY AND CAR: THE ERA OF PATASSÉ AND FRENCH 'WITHDRAWAL'

Patassé's triumph at the polls culminated in an almost immediate rupture with the former colonial power. In 1993, French economic support to CAR was cut suddenly, including wages for soldiers. While Patassé cried foul, French assistance to Africa was now being exercised through multilateral organisations and CAR's neighbouring states.

At the domestic level, the post-1993 multiparty democracy era revealed serious ethnic and regional differences in CAR. The message voters expressed was that the political elite needed to form a coalition in order to heal and equitably run a peaceful country.

The early programmes of the new regime appeared to focus on revenge, reversing the footprint of Kolingba and dominance of the Yakoma, and attempt to reassert competing ethnic interests of the Gbaya, Sara and Kaba. This was also the fate of other Yakoma in senior and lucrative government posts, who were dismissed and replaced with those perceived to be loyal to Patassé.

Patassé relieved Kolingba of his military rank and charged him several human rights violations. Other units were also purged, dismissing or reassigning to FACA over 200 former presidential guard security personnel. In retrospect, the actions of the new civilian president demonstrated sentiment and party leadership that was clearly unhappy with its experience since independence. Distrustful of FACA, Patassé deployed the standing army outside the capital, into the interior and inhabitable border areas, while keeping his gendarmerie-paramilitary force and the new Unité de sécurité présidentielle (USP).

However, even as this was taking place, evidence that this would give birth to the seeds of rebellion and mutinies by the rank and file was beginning to emerge. USP and other militia loyal to Patassé clashed with the outgoing elements established by Kolingba. This development reflected the temporary nature of CAR military units, whose loyalty and professionalism was not viewed beyond the reign of a particular leader.

Under Patassé's rule, major mutinies began, which forced the participation of France in their resolution. This remains at the heart of the current military vacuum in CAR.

A series of rebellions wracked Bangui in 1996: the first on 18 April, followed by a second on 18 May, a third on May 26, a fourth on 15 November, and yet another on 6 December 1996. It began with an estimated 200 to 300 soldiers who demanded their wages be back-dated to 1992/93. As the unrest continued, the demands escalated to include political matters and calls for Patassé's resignation. Several people on both sides were killed, while others received severe injuries during the clashes. In reaction, the French intervened with Operation Almadin I, II and III, during which time Paris mediated and settled the outstanding wages, and compelled Patassé to grant a general amnesty. France also expanded mediation to include neighbouring Gabon, Burkina Faso, Chad and Mali.

Patassé became paranoid, determined to eliminate the mutinies and its participants. In undertaking this, cruel executions by forces loyal to Patassé ensued, leading to an estimated 20 000 Yakoma FACA soldiers fleeing into the forests. Fearful of the reaction of France, Patassé sought to strengthen his security and the presidential guards. He created Force spéciale de défense des institutions républicaines (FORSIDIR), and accepted 300 personal guards from Libya and Jean-Pierre Bemba's forces from DR Congo.

MILITARY COUP D'ÉTAT WITHOUT FRENCH ASSISTANCE: FRANÇOIS BOZIZÉ (2003–2013)

The onslaught on Patassé continued and succeeded on 15 March 2003, when Bozizé seized power, leading a coalition of the Kwa Na Kwa (KNK). It is therefore true that Bozizé ran a strong militia group outside FACA. Once in office, Bozizé appointed his son, Jean-François Bozizé, in charge of the Ministry of Defence, and an old military-academy friend, General Antoine Sambi as Chief of Staff. However, even as Bozizé sought to consolidate power in Bangui, the civil war in the countryside escalated, with Michel Djotodia leading the Union of Democratic Forces for Unity (UFDR), also known as the Séléka 'alliance'.[3]

Bozizé's reign sought to reverse Patassé's gains and ended up committing similar if not worse atrocities. In 2006, the presidential guard and army were accused of regularly extorting from the public, torture and undertaking summary executions in a context where no local or national judiciary was in place. In order to fund his force, Bozizé employed proceeds from mineral contracts entered into with China, Libya and South Africa.

The impact of the repressive excesses was that an estimated 150 000 people became internally displaced, fleeing from state-sponsored violence. In response, French forces relocated from Bangui to Abidjan, Dakar, Djibouti, Libreville and N'Djamena, operationally supported by the Paris-based Force d'action rapide (FAR).

THE PHANTOM STATE – FROM ZARAGUINAS[4] TO SÉLÉKA REBELS: MICHEL DJOTODIA (2013–2014)

Michel Djotodia's Séléka forces attacked and occupied bangui in January 2013, forcing Bozizé to flee to the DRC. On assuming power, Djotodia suspended the constitution, dissolved parliament and announced that he would rule by decree and hold elections after three years. However, even after taking power, the violence continued to increase andtook on a sectarian characteristic between the Christian Anti-balaka and the Muslim-inspired Séléka. Anti-balaka perceived themselves as local vigilantes, ex-FACA and other Christian forces, largely using machetes for self-defence. Furthermore, sentiment against Islamic states was growing and this soon created sufficient momentum and intense pressure from the international actors to force Djotodia to relinquish power. On 10 January 2014, the Economic Community of Central African States (ECCAS) forced Djotodia to relinquish office, accusing him of failing to bring about peace and, instead, exacerbating the situation.

ANALYSIS

This civil-military relations case study of CAR since independence in 1960 reveals important trends that should guide us to develop new policy guidelines for the establishment of sustainable defence and security institutions in multiparty democratic Africa.

While CAR has emerged as the epitome of success of French-Africa post-colonial policy, the subsequent stepping into the breach by neighbouring countries has meant that nothing has changed.

Within the CAR political elite, the role of the military in politics is best revealed by looking at the reign of the six presidents since independence – Dacko, Bokassa, Dacko, Kolingba, Patassé, Bozizé and Djotodia – before Catherine Samba-Panza took over as interim president in January 2014.

On assuming power, each adopted a familiar pattern:

- Suspending the constitution or, in Patassé's case, introducing a new one two years after winning the elections in 1993, which has had little or no impact.
- Suspending the National Assembly and concentrating power around the presidency.
- 'Reforming' government and the civil service in line with intentions to displace sitting ethnic groups, and allow their own privileged patronage and access.

- Not trusting FACA and creating at least two units around the presidency, commanded by separate officers who reported directly to the president.

FACA became marginalised, and was deployed largely in the interior and outside the capital. This approach to the military establishment, at least until 1993, enjoyed the full support of the French. France had Mantion in place and paid the salaries of the miniscule force that complimented the physical presence of French forces in Bangui.

In order to overcome this elaborate security arrangement, Kolingba, Patassé, Bozizé and Djotodia worked with neighbouring state governments and rebel groups, including armed professional poachers and mercenaries from Darfur, Sudan and the Congo, against the sitting governments.

When the French stopped paying soldiers' salaries in 1993, amid a repressive campaign by Patassé to remove the Kolingba's dominant Yakoma, debilitating mutinies broke out resulting in limited French intervention and an inability to pursue an independent and autonomous post-colonial policy in Africa. Faced with receding power and influence, CAR's neighbours, Chad and Libya, became increasingly assertive, participating directly in he country's affairs and working with Patassé, Bozizé and Djotodia.

When interim president Catharine Samba-Panza took over in January 2014, the country had no rule of law, no judiciary and a dysfunctional civil service; FACA had imploded leaving the Anti-balaka and Séléka fighting. Alarmed at the situation, the AU intervened and later suggested the UN establish a robust peacekeeping force to bring about peace and stability in CAR.

Is CAR a phantom state? Part of the answer lies in the strategic politico-economic and Cold War sphere of interests, and the aggressively successful implementation of the La Baule françafricaine policy; the connection of this policy with the political elite class; the naivety and mendacious mentality of Dacko, Bokassa, Kolingba and others, soon taken advantage of by neighbouring state leaders; the existence of CAR in a particularly violent neighbourhood; and the fear of each regime, resulting in the deliberate weakening and marginalisation of FACA, has, after 55 years, delivered one of Africa's most fragile states.

This chapter is not designed to offer prescriptive recommendations on the way forward in reviving and consolidating the state in CAR. Its main purpose is to offer insight on what has led to the current state of affairs, where a country has no credible standing force after decolonisation. If the reasons and practice of what has led to the current crisis are fully understood, a solution can be found. Although CAR has been reduced to phantom status, this can be easily overcome with the concerted effort of locals supported by the AU and the Multidimensional Integrated Stabilization Mission in the Central African Republic (MINUSCA), which is already in place.

NOTES

1. *Operation Barracuda* was launched on 20 September 1979 to remove Emperor, Jean-Bedel Bokassa and reinstall David Dacko.

2. Michel Djotodia had been Bozizé's consul in Darfur, based in the town of Nyala, during which time he established working relationships with bands of mercenaries, professional poachers, diamond and gold smugglers from across the Sahel region, including Chad and Sudan.

3. Seleka 'alliance' partners included *Convention des Patriotes pour la Justice et la Paix* (CPJP), *Convention Patriotique pour le Salut du Kodro* (CPSK), *Union des Forcees Democratique pour le Rassemblement* (UFDR).

4. 'Zaraguinas' refers to bandits that came across the porous borders of Chad, Sudan, DR Congo and Uganda to roam and plunder in the CAR.

REFERENCES

African Development Bank. 2014. *Ending Conflict and Building Peace in Africa: A Call to Action – Report of the High Level Panel on Fragile States.* Tunis: African Development Bank.

Agger, K. 2014. 'Behind the Headlines: Drivers of violence in the Central African Republic (CAR)' at *http://www.enoughproject.org*. Accessed 30 December 2014.

Aldrich, R. n.d. 'Decolonization, the French Empire and sites of memory' at *http://www.port.ac.uk/special/france1815to2003*.

Anon. 2007. 'Operation Boeli – French Aid Mission to FACA' in *Africa Research Bulletin: Political, Social and Cultural Series*, Vol. 43:12, pp. 16909A–16910. Published online. Accessed 30 December 2014.

Dolek, C. 2008. 'From Francafrique to Eurafrique with Sarkozy: Not much of a difference?' in *Journal of Turkish Weekly*, 11 March 2008 at *http://www.turkishweekly.net/*. Accessed 3 January 2015.

Hovil, L. 2014. 'Why are African conflicts so often misunderstood?' African Arguments at http://africanarguments.org/2014/02/10/why-do-we-continually-misunderstand-conflict-in-africa-by-lucy-hovil/. Accessed 14 December 2014.

International Crisis Group. 2007. 'Central African Republic: Anatomy of a Phantom State' in *Africa Report* No. 136, 13 December 2007.

Kalck, P. 1971. *Central African Republic: A Failure in Decolonization.* New York: Praeger. p. 1.

Martin, G. 1995. 'Francophone Africa in the Context of Franco-Africa Relations' in Harbeson, J.W. & Rotchild, D.S. (eds). *Africa in World Politics: Post-Cold War Challenges,* 2nd Edition. Boulder: Westview Press. pp. 163-88.

Martin, G. 2000. 'France's Africa Policy in Transition: Disengagement & Redeployment' in in Harbeson, J.W. & Rotchild, D.S. (eds). *Africa in World Politics: Post-Cold War Challenges,* 2nd edition. Boulder: Westview Press.

Panter-Brick, K. 1988. 'Independence, French Style' in Gifford, P & Louis, W.M. (eds). 1998. *Decolonization and African Independence: The Transfers of Power, 1960-1980.* Westview: Yale University Press. pp. 73-104.

Reuters News Agency. 2013. 'Bozizé Ouster is Latest Power Grab in Africa's "Phantom State"'. 25 March 2013. Accessed on 30 December 2014.

Somerville, K. 1990. *Foreign Military Intervention in Africa.* London: Pimnter. Chapters 2 and 3.

Somerville, K. 2014. 'Is the Central African Republic an artificial state?' Africa-News & Analysis at http://africajournalismtheworld.com/2015/01/01/. Accessed 30 December 2014.

Stapleton, T.J. 2013. 'The military and violence in Central African Republic (CAR)' in *A Military History of Africa The era of independence: From the Congo Crisis to Africa's World War.* California: Preager. pp. 216-224

Titley, B. 1997. *Dark Age: The political odyssey of Emperor Bokassa.* Montreal: McGill – Queen's University Press.

Zapata, M. 2012. *Central African Republic (CAR): Mutinies, Civil Wars and Coups, 1993-2003.* Enough Project Part I, Washington DC: Centre for American Progress.

Chapter 8

Civil-Military Relations: Perspectives in South Sudan

by Sunday Angoma Okello

There are inadequately detailed explanations and analyses of civil-military relations (CMR) that attempt to underpin South Sudan's experiences of the tragic collapse into civil war on 15 December 2013, known as 'Dark Sunday'. In theory, civil-military relations have contending views to post-modernist and neo-Marxist explanations, pitting the context of transformation of the international order in Africa against the local context. In practice, very little support is offered for understanding the inseparable relations between the civil population and the military, or the cauldrons of instability that continue to hamper the new state. The methodology orientation asked whether CMR perspectives could explain the tragic collapse. Perspectives, interviews and document analysis capitalised on the civil war following the changed perceptions of the ruling Sudan People's Liberation Army/Movement (SPLA/M) in relation to its population (ICG, 2014). The perceptions of international communities are aimed at creating a modern and democratic governing state, and attaining liberal peace in post-independence South Sudan. However, the United Nations Mission in South Sudan (UNMISS) is perceived as weak in coordinating civil-military relations to reach a common understanding of building state institutions. Sovereignty and violence contend modernity. SPLA/M capitalised its rebel governance using multiple traditional and local structures, and social authorities, which engaged, generated, negotiated, contested and strategised society. These structures and authorities have an ethno-political mind-set, with sources of mobilisation and militia recruitment producing primarily a militarised civil population. This chapter finds that a militarised population, whose CMR is hard to distinguish, directly affects democratic governance in a state such as South Sudan. Any alternative assumptions may package inconsistent realities. CMR in South Sudan is far more completed, implicating governments and opposing parties, civil society, regional actors and regional mechanisms such as the Intergovernmental Authority on Development (IGAD), the continental mass of the African Union (AU) and the international institution, UNMISS. Relying on sovereignty, gained independence is historically, logically, analytically and theoretically displacing CMR.

BACKGROUND AND CONTEXT

Violent internal conflict broke out in the Republic of Sudan on 15 December 2013, when the long-standing tensions within the country's ruling party, the Sudan People's Liberation Movement (SPLM), boiled over into armed civil conflict in the nation's capital, Juba. Like many post-colonial countries in Africa, South Sudan joined the civil war discourse. Before and after the Cold War, more than 80 violent changes of governments took place between the decades of Africa's independence, from 1960 to 1990 (Adebayo, 1999: 3).

Although many argue that Africa's civil wars are on the decrease compared to the post-independent Sub-Saharan African (SSA) countries, which had fewer civil wars prior to the Cold War collapse in the 1980s, South Sudan emerged with very intense and violent civil war. The split between the SPLA forces loyal to the government of president Salva Kiir Mayardit, and former vice-president Riek Machar Teny-Dhurgon, led to serious clashes and deaths. On 16 December 2013, Kiir, clad in military uniform, addressed the nation and announced that there had been an attempted military coup d'état.[1] He accused the former vice-president of being behind the attempted *putsch*.

In turn, Machar, speaking from his hiding place, denied that he had been behind the insurrection, or that there had been an attempted coup d'état at all: 'There was no coup. What took place in Juba was a misunderstanding between presidential guards within their division. It was not a coup attempt. I have no connections with or knowledge of any coup attempt.[2,3] The trading of accusations and counter-accusations worked on the minds of the civilian population. The 'loyalists' were pro-Kiir – true and committed SPLA/M historical followers – and the 'side-changers' were followers of Machar, who had a history of tearing SPLA/M apart in 1991.

Mistrust is grounded in the historical moral values of the movement: that members should pay absolute commitment and not abandon the movement at any time. Side changers have always been viewed as those who defy the movement and may continue to defy the rule of the true 'comrades' in struggle. This new set of perspectives remained strong in the foundation of hatred leading to the polarisation of the people of South Sudan, with pro-Machar against pro-Kiir, and, to a greater extent, Nuer against Dinka. Following this historical background and context, violence spread rapidly among security forces in Juba, engulfing entire neighbourhoods. Within days, hundreds of civilians died in Juba alone, and the number of deaths in other cities was estimated at between 50 000 and 100 000 people (UNMISS, 2014; APF, 2014). Some 100 000 people sought refuge inside UN-protected bases and over two million people sought refuge in neighbouring Uganda, Kenya, Ethiopia and Sudan (APF, 2014).

There is a regional dimension to the emergence of intrastate conflict in South Sudan. The conflict transgressed from its internal, regional framework to an international context. The outbreak of civil war in South Sudan was not surprising in the eyes of post-Cold War analysts; according to Beer (2006: 119), the emergence of intrastate conflict post-Cold War has posed a threat to international peace and security, mostly developed in the context of transformation of the international order. South Sudan registered into the international order. Doyle and Sambanis (2000: 779–801; 2006) have established criteria that a civil war must meet: the war causes more than 1 000 battle deaths; the war represents a challenge to the sovereignty of an internationally recognised government; the war occurs within the recognised boundaries of the state; the war involves the [government] as one of the principle combatants; and the rebels are able to mount an organised military opposition to the government and to inflict significant causalities on it.

IGAD has been leading the failed mediation process in South Sudan since 3 January 2014. Its efforts are being supported and influenced by regional and international actors, and the IGAD-led mediation peace process has had a direct impact on civil-military relations inside South Sudan. IGAD member states, the AU, UN, European Union (EU), China and the troika countries (Norway, United Kingdom and United States) are all party to the talks. However, the mediation process has not been finalised despite the warring parties signing successive agreements. The Cessation of Hostilities Agreement (CoHA) signed in January 2014 was broken several times, and the latest agreement, signed in February 2015, has not stopped the conflict. Similarly, the commitment of the negotiating parties in reaching a final agreement by 5 March 2015 was not realised. This has made the current IGAD-led mediation efforts in South Sudan tiresome and challenging, and a frustration to the hope for peace among the South Sudanese civil population.

CMR in South Sudan has dimensions implicating regional, cross-border military intervention, with hard resources provided to Kiir's government by Uganda. The IGAD-led mediation process, now transformed into an IGAD-plus format, has attracted international preventive diplomacy perspectives. IGAD-plus is still anchored on the first IGAD mediation attempts to broker peace among warring parties. Both processes emphasise the civilisation of the conflict in the overtones to stopping violence and resorting to building a democratically modern state. It is argued that these discourses would, in fact, set foundations for the fluidity of living in 'cold-peace' and for the explanations driven by liberal peace agendas. The focus on the over-emphasised enemy-image, of 'us against them', has reinforced negative CMR, especially when it comes to ethnically impervious misrepresentations and under-representations of the undemocratic governance in South Sudan. For example, Greater Equatoria, Greater Upper Nile and Greater Bar el Ghazel are fractured along the above-mentioned lines. More so, the regions have been vying for a hegemonic show of biceps, albeit diplomatically, but with a firm gaze towards federalism.

The notion of neutrality, access to vulnerable populations and the conduct of operations is required to address the complex humanitarian catastrophe influencing CMR. There have been strong calls from international actors to end the violence and associated human rights violations and abuses. At the end of April 2014, the UN High Commissioner for Humanitarian Rights and Special Advisor to the Secretary-General on the Prevention of Genocide visited South Sudan, and met with the conflicting parties: the government of South Sudan and the Sudan People's Liberation Movement-in-Opposition (SPLM-IO). They briefed the Security Council on 2 May 2014 about their visit, and this was followed by a visit of the UN Secretary-General on 6 May 2014. On the same day, the US imposed targeted sanctions on two individuals: one associated with SPLA/M and the other with the SPLM-IO.

In summary, South Sudan's internal disorder can be put in four transitional contexts prior to 15 December 2013. Firstly, SPLA/M fractured internally and needed to move from being a liberation movement to governing an independent state, following a more liberal peace agenda. Secondly, the politics of war needed to be shifted both physically and psychologically towards politics of peace, following the civil (democratic) governance paradigm. Thirdly, the notion of moving away from one united Sudan, which remains firm in the minds of the Sudanese, and not let South Sudan go, required a new set of relations between the inhabitants of the two Sudans. And fourthly, a combination of all three was needed to underpin the fractured leadership.

Minutes from meetings held in Rumbek in 2004 suggest that John Garang was leading a divided SPLA, lost between allegations and suspicions of assassinations, corruption and disregard for the will of the people of South Sudan.[4]

In all four transitions, the relations between the military, SPLA and the militarised civil population in South Sudan have been heavily affected. Many believe that civil-military perspectives have changed for the worse compared to the liberation war of the past 35 years, before South Sudan obtained independence. Many members of the rebel SPLA/M are perceived as corrupt and embarked on resource extortion from public office. Therefore, the perceptions of CMR, contrasted with the current antagonistic parties, are mostly along ethno-political rigmaroles and ethnic-based dimensions. These have made the conflict difficult to extirpate.

Regionally and internationally, skewed political factionists among South Sudanese elites also tramped up the current violence. Gurr and Harff (1994), and Wimmer (1997), argue that the intrastate conflict in most of SSA widely embroiled ethno-political rigmaroles, ethnic-based propaganda entrepreneurship, and political levering of power. The contextual analysis dictated that the SPLA/M, as can now be seen, were motivated by the hypothetical unity in the grievance against Arabs (as a people) and Moslems (as a religion) brought into post-independence governance. SPLA/M continued to administer its primordial hatred and revenge, and the elimination of the demo-pessimistic elements. It continued to follow the concept and ideology of liberation war, working up the minds of civilian support in its attempt to govern. The shock, which would be felt at top leadership, and which led to the violence outbreak, gathered the general perceptions of ethnic group affinity and group protectionism.

METHODOLOGICAL ORIENTATION

Does the CMR perspective explain the tragic collapse of the new state following the eruption of internal conflict in South Sudan in December 2013? Drawing insights from my work in South Sudan for over 20 years, more specifically, in the two years up to the first week of December 2013, I observed diverging and sometimes converging contentions in CMR. Some had theoretical contestations. I found that Post-Modernist and neo-Marxist views were initially converging in the way South Sudanese wanted to have democratic governance in the new state. However, CMR posed questions that implicated the search for democratic governance, state building and preventive diplomacy in ending the civil war. The implications come from the liberal peace paradigm that the US and Norway would have moulded opinions about forming the new state.

Documentary analysis has been sought widely to underpin the explanations linking the relationships between militarised militia armies, whose outlook has the cosmetic acts of a national army, the SPLA, and the highly militarised civil population. Internet-based research (Nhoma 2006) was used to address the notion of CMR.

Ten isolated interviews were conducted with key people from South Sudan over a period of five weeks from the beginning of April to mid-June 2015. Telephone interviews were conducted with over 20 people charting out the perspectives of the civilian population in South Sudan. Face-to-face meetings were conducted with ten policy makers at government level and regional actors of IGAD. Attempts to reach the officials, more specifically the Social and Political Affairs Department of UNMISS were limited to only a few officials, but a lot of material published by the UN and other related agencies was used.

THEORETICAL UNDERPINNINGS

CMR can take the form of a classical liberal idea of understanding how governing societies operate. Dean (2007) argues that a classical liberal idea assumes there are relationships between an agency of political rule and administration, commonly referred to as a government, and a sphere external to that realm, society or civil society; and a set of purposes and means for the action of one upon the other. The case of South Sudan has raised contentions whenever international intervention in the fragile state and conflict-affected parts of the country required detailed theoretical explanations. The difficulties are partly contributed to by the lack of clarity and the amorphous interface and relationships between a militarised civilian population and a militia-type army appearing as a national army.

Attempts can be made to view the dominant narratives and theories that evolved towards the beginning of the 21st Century. Didier Pe'clard Mechoulan (2015) argues that the narratives and theories that account for civil wars in Africa converge around the idea that the upsurge in violence is aligned to state failure or decay. In SSA, more specifically South Sudan, post-Cold War political analysts have continued to forward their bloc politics of post-colonial state building and democratic governance arguments. They view conflict as almost always framed according to neo-Marxist dependency theory, modernisation theory, or simply according to Marxist narratives of class domination and peasant emancipation, or revolutionary movements and counter-insurgency (De Soysam 2001).

These analyses generalised the discourse of conflict and wars in China and Vietnam with embedded policy imperatives that reinforced the premises of competing propositions of building a modern state for SSA, and forging stronger relationships between the civil population and the military. The dangers of the explanations assume that the absence of violence was often interpreted to mean that there are sometimes disregarded objective ethnic-politics and ethnic-based propaganda entrepreneurship, political levers to anchor on power, corruption and resource extortion, justice-seeking groups, primordial hatred and revenge, and demo-pessimistic elements.

Following the dominance of the narratives and theories, the CMR approach has been impacted upon and picks up a dual orientation to conventional writing on violence. Tilly (2006: 8) argues that analysts of violence commonly construct the motives, interest, circumstances or beliefs of one actor at a time, then divide between condemning or defending the actor. After major clashes, South Sudan's 'Dark Sunday' was registering an end to the transition of joy obtained from the successful battle with Sudan that brought independence. This was cocooned within the disintegrated army (militias) to mean one army, but provided conducive acceleration to past divisions.

The transformation of the power of violence into legitimate domination (Schlicte, 2009) was part of the new wave of politics of collective violence in South Sudan, and yet it was termed 'misunderstanding between the government's presidential guards'. This 'misunderstanding' also broke the bond that brings the civil population together with the military, which serves to safeguard the nation and is, itself, a non-differential part of society.

South Sudan's violent conflict is an expression of the weakness, disintegration and collapse of political reform after independence, and the guerrilla movement SPLA/M. The movement carried forward the ideological armed wings and contending behaviours of revolving militia groups. It was easy to pit against each other. Cramer (2006) refers to such transitions as a 'blank state approach'. Many have refuted Cramer's arguments as burdened by reductionism, and we therefore need to move beyond the search for motives that bring out militarised civil populations from the politics of civil war.

By arguing that civil wars are part and parcel of processes of state formation, the political order of the South Sudan government is still heavily influenced by its rebel background. In some ways that may help us to understand the perceptions of the civilian population, and at the same time strike a common balance between civil wars and developing state institutions where the politics of armed militia groups predominates (Schlicte, 2009). Mampilly (2011) argues that the success of rebels depends on their ability to rule. The relations between the current South Sudan government, the SPLA, with the civilian order and governance has long been associated with violence, a high probability to turn to warfare, and dilemmas in addressing and thus legitimising actions.

SPLM/A continued to manipulate civilian perspectives and defined CMR in the mundane and theoretically inclusive politics of post-independence 'big-tent' policy of government. The 'big-tent' policy assumed armed militia-military, military-military and military-civilian relations. In reality, very strong ethno-political relationships with an individually militarised civil population assumed that good governance and state building would be put in place. Popular explanations that stress democratic governance against competing propositions of building a modern state disregarded questioning qualities of leadership. The explanations are sometimes based on the merits of post-modernisation and neo-Marxist viewpoints. More explanations are that South Sudan's return to civil war executed a 'new age of national security' generated by a fight for power, failure to address internal political party reform democratically, and survival. 'Dark Sunday' started trading on a disputed allegation that the government foiled a coup attempt, placing the incidence within the contesting strand of political discourse of protecting the undemocratic process to reform the SPLM party. According to Mampilly (2011), such a discourse would also be considered motivation to arrest other political opponents. As a result, the spiralling of fights in the major state capitals of Jonglei (Bor), Upper Nile (Malakal) and Unity (Bentiu), widened the relationship gap between the civilian population and the military. The government is caught in between.

Following the post-independent civil war in South Sudan, CMR has become part of human violence that may be understood in three ways: idea people, behaviour people, and relation people. South Sudan failed to address its human affairs, let alone its political affairs. Idea people following SPLM agency missed out on the consciousness of human action that could have served as a basis to claim that it had improved its CMR. The civilian population expected the new state to carry with it the common beliefs, concepts, rules and values to reshape societal impulses.

Instead, SPLM ideas and actions to establish social relations in the country after independence decayed and polarised expectations. Ideally, the perspectives are antagonising the government and SPLM-IO as anti-peace efforts that failed to stop property destruction, looting, killing, rape of innocent civilians and, above all, deprived an interpretation of civil liberty. Acts and intended acts of genocide, deterred terror, which should have paved the path to justice and mitigation of violence from brawls, were both implicitly and explicitly causative to the weakening of CMR. South Sudan was advised to learn from the previous post-colonial states of Africa but such views followed the liberal peace-building 'toolkit' approach (Newman, Paris and Richmond, 2009; Paris, 2004). Moreover, the debate on civil wars moved from the quest for rebels' motives and the origins of violence to a thorough analysis of the political dimensions of life during civil war (Arnaut and Hojberg, 2008). This was a transition that referenced fighters and politicians to strengthen their collective violence that later defined new battlefields and ethnic frontiers, engineered from uncoordinated but autonomous motives, impulses and opportunisms, with full-scale aggressive actions.

Aggressive action of the civilian population towards the military in South Sudan has also been apparent, mainly in the address to fulfil human needs. Tilly (2006: 5) argues that human beings employ aggressive means to acquire mates, shelter, food and protection once threatened. The propensity to adopt these aggressive means entered the human heritage. And yet other generated needs and incentives are domination, exploitation, respect, defence, protection or security, which underlie collective violence (Tilly 2006: 5). Two factors are clear from Tilly's arguments: CMR become a socially imposed control over motives and socially created opportunities express the motives.

In South Sudan, the relations between civil populations and the military were remembered within the collective violence that failed to project meaningful and peaceful conversations from peace talks, including the Comprehensive Peace Agreement (CPA) in 2005. Concessions to influence the propensities of groups to have irreducible distinctive properties to stop the war were futile. Many analysts argue that the conflict defined the complaints within SPLM, but it is also prudent to state that the complaints defined the conflict. Marxist narratives gain ascendency given the particularity of time and space, based on who is able to effectively organise violence, and division was expected.

According to Varshney (1997):

> It is impossible to establish the truth ... about cause and effect of communal violence. Contemporary communal violence has become horribly tangled in discursive 'contestation' and politically manipulated 'representations'. Indeed facts and representations cannot be separated. It is not that facts do not exist, but that the most important facts necessary to make causal arguments simply cannot be called the morass of representations.

Classic Marxists derived shared interests, especially from relations of production, but then saw interests as determining both prevailing ideas and interest-oriented behaviour. To some extent, violence in South Sudan society is viewed as generally resulting from within the promoted class interest. Marxists tend to prioritise relations, but a combination of relations, ideas and behaviours interact in South Sudan's case.

CMR AFTER THE MID-DECEMBER 2013 CONFLICT

CMR in South Sudan is overburdened by the use of force, violence and revenge attacks. However, the use of force does not necessarily mean violence and war, and rather includes deterrence, alliances, cohesion, mass internal displacement, and systematic punishment with sometimes unwarranted rewards. In South Sudan's historical and political life, and in the ongoing civil war, social polarisation along 'we' versus 'they' is clearly divisive. As mentioned previously, it became clear that the escalation of the war took an ethno-political spark. This attribution to the 'good' motivations for either side for purposes of seeing each other's side as wholly evil has compounded stereotyping and ethno-political conflict in the country.

Certainly, the psychological dynamics of war on both sides is also assuming the image of who is the real enemy (Keen 1984; Carlton-Ford and Ender, 2011; Hauss 2011). According to Goldstein (1999), military force is one of the most important elements of national power, at least in the long run, not applicable to the state of relinquishing the job descriptions of obedient SPLA soldiers. In practice, well-paid soldiers have tended to fight better, imbued with moral favour for the cause. Goldstein (1999) cites Chairman Mao Zedong of China who once stated that 'All power grows out of the barrel of a gun', and adds that 'Stalin once dismissed the opinion of the Pope with the retort: "How many divisions or armies does the Pope have?"'

It was apparent that, after South Sudan's independence, the perspectives of the majority of the civil population pointed to tackling under-development, which was dominated by military stewardship. However, difficulties in realising militarised CMR are argued against the lack of democratic process, militarised civil society, ethno-political conflicts based on tribalism, a high rate of illiteracy, an undiversified economy, and poor infrastructure and social services. Ethnic tensions between groups and underdevelopment are also addressed as parts of the hidden dilemmas to state formation, which many were looking to in the process of state building. The majority of these demands have fallen into the basket of disregard of what was called 'The Pope's Army'.

State building did not exist in South Sudan during the 35 years of war. In the five years of transition, after signing the CPA in 2005, while state construction was beginning, the multiple structures of traditional and local authorities continued to forge stronger tribal structures and social authority that linked the civil population to its local militias. Traditional structures had a very limited unifying force on nationalism, rather concentrating on achieving its objective of protecting tribal groups. Major tribes have regarded each other as interlopers, rivals and/or enemies of the liberation struggle that self-ascribed military positions and consolidated political and financial privileges. The arrogance, dominance, fierce conflicts and power struggle from within has derailed the foundation set for state building and peace building.

As the tensions and civil surge takes centre stage, lack of development is not be entirely blamed on lack of good governance. Governance delayed is democracy denied to the innocent citizen. A more tenacious solution to conflict relies on traditional democratic peace. The leaders in South Sudan failed to transparently observe its basic democratic start by reforming the rebel party to independent national representation. The democratisation process hardly took shape within the less than three years of self-rule. The expectations of many have been expressed in the discourse of a 'regrettable situation'. There has been a lack of unified political will from opposing leaders to resolve internal frictions. Going back to the battlefield within three years has failed the test of peace. The opposition movement took control of Bor, Bentiu and Malakal. the latter two cities particularly important for the oil industry (Koos & Gutschke, 2014).

The incidental political tensions that 'triggered' military clashes is not new. There have been persistent divisions, clashes, defections and unifications, local raids and counter raids throughout the history of SPLA/M. However, differences can always be seen in how previous clashes are addressed. The fights escalated past political, military and ethnic issues. Many have already discounted the possibility that there was a coup attempt, and view it more as a political hoax that Kiir wanted to use to get rid of his fierce political opponents. Although the two biggest tribes of South Sudan, the Dinka to whom Kiir belongs, and the Nuer from where the vice president originates, dominate the military and public service, other political opponents who were accused of colluding with the foiled coup attempt come from different tribes. However, frictions between these two tribes have always raised the passions of revenge, arising from deep-seated hatred, fears, insecurities and the ever-boiling aggressiveness of well-armed militia on both sides. These have had huge implications on ethno-political tensions and discourses, of which the views of civilians who belong to one side would want to transform its civilian support to military protectionism.

Ethno-political discourses have been characterised by the lack of trust or transparency between the two leaders who stand at the hub of providing leadership to strengthen political institutions in the country, or the tribes. The institutional establishment, including pressure groups and opposing political parties, is also handicapped. Even if they exist, opposition parties and strong civil society groups have not managed to place demands on the government without persecution and/or 'elimination'.

CMR BASED ON ECONOMIC DEVELOPMENT

CMR is based on economic development in South Sudan. The conditions have been dictated according to the correlations between wealth, democracy and the military. An increase in wealth from oil has made competition for other resources less desperate. Currently, this notion seems to be changing in South Sudan because the correlation cannot be equated to fighting for oil revenue only. It is partly being advanced as a cause of the current internal conflicts, and yet tribal affinity is much stronger. Greater wealth is believed to strengthen the resources of the country, but it is also strengthening those leaders who tow tribal lines. Economic growth in South Sudan has been difficult to specify, partly because of mismanagement of national funds, austerity measures and external influences.

In a report prepared by Frontier Economics, in collaboration with the Center for Peace and Development Studies at Juba University, and the Ugandan Center for Conflict Resolution, if the conflict continues for another one to five years, it will cost South Sudan between USD22.3 billion and USD28 billion.[5] The report states that, if the effect of the conflict is measured over 20 years, to allow for flow-on effect, the loss is even greater, at between USD122 billion and USD158 billion.[6]

Other influences include foreign governments, institutions and individuals that have supplied ideas and offered inducements, as well as sanctions or the threat of them.[7] Pinkney (1993) argues that some of the influences have only been indirect but, all in all, democracy cannot be imposed. Although many South Sudanese would want to accumulate a lot of wealth for themselves, mostly army generals and those in high political positions, CMR has tended to favour army generals more. The majority of South Sudanese have been left to face the problems associated with political attitudes and tribally affiliated behaviours, with the military setting the base.

Following the central argument advanced by modernisation theorists, solving these problems should be the shaping factor for socio-economic growth. Democracy requires a willingness to accept government consent as a means of resolving conflicts. South Sudan's political elites failed to agree on the rules of their political games, and instead took the rough route to civil war and national disintegration. The rules have apportioned non-elites and political institutions to vary in their perspectives and relationships. In other words, politicians and the military do not have sharp distinctions in their relations, operations and formation. According to Pinkney (1993) institutional establishments should include pressure groups and opposing political parties who place demands on the government. In South Sudan, the problem can be understood well if one looks at the dangers that institutional determinism poses, where the role of economic development at grassroots levels tends to be relegated and overshadowed by external influences.

It is not surprising that the realities of South Sudan's post-independence is tied to the acute need for speedy economic and infrastructure developments – a way to reap peace dividends and enforce stronger relations between SPLA/M and different ethnic groups. The country's economy is not as diversified as it could be to meet its internal and external demands. According to a 2012 World Bank report,[8] South Sudan's economy continued to depend on the 98% of the country's total revenue from oil. During less than three years of independence, South Sudan had an inadequate 2% source of revenue when it closed oil exploration for nearly one-and-a-half years. The country was run under austerity measures, a time when the global financial crush was hitting major world economies in Europe and the US. NGOs and other international agencies pursued the demand for speedy post-independent governance and democratisation processes to consolidate state and peace building. Some NGOs and international agencies felt they laid the foundation and were the pacesetters to implement the liberal peace paradigm of operationalising modern state-building policies. Their continued existence and influence cannot be ignored in CMR.

Economic and good governance pressures came from the top-down and the bottom-up, clamping the leaders in between. These pressures were to be overcome by the provision of leadership, but all SPLA/M leadership originated from within the former rebel military forces and the economy remained undiversified.

Many South Sudanese believed, during the eight years of Kiir and Machar working side by side, that not building relationships with the military and civil population was a lost opportunity. Instead, the party remained polarised, with 'loyalists' holding the absolute moral values of SPLM/A, and 'side-changers' who were assumed to be working with the new cause, post-independence.

In order to diffuse triggering factors, Kiir always presented himself as a controversial leader by accommodating all side-changers, the once-termed enemies of the popular movement. Machar and other side-changers characterised the president as an agent who was slowly personalising power in the country. In both cases, the trading of accusations was used to technically assert power and polarise communities. The formation of elites also took shape, along with massive wealth accumulation.

Kiir was hailed by the international community and the people of South Sudan when, on 3 May 2012, he wrote a letter to 75 government officials and eight foreign governments in an attempt to recover an unaccounted for USD4 billion lost to corruption.[9] Kiir was able to appeal to his 'comrades' directly when he said in his letter: 'We fought for freedom, justice, and equality. Many of our friends died to achieve these objectives … Yet, once we got to power, we forgot what we fought for and began to enrich ourselves at the expense of our people.'

The South Sudanese traditional structures, cultural affinities, and treating 'comrades' as brothers in the struggle, exposed some people, but international communities who were also requested to return money were not emphasised. The letter was widely regarded as the rational assumption of the president that South Sudan should operate as a modern state, with functioning institutions and without corruption. He immediately assigned the Anti-Corruption Commission to recover approximately USD60 million in stolen public funds. Some who received the letter felt agitated and felt that the president was referring to them as thieves.[10] A rift emerged, leaving analysts with less knowledge about how multiple social structures, militarised politics and tribal affinity function in South Sudan.

In another rare incidence, cash was stolen from the president's office, despite tight security provided by the president's protection unit in the compound. The investigation committee presented a report stating that the suspects broke into the accountant's office and had stolen approximately USD57 000, of which USD14 000 was not recovered.[11]

CMR BASED ON SOCIAL DEVELOPMENT

Debacles and legacies of many years of democratic political trends have been signalled as lessons learnt from previously independent African states. These warned against internal political tensions, and cultural and tribal pluralism. The lessons and trends reinforced the realist dictum towards attitudes disparaged by salient ethnic nationalism, and warned against reinforced politics of hatred and suspicion that makes groups subject to Machiavellian manipulation.

Many have examined the temperament of statesmanship to play a role in state building and governance based on Thucydides' 'true realism', advanced 2 400 years ago. According to Morgenthau, in order to improve the world, it is important to work with forces inherent in human nature (self-interest, fear, incessant fear and coercion), not against them. Realists cannot believe any longer that international institutions by themselves are crucial to peace, without reflecting on the balance of power of other states, which is a good place to start analysing state building and governance in South Sudan. After independence, state building and governance in most of SSA did not consider that gaining power can limit power from former colonialists, neighbouring states, or from within. South Sudanese CMR has become a victim of this demise.

Many authors have analysed social relations based on modernisation, neo-Marxist failure of the state, and post-modernist perspectives. Social relations and social contracts are considered acts of ruling or controlling an independent state or its citizens with state authority. With respect to CMR, peace building in South Sudan needed to work within a system of governance driven by the function of good leadership and, in conducting state affairs, to influence or determine the course of action.

The 1998 World Bank report refers to governance as the exercise of political power to manage a nation's affairs ... [and] dedicated leadership who can produce quite a different outcome. The report adds that it requires a systematic effort to build a pluralistic institutional structure, a determination to respect the rule of law, and vigorous protection of the freedom of the press and human rights (World Bank, 1989). These are pillars of social relations and social development that are minimised in today's South Sudan.

The role of social relations in understanding CMR in South Sudan is sometimes informed by the conditions that favour discussions relating to the early formation of democratic processes. According to Dahl (1998) democracy prevails where there is effective participation of the citizens in the political life of a country; equality in voting; people have an enlightened understanding of what their actions leads to, control is exercised over the agenda, and adults are included in the democratic process. Undesirable consequences like tyranny have to be avoided, essential rights need to be guaranteed, general freedom and self-determination with moral autonomy must prevail, as does precipitated human development, protection of essential personal interest, political equity, prosperity and peace (Dahl 1998).

The five years of transition after signing the CPA in 2015 attempted to set the pace for social relations in South Sudan. However, the traditional structures that grounded stronger tribal structures, and authority to govern the people, played a lesser unifying force vat national level. Van de Goor, et al. (1996) refer to Mazrui's 'multiple structures of authority' as a form of understanding this kind of state building, which can play a role in moving society from military politics to civil politics. Major tribes regard each other as interlopers, rivals and/or enemies, with self-ascribed military positions, and political and financial privileges. The arrogance and exploitation to dominate power has brought tension, fierce conflict and power struggles from time to time.

According to the Minorities at Risk Project, ethnic groups have been involved in more than 70 protracted conflicts around the world (Banseka, 2005). While many authors, mainly of political background, refute the notion that ethnicity can be a cause of conflict in SSA, the case of South Sudan has clear traces of ethno-political conflict. Tribal groups in South Sudan have defined themselves using ethnic criteria to make claims on behalf of their collective interests against, first, the Khartoum government which colonised them, and now the state and the other internal political groups and/or ethnic groups. After independence, political party formation added to the reciprocity and the level of animosity and violence between ethnic groups. It has raised the emotional potency of conflicts, disposition to arouse deep-seated anxieties, fears and insecurities, and the degree of aggressiveness.

Tribal conflicts in South Sudan are protracted and have been bloody amid the apolitical trend of turmoil and tension. These are happening irrespective of the lenses put on by the traditionalists versus modernists, monarchists versus republicans, leftists versus rightists, centrists versus rightists, socialists versus capitalists, and secularists versus religious fundamentalists. Political and military encounters in South Sudan fiercely target power domination and resource accumulation in favour of one's own tribe. The case of South Sudan's democratic process is unique, and must be examined through various theoretical lenses that focus on state building, democratic governance and the psychology of society and the army.

CMR BASED ON IGAD-LED MEDIATION PEACE TALKS

South Sudan has a long history of engagement with IGAD. Mediation efforts began in Sudan in September 1993, aimed at stopping the ongoing civil war between the central Sudanese government and the SPLA. Peace-talk initiatives in Sudan started before the agency revitalised at the Addis Ababa summit (Healy, 2011). When the Sudananese government did not accept the IGAD proposal, because it was against the right to self-determination, the bond between the people of the South became even stronger. Eventually, the peace-talk sessions in Sudan had to be officially adjourned (ISS, 2004a).

In July 2000, the second phase of the IGAD-led mediation process was launched, and there were subsequent round of talks held under the new arrangement. These continued until July 2002, which resulted in the signing of the Machakos protocol (ISS 2004b). This provided a platform for the signing of the 2005 CPA, which gave South Sudan regional autonomy to administer itself. The agreement also provided a platform for a referendum that led to the independence of South Sudan in 2011 (Healy 2011). However, Young (2007) states that, despite its success, the IGAD mediation process in Sudan had many challenges and weaknesses, including the narrow focus of the peace-talk sessions, impartiality, lack of inclusivity throughout the process, failure to emphasise the influence of the international community, lack of trust and understanding between the warring parties, viewing media as an enemy, and a lack of institutional weakness. These are some of the factors that SPLA carried with them into their post-independence civil war.

Following the IGAD-led mediation process that started on 3 January 2014, now advanced to IGAD-PLUS mediation, bonds that loosely existed between Kiir and Machar have remained circumstantial.[12] These have had a significant impact on the rift between the people and military operations that continued to kill, maim and displace civilian populations.

A recent decision passed by the chairperson of the African Union Commission aimed at further strengthening the AU's contribution towards ending the conflict in South Sudan and the untold suffering inflicted upon the civilian population. The Commission was working towards the early operationalisation of the AU High-Level Ad Hoc Committee, established by the Peace and Security Council (PSC) at its 474th meeting on 5 December 2014,[13] in order to enhance Africa's support of IGAD mediation efforts. However, the Committee, which comprised of the heads of state and governments of Algeria, Chad, Nigeria, Rwanda and South Africa, met on the margins of the AU Summit held in Johannesburg, South Africa, in mid-June 2015. The outcome has not shown progress, but did change CMR for the worse and war ensued.

IMPLICATIONS OF CMR IN SOUTH SUDAN

CMR in South Sudan implicates the governance and democratisation process. Perspectives suggest that this is happening according to the demands and supply of state and peace building. The inspiration to build a state and set up good governance in South Sudan after it gained independence has grounded innovations from the military and political struggle of the SPLA/M. The reality of independence stagnated economic gains by fully utilising oil revenues that contribute 98% of the country's total revenue.

Modernisation theory bases on the economic developmental theoretical debate, which can be attributed to John Maynard Keynes, were followed by the practical insights contained in the Marshal Plan. South Sudanese political leaders, institutions and the civil population are included in the examination of this theory. Amid the joy of independence and setting on track the process of state building, the citizenry's demand for the provision of goods and services is increasing. Developing a good governance system, locally and globally, will attend to the accelerated needs of the economy.

The independence of South Sudan was accompanied by global austerity measures. Among the demands that the government should have dealt with are issues of CMR. The role of the state to deal with internal community conflicts and coordinate service provision remained limited. The implication of this theory is seen in the demand that assumes South Sudan is a functioning state with cohesively netted social activities, without giving due consideration to the lack of and/or having only meagre capital and human resources. In this respect, modernisation theoretical underpinning has assumed that South Sudan is supposed to function as a state with pre-existing established institutions, and, therefore, the heavily militarised civil society would render democratic governance in making CMR work. The growth in the national political institution has created animosity among ethnic groups. The basis for this is that multiple local structures of governance and social authority are the most known in South Sudan, but are not being considered.

The political system and idea in South Sudan about how a country should function oscillates between the levels of post-independence governance structure compared to the transformed SPLA/M governance system. The variation does not only lie in the transformation of SPLA, but also in the possibility and capacity to establish good governance and democracy from the centre to allow state building to bear fruition. The assumption here is that the decision-making body of civilians and civil society organisations would be strengthened.

Recently, the notion of state building demonstrated sideline advocacy for local to national structural-functionalism following on the SPLM political party reform. Such thoughts assumed that the political system could provide better political development of the country, but failed to understand the role of individuals and the ethno-political arrangement in country. In both cases, the state seems to be used as an arena where social forces are competing for power and resource allocation.

There is a common belief held by economists and politicians that modernisation can or should move South Sudan forward from its independence to the next development stage, with its focus on the would-be state, governance, political party formations and who should govern. According to Leys (1995) and Shivji (1975) much emphasis is placed on the fact that the control of the state in Africa was exercised not by an independent and assertive class of capitalists, but by a compracor or bureaucratic bourgeoisie, which may use its control of the state to feather its nest with the help of access to public funds.

Development peace theorists suggest that there is a curvilinear relationship between development and political conflict. But this argument applies only to internal forces that tend to happen during state formation, without considering the external capital. It further fails to determine the level of economic or political development that can be attained, and yet ethno-politics, ethnicity and power struggle lies at the centre of state building and governance.

Neo-Marxist theoretical explanations would put it that understanding the state in Africa was not really controlled by domestic forces in the first place, but by the agents of international capital. Like most African state policies, South Sudanese governance policies have been designed by NGOs and international agencies, which, to a greater extent, were dictated by international capitalism. Some of the policies focused more on benefits aligned towards multinational corporations. The resultant effect is grounded on the vision that political and institutional development of South Sudanese society will be determined by material forces – oil revenues as it stands. The state and the leaders are an integral part of society, but also with different classes whose instrument to use power and domination create class, accumulate capital, and consolidate power and domination.

This position can easily be challenged by opposing groups who are side-lined from power, not part of the gains from the material forces, and have no share of the dividends of peace from the long years of liberation struggle. It has already been demonstrated in South Sudan that the instrument of power and domination may oppose overall governance and institutional development, thus denying the local population and civil society group participation. The contention of believers of Neo-Marxist theory implicates South Sudan, that, using the state, it is hindering political participation, acting less to create wider participation within the public policy exercise, institutional and plural governance development. Such a position may push the governance system to portray the state to act as an agent that is failing to solve its civil society and grassroots problems. In a theoretical sense, this is a very vulnerable position for governance as resistance can be generated or render state's situation to portray that it has failed to live up to the expectations of its people. Many authors accept that, should the state fail to make some positive differences in human and material development, the basis for arguing in support of failure of the state theory holds.

An American organisation, Fund for Peace (FFP) has identified some of the above reasons to rank South Sudan as a failed state (Taft, 2014). Their measured index relates to demographic pressures, group grievance, human flight, uneven development, poverty and economic decline, legitimacy of the state, public services, human rights, security apparatus, factionalised elites, and external intervention. An aspect that has not been considered is that failure of the state theory, whose arguments are based on administration theorists, also argues for bureaucratic reform. Further, administration theorists who are also economists maintain that market failure in a failed state is due to over-regulation and a rent-seeking attitude of state leaders.

However, South Sudan is too young to undergo bureaucratic reform and follow over-regulation and rent-seeking attitudes of the leaders. Although elements of corruption among top government officials exist, FFP did not exhaustively measure the case of South Sudan. FFP emphasised the theory that explains the state use of power as a tool for solving problems facing the society (Adebayo, et al., 1999). Partly, they look at the ineffective control over other groups in society, making the state to be seen as promulgating without adequate enforcement mechanisms to comply with the democratic norms of governing a militarised society. This has only triggered arguments that the prominence of patronage is actually rolling out into the failure of state theoretical discussions in South Sudan's case. The general trend is following on the blame posited on the role of the state and governors in the country. The logical trend would be to make a weak comparison of state building with the strengthening of civil society groups as a means of understanding CMR better.

Where there is increasing personalisation of power relations, and as the notion of the state as an instrument of technical rationality drifts away, the need to formulate alternative structures of governance and administration is hard. In South Sudan, multiple traditional structures and cultural affinities which are being challenged by pre-modern values are only acting as underlying rational assumptions that South Sudan can be a modern state with its functioning institutions operating fully after it achieved independence. South Sudan is, in this context, analysed as a state with universal phenomenon, without analysing its local context and the factors and conditions that the SPLA/M went through. This has created a burden on the discussion surrounding CMR.

On the one hand, post-modernists argue that state building and governance should be seen through the lens of institutional universalism while considering cross-cultural societies. The argument bases more on empirical substance than epistemological or theoretical justifications. The reason lies with some academics that claim subversion of the dominant paradigm of state building and governance, arguing that there is no truth and that everything is relative. They argue that states and governance should be studied in a special context so as to guide our understanding of the complexities of governance. While academics are not irrelevant, South Sudan is building CMR bridges in its attempts to build the state. It is following ethno-political lines.

Academics are picking up public policy issues, while politicians are picking up concepts and theories from the realms of academics. But key issues of state building and governance in South Sudan have not transformed its course from the ethno-political sources of conflict, now that the fight against Khartoum for political independence has been achieved. In any case, joining laws and violence threatens the principles of sovereign nomos with distinction (Agamben 1998: 31). The practical reality in South Sudan is that there exists some cultural links to sovereignty described by Mbembe (2003) as necropolitics.

The explanations of CMR after the mid-December 2013 conflict took a political twist, while others and, what can be observed on the ground, lean more towards ethnic confrontations between Nuer-led opposition, and Dinka–Government-based confrontations. There is a dysfunctional political system that made the war a classic division of powers in the legislative, executive, and judicial branches of government. On the one hand, the seemingly 'federal' run states' apparatus considered the cultural and regional differences within the country. Fusing the two systems into a rebel-run type of governance made it impossible to strengthen the CMR in post-independence governance. The challenges from the unfulfilled CPA doctrines of 2005 are another added factor. These can be backtracked to the historical distrust between the Dinka and Nuer people.

CMR based on economic development in South Sudan often faces a dilemma, especially when dependence on oil remains central to the life stream of the people and the economy. It is commonly called the 'resource curse'. The glue that had to mend relations between the citizens and the government, lacked proper taxations, provision of public goods, public service, and development policy to improve the living standard of its people. Instead, the country has been concerned with its internal competitions over rent seeking and access to resources and power. The instability and continued violence has had serious impacts on vendors and small retail businesses, thus disrupting the roadside economic activities that blended many ethnic groups.

CMR based on social development is registering decay, following the serious impact of the civil war. The humanitarian crisis has not diminished. While the government has sometimes been blamed for stalling and/or blocking humanitarian access, the rebel opposition does the same.

The initial stages of the IGAD-led mediation peace talks presented a glimmer of hope among the civilian population in South Sudan. However, the IGAD peace processes are viewed differently now. Many believe that IGAD member states had self-interest in the South Sudan conflict. The international actors have also registered frustration with the process, partly because of its historical and financial support. Several states, including the US, Norway, UK and the European Union threatened to impose sanctions on the South Sudanese government and the Machar rebels if they continued to undermine the peace process by not engaging constructively with the cease-fire.[14] The hybrid IGAD-PLUS process has mirrored a wait-and-see perspective of the already skewed perceptions of the civilian population in South Sudan. The government and the Machar rebel opposition have shown disregard for IGAD-PLUS, offering no leeway for the resolution of the conflict.

Analysts like Riker (1962) have argued that this kind of act conforms to the theory of behaviour to increase the power balance, which, in turn, results in bandwagoning. Bandwagoning is therefore a tendency for weak states to seek alliance with the strongest power, irrespective of that power's ideology or type of government, in order to increase their security. Uganda has been bandwagoned into the South Sudan conflict.

CONCLUSION

This chapter has explained the expository CMR perspectives in South Sudan. CMR is no more than a theory in South Sudan. The perspectives have clearly shown that the relations have primarily contingent populations to the varying capabilities, doctrines, procedures and understanding of state building, governance, democracy, humanitarian and development issues. The SPLA/M have remained with the misnomer of the past that walked them into the disastrous war. The fusion between the military, political groups and civil population has not played to the advantages of the new state, so as to create a firm basis for forming strong governance.

The political power struggles between Kiir and Machar wedged the relationships between the SPLA loyalists and breakaway factions. While on the one hand the civilian population continues to bear the burden of the war, other factors like food insecurity, health and lack of clean drinking water have distanced the population from the government and the military, where the disasters may be originating.

In the short and long term, economic pressure and its consequences will treat South Sudan very harshly. With all eyes fixed on oil revenue, the war is primarily playing out in oil-bearing areas, which may at some point diminish access or result in total cut off. Trade will suffer as many offices close down and salary remittances will continue to impact on performance, encourage corruption, increase prices of essential commodities and discourage the commitment of civil servants to serve the country.

Fighting a major war, and moving into civil war, is costly in terms of loss of lives and income. These costs greatly reduce a country's tolerance for undertaking another war, but there has been no sign of war weariness among the South Sudanese.

IGAD and its IGAD-PLUS formation can draw otherwise neutral parties into opposed coalitions and control over the militarised population may discourage aggression and win favour of the civilian population. But this intervention poses challenges to sovereign interference of the state, despite countries like Uganda already being party to the intervention. Both sides fighting in South Sudan have played by the rules for rivals in balancing the process of staying vigilant, seeking allies whenever they could not match the armaments of an adversary; remained flexible in making alliances; played charitable understanding of the humanitarian crises; and opposed any state that supported hegemony of the other.

CMR in South Sudan had an exciting and challenging beginning. The population welcomed the new nation with much more than a fleeting excitement of its freshness as a part of sovereign state. However, the path of statehood and nationhood became a very uncomfortable one. The relationship between the military and the civilian population is either edging in a deadly direction or is becoming more militarised. Both paths offer no credit for improving CMR.

NOTES

1. *See* 'South Sudan: Kiir Says Ready for Dialogue with Machar' in All Africa, 19 December 2013. Available at http://allafrica.com/stories/201312190258.html. Accessed 29 May 2015.

2. Ibid.

3. For details *see* Apuuli (2014).

4. The Rumbek meeting minutes were classified as highly confidential, which barred them from being shared in the public domain, until recently, when fighting broke out in South Sudan, when photocopies of the document became a 'public secret'. Much of what is contained in the document reveals the depth at which SPLM/A were divided and lacked a unified center of command and leadership from John Garang.

5. 'The Cost of War:An estimation of economic and financial costs of ongoing war'. A report prepared by Frontier Economics, in collaboration with the Center for Peace and Development Studies, Juba University, and the Ugandan Center for Conflict Resolution on South Sudan, looking forward from January 2015.

6. Ibid.

7. The details and modalities of the sanction proposal is suggested in the Draft United Nation Security Council Sanction Report, Version 6, January 2015.

8. The 2012 World Bank Report has detailed trends on how South Sudan's economy may be declining.

9. Details of the two-page document and a letter to the Anti-Corruption Commission is available at http://paanluelwel.com/2012/06/01/letter-from-president-kiir-on-corruption-4-billion-dollars-stolen/; also reported at http://www.sudantribune.com/President-Kiir-demands-S-Sudan,42785. Accessed 20 April 2015.

10. Ibid.

11. *See* 'Millions in cash money stolen from President Kiir's office in Juba' in *Sudan Tribune*, 27 March 2013. Available at http://www.sudantribune.com/spip.php?article45984.

12. See series of IGAD press releases/articles, available at http://www.igad.org, accessed May 2015.: 'Parties sign implementation matrix and agree timetable for implementation of cessation of hostilities in South Sudan', 9 November 2014; 'IGAD-led peace talks on South Sudan continue in Bashir Dar', 22 September 2014; 'South Sudan peace talks make progress, adjourn for consultations', 3 October 2014; 'President Salva Kiir and Dr Riek Machar sign a landmark agreement to end the conflict in South Sudan', 9 May 2014; 'Direct Phase II of the IGAD-led South Sudan peace process resumes in Addis Ababa', 25 March 2014; 'Press release from IGAD special envoys to South Sudan peace dialogue', 3 March 2014; 'Direct negotiations between South Sudanese parties', 6 January 2014; *Intergovernmental Authority on Development Profile* (2004).

13. The Chairperson of the Commission of the African Union (AU), Dr Nkosazana Dlamini-Zuma issued a press release on 2 June 2015 in Addis Ababa announcing the appointment of former president Alpha Oumare as AU High Representative for South Sudan.

14. The most comprehensive account of the war, suggesting that it is ethnic based, was first released by the ICG in 2014: 'South Sudan: A civil war by any other name', Africa Report No 127. Available at http://www.crisisgroup.org/~/media/Files/africa/horn-of-africa/south%20sudan/217-south-sudan-a-civil-war-by-any-other-name-.pdf.

REFERENCES

Adebayo, A. (ed.). 1999. *Comprehending Mastering African Conflicts*. London: African Centre for Development and Strategic Studies (ACDESS) and Zed Books.

AFP. 2014. '50,000 and not counting: South Sudan's war dead', 15 November 2014. Available at http://releifweb.int/report/sputh-sudan/50000-and-not-counting-south-sudans-war-dead. Accessed 19 May 2015.

Agamben, G. 1998. *Homo Sacer: Sovereign Power and Bare Life*. Translated by D. Heller-Roazen. Standford, CA: Standford University Press.

All Africa. 2013. 'South Sudan: Kiir says ready for dialogue with Machar', 19 December 2013. Available at http://allafrica.com/stories/201312130258.html. Accessed 29 May 2015.

Apuuli, K.P. 2014. 'Explaining the (il)legality of Uganda's intervention in the current South Sudan conflict'. Published online by African Security Review, 23 September 2014. Available at http://www.tandonline.com/loi/rasr20. Accessed 29 May 2015.

Arnaut, K. & Hojberg, C.K. 2008. 'Gouvernance et ethnographie en temps de Crise: Del'e'tude des Orders e'mergents dans l'Afrique ente guerre er paix' in *Politique Africaine*, Vol. 111.

Banseka, C. 2005. 'Development for Peace: In search of solutions to conflicts in Sub-Saharan Africa'. Diss (2002) Boca Raton, Florida.

Beer, D. 2006. 'Peace-Building on the Ground: Reforming the judicial sector in Haiti' in Keating, T. & Knight, W.A. (eds). 2006. *Building Sustainable Peace*. New Delhi: Academic Foundation, United Nations University Press.

Beer, S. 1966. 'An operational research method approach to the nature of conflict' in *Political Studies*, 14(2): pp. 119–132.

Carlton-Ford, S. & Ender, M.G. (eds). 2011. *The Routledge Handbook of War and Society: Iraq and Afghanistan*. New York: Routledge.

Cramer, C. 2006. *Civil War is Not a Stupid Thing: Accounting for violence in developing countries*. London; Hurst & Co.

Dahl, R.A. 1989. *Democracy and its Critics*. New Haven: Yale University Press.

Dahl, R.A. 1998. *On Democracy*. London: Yale University Press.

De Soya, I. 2006. 'Do foreign investors punish democracy? Theory and Empirics, 1984–2001' in *Kyklos*, 59(3). Available at http://www.svt.ntnu.no/iss/Indra.de.Soysa/POL3503H05/jakobsen%26desoysa. pdf. Accessed 15 June 2015.

Dean, M. 2007. *Governing Societies: Political perspectives on domestic and international rule*. London: McGraw Hill.

Didier Pe'clard Mechoulan, D. 2015. 'Rebel governance and the politics of civil war' (working paper). Bern: Swiss Peace Foundation.

Doyle, M.W. & Sambanis, N. 2000. 'International Peace-Building: A theoretical and quantitative analysis' in *America Political Science Review*, Vol. 94, pp. 779-801.

Doyle, M.W. & Sambanis, N. 2006. *Making War and Building Peace: UN Peace Operations*. Princeton: Princeton University Press.

Goldstein, J.S. 1999. *International Relations*. New York: Pearson Longman.

Gurr, T. & Harff, B. 1994. *Ethnic Conflict in World Politics*. Boulder: Westview Press.

Hauss, C. 2011. *International Conflict Resolution: International relations for the 21st Century*. New York: Continuum.

Healey, S. 2011. 'Seeking peace and security in the Horn of Africa: The contribution of the Inter-Governmental Authority on Development' in *International Affairs*, 87(1): pp. 105–120.

Institute for Security Studies (ISS). 2004a. 'The peace talks' sessions in Sudan with SPLA officially adjourned'.

Institute for Security Studies (ISS) 2004b. 'Machakos Protocol'.

International Crisis Group (ICG). 2014. 'South Sudan: A civil war by any other name', Africa Report No. 217, 10 April 2014.

Keen, S. 1984. *Faces of the Enemy: Reflections on the hostile imagination*. New York; Harper & Row.

Koos & Gutschke. 2014. 'South Sudan's newest war: When two old men divide a nation' (working paper).

Available at http://info.southsudanngoforum.org/dataset/koos-and-gutschke-2014-south-sudan-s-newest-war. Accessed 15 June 2015.

Leys, C. 1975. *Underdevelopment in Kenya: The political economy of neo-colonialism*. Berkeley: University of California Press.

Mampilly, Z. 2011. *Rebel Rules: Insurgent governance and civilian life during war*. New York: Cornell University Press.

Mbembe, A. 2003. 'Necropolitics' in *Public Culture*, 15(1): pp. 11-40.

Newman, E., Paris, R. & Richmond, O. (eds). 2009. *New Perspectives on Liberal Building*. Tokyo: United Nations University Press.

Nhoma, G. 2006. 'Actor/Actant-Network Theory as emerging methodology for environmental education in South Africa' in *South African Journal of Environmental Education*, 23(1).

Paris, R. 2004. *At War's End: Building peace after conflict*. Cambridge: Cambridge University Press.

Pinkney, R. 1993. *Democracy in the Third World*. Philadelphia: Open University Press.

Riker, W.H. 1962. *The Theory of Political Coalitions*. New Haven: Yale University Press.

Schlicte, K. 2009. *In the Shadow of Violence: The politics of armed groups*. Chicago: University of Chicago Press.

Shivji, I. 1975. *Class Struggle in Tanzania*. Dar es Salaam Publishing House, Tanzania.

Sudan Tribune. 2013. 'Millions in cash money stolen from President Kiir's office in Juba', 27 March 2013. Available at http://www.sudantribune.com/spip.php?article45984). Accessed May 2015.

Taft, P. 2014. 'Statehood or Bust: The case of South Sudan'. Available at http://library.fundforpeace.org/fsi14-southsudan.

Tilly, C. 2006. *The Politics of Collective Violence*. Cambridge: Cambridge University Press.

UNMISS. 2014. 'Conflict in South Sudan: A human rights report'. Available at http://www.unmiss.unmissions.org/Portals/unmiss/Human%20Rights%20Reports/UNMISS%20Conflict%20in%20South%20Sudan%20-%20A%20Human%20Rights%20Report.pdf.

Van de Goor, L., Rupesinghe, K. & Sciarone, P. (eds). 1996. *Between Development and Destructruction: An enquiry into the causes of conflict in post-colonial states*. London: MacMillan

Varshney, P.K. 1997. *Distributed Data Fusion for Network-Centric Operations*. New York: Springer.

Wimmer, A. 1997. 'Who owns the State? Understanding ethnic conflict in post-colonial societies' in *Nations and Nationalism*, 3(4): pp 631–666.

World Bank. 1989. *Report on protection of the freedom of the press and human rights*. World Bank Publication.

World Bank. 2012. *South Sudan's Economy*. World Bank Publication.

Young, J. 2012. *Sudan IGAD Peace Process: An Evaluation*. Institute of Governance Studies, Simon Fraser University, Vancouver.

Chapter 9

Civil-Military Relations Dynamics and the Prospects for a Democratic Developmental State in Zimbabwe

by Gorden Moyo

INTRODUCTION

This chapter sets out to interrogate the phenomenon of a democratic developmental state (DDS) within the discursive context of civil-military relations (CMR) in Zimbabwe. Extant literature dating back to the classical East Asian style developmental states is conspicuously silent on the relevance of the epistemic and ontological designs of CMR as development imperatives in the developing world. Yet a cursory analysis of the political economies of most African countries, including Algeria, Angola, Burundi, Eritrea, Gabon, Nigeria, Rwanda, Togo and Uganda, points to the omnipresence, if not omnipotence, of the retired and serving military officers in vital state institutions, political economy, and public leadership. This specter is also provably recursive in Asia and the Middle East, where countries such as Myanmar/Burma, Indonesia, Pakistan, Thailand, Syria and Turkey, have been repeatedly prone to and indeed sustained by the executive-military oligarchies. Similarly, in Latin America's emerging democracies, senior military corps continue to play an integral role in the political and economic spheres as members of the ruling politico-military alliance.

Not to be outdone, the Zimbabwean military institution has been progressively expanding its influence and visibility in the political economy over the past three-and-a-half decades. Viewed from this context, the military has a bearing on the project of institutionalising a DDS in that country. As will be illustrated in the rest of this assessment, the increasing commercial orientation of the military, through survival tactics, political motivation or institutionalised commercialism, is a specter that has been ossified and made a permanent feature in Zimbabwe today. While the military's increased involvement in politics, economy and commercial enterprises may only be a few decades old, the military now runs large swaths of both illicit and legal businesses, ranging across hunting safaris, housing, informal trading, farming and mining companies. Evidently, the military in Zimbabwe has made deeper inroads into the political economy; this is not in the national interest, but in the interest of ensuring regime survival, whose beneficiaries are the political elites, the military themselves and their families, and not the general citizenry.

This discussion is predicated on three broad theoretical and empirical observations concerning the military and democratic governance. First, it is argued that Zimbabwe has been captured by a coterie of military officials: the Joint Operations Command (JOC), which now dominates most crucial state institutions, including state enterprises and para-statals (Zimbabwe Institute, 2008; Chitiyo, 2009; Rupiya, 2013). Together with the political elite, this military oligarchy exhibits Stalinist tendencies, neo-praetorian paradigms and neo-patrimonial practices, all of which are inimical to the institutionalisation of the norms and principles of a successful DDS. Second, some prominent scholars posit that Zimba-bwe's executive-military alliance is symbiotically connected by the history of the liberation struggle, ideological orientations, clientelist-patronage network, and by acts of impunity in the post-liberation era (Moyo *forthcoming*). This executive-military partnership has repro-duced colonial matrices of power, being and knowledge which militate against the core values of a DDS, such as genuine citizen participation, citizen empowerment, citizen own-ership and public accountability (Moyo, 2013). Third and final, the construction of a DDS as portrayed in the available literature takes as a given the Huntingtonian's 'objective civil-military relations' model (Huntington, 1957). Yet in most countries that gained their inde-pendence through an armed struggle, such as Angola, Mozambique and Namibia, CMR do not appear to be conforming to the western traditions of civilian control. Instead, subjective CMR seem to dominate state-military relations in these countries. In the final analysis, the three fundamental assumptions made in this contribution seem to suggest that the military in Zimbabwe is more of an albatross weighing heavy on the effort towards the construction of a DDS. While the military is not the only institution in Zimbabwe that makes rapacious and disproportionate grab for resources, power and influence, there are two major reasons to focus on it. First, its power means it can be much more effective in grabbing resources. Second, there is a lack of transparency in military transactions as the relevant data is rou-tinely stated to be confidential.

This chapter is divided into seven sections. The first section provides an overview of the notion 'civil-military relations' as deployed in this contribution. The second section examines the historical trajectories of CMR in Zimbabwe. Pertinent to this discussion is the role of nationalist-continuist discourse in the democracy and development project in

Zimbabwe. The third section discusses the logic for a DDS in the context of the 'coercive and redistributive mechanisms' pursued by the executive-military oligarchy. The fourth section concentrates on the interface between the military sector and the civilian population – specifically the manner in which the executive-military alliance has defined its role and dominated all the sectors of the state, thereby erecting the barriers against the possibility of constructing a successful DDS in Zimbabwe. The fifth investigates the pervasive party-military relations which tend to exclude other stakeholders in the public spaces in Zimbabwe. The sixth section interrogates some of the prospects for transforming CMR in Zimbabwe in order to catalyse the incubation of a DDS. The seventh and final section presents the concluding remarks of this chapter.

CONCEPTUALISING CMR

For the purposes of this study, CMR refer to the web of relations between the military and the society within which it operates (Rupiya, 2005; Luqman, 2011). More generally, 'matters of civil-military relations involve issues such as the attitudes of the military towards the civilian society, the civilian society's perceptions of , and attitudes to the military, and the role of the military in relation to the state' (Ebo, 2005). Such relations encompass all aspects of the role of the military: professional, political, social and economic. To be sure, the discussion here views CMR in broad terms, that is, civilian-security relations rather than simply focusing on CMR in the narrower institutional sense of the concept.

It is crucially important, right from the outset, to distinguish between the two widely advertised models of CMR in literature, namely 'objective' and 'subjective' civilian controls. These two models have been widely discussed by scholars such as Huntington, Jawonitz and Finer. As observed by Cleary (n.d.), 'although these three men were apt to criticise each other on aspects of their respective theories, they were essentially in agreement that stable, democratic civil-military relations were more likely if the military was professional, reflective of the society it served, and believed in an explicit principle of civil supremacy'. In essence, their theories of objective and subjective control are premised on the Clausewitzean trinity, that is, people, army and government (Cleary, n.d.). It would appear that, in Zimbabwe, the ruling party-military relations are fused, government/executive-army relations are symbiotic, but the people-army relations are frosty. While objective civilian controls exist on paper, in practice the subjective civilian controls dominate the relations in that country.

By definition, objective control refers to those mechanisms of a formal, constitutional and legalistic nature operating externally to the military establishment and embodying the political and constitutional pact entered into between the state and the armed forces (Huntington, 1957). Arguing on the same lines Naidoo (n.d) contends that objective civilian control will be at play:

> ... when the civilian and military institutions are distinct from each other; when the institutional boundaries that separate the civilian and military spheres of activities and functions are clearly demarcated; when the civilian authority makes policy that the military implements; and where the military's participation in policy making is limited to security and defence issues and obtained through civilian and not military initiative.

This tradition is rooted and common in mature democracies such as the USA, UK, France and Germany (Huntington, 1957). Viewed from this perspective, the military is assumed to willingly accede to civil control as enshrined in the national constitution, defence and security policy frameworks, as well as in the norms and values of liberal democracy. This is hardly the case in Zimbabwe. To gain a better understanding of the role of the military, it is important to bear in mind its pivotal place at the origin of the post-colonial state of Zimbabwe, and to grasp the strength of the military connection to the war of liberation. Basically, Zimbabwe has a political army that believes itself to be the custodian of the country's independence, national interest and national integrity. In addition, the military believes that it has an onerous role of keeping the nationalist movement the ruling party ZANU-PF in power. Under these circumstances, objective civilian controls are subservient to the more practical and pragmatic subjective civilian controls.

By definition, subjective control model is an antinomy of the objective paradigm. It states that civil supremacy is assured through the deployment of various non-democratic tactics such as ethnic manipulation, divide and rule, co-option of influential military figures, indoctrination, instrumental pay-offs, bias recruitment, promotion and posting of loyal officers, party penetration of the leadership echelons of the military sector, and establishment of security counter-balances to the influences of the armed forces in the form of the presidential guard (Williams, 1998; Rupiya, 2005; Luqman, 2011). In short, subjective civilian control is achieved when the distinction between the government and the army has been lost. This present contribution argues that patronage-based military control is a norm in Zimbabwe today.

As a matter of principle, the military in Zimbabwe is prohibited by law from participating in politics. They can exercise their democratic right to vote, but are not permitted to hold office in any political party or political organisation. However, in practice, several generals are represented in the various ZANU-PF party structures. As will be illustrated, 'the ideology that power comes from the barrel of the gun and that the gun is subordinate to the former is a notion that has since been transferred to the present governmental machinery without reorientation' (Rupiya, 2005). This situation accounts for the firmly entrenched executive control of the military, as well as for the incestuous and non-transparent nature of CMR that represents resistance to the introduction and of evolution of democratic CMR in that country.

HISTORICISING CMR IN ZIMBABWE

The discussion here begins with a brief exploration of Zimbabwe's complex politico-military history. For one to gain a more nuanced understanding of the implications of CMR on the DDS construction, one needs to unpack grammar from the colonial, liberation struggle and post-liberation vantage points. Clearly, the current CMR in Zimbabwe represents the continuity of authoritarian governance systems passed on from the then Rhodesia to Zimbabwe. In this regard, the achievement of the juridical freedom in 1980 only changed the composition of the managers of the state and not the character of the state, which remained much as it was in the colonial era.

At independence in 1980, Zimbabwe inherited repressive state security apparati geared towards the protection of the colonial regime (Hendricks & Hutton, 2009). In fact, the raison d'être of the colonial military establishment was state security as opposed to human security. Bluntly put, the major function of the colonial state military sector was to hold down a conquered and beleaguered people. Under these circumstances, citizen participation in policy making, decision making and elections were not just impossible, but also criminalised. The military was an instrument of subjugation, violence and intimidation. This assertion is confirmed by Ndlovu-Gatsheni (2013) who argues that, as in all colonial encounters, 'coercion rather than consent formed the DNA of colonial governance' in the then Rhodesia. Apparently, this colonial culture of impunity, lack of accountability, coercion and violence has been inherited by the post-colonial state managers in Zimbabwe, root, stalk, and leaf.

Similarly, the liberation struggle left negative imprints on the current CMR in Zimbabwe. Observers note that the armed struggle produced a violent culture of intimidation and fear within the ranks of the liberation movement and among their social base of peasant supporters (Moyo, 1993). Moreover, the armed struggle lacked a guiding moral ethic and was thus amenable to manipulation by unscrupulous nationalist-military alliance which personalised the liberation war for its selfish ends to this day (Moyo, 1993). To this end, the Zimbabwean military acts rather like a single-party regime that cannot tolerate any opposition to its monopoly position. The dominant culture of coercion remains deeply ingrained among the ruling elite, and largely accounts for its persistent intolerance towards democratic transition in that country. Besides, the military has subsequently mythologised its role in the independence struggle and now sees itself as the creator, guardian, protector, warrantor, guarantor and underwriter of the Clausewitzean 'trinity' of the ruling party ZANU-PF, the state and the executive branch of government.

Notwithstanding the legal and constitutional provisions for civilian control, Zimbabwe's liberation era CMR has had a profound impact on the country's body politic, reflecting a much more integrated executive-military structure than appears in the texts (Rupiya, 2005). Not surprisingly, the executive-military diarchy has been using its hegemonic political power to maintain, and in some cases to expand, the colonial matrices of power such as the Public Order and Security Act (POSA) and the Criminal Law (Codification and Reform) Act to suppress the political activities of the citizens. The colonial matrices of power, being and knowledge have contributed to the development of the executive-military oligarchy that is assigned wide discretionary powers and is subject to little parliamentary oversight and public accountability in Zimbabwe today. Almost invariably, the Zimbabwean military makes frequent reference to the legacy of the liberation struggle, but rarely invokes any respect for the rule of law. This is not surprising, since the rule of law would imply that the military is just one institution among many, and should not be in overall control of the levers of state power.

Viewed from this perspective, CMR in Zimbabwe is a complex fusion of the colonially inherited, the liberation struggle inspired paradigms and the post liberation political exigencies. Clearly, ZANU-PF, having been a militarised liberation movement, has failed to demilitarise itself, not only in practice, but also in attitude, culture and style of management of civil institutions and the state at large. In short, the ZANU-PF-led government readily assumed the resilient colonial and military oriented structures and strictures left by the retreating Rhodesian settler state, with serious implications for democracy, human rights and human security and, most importantly, to the project of institutionalisation of a DDS in Zimbabwe.

Consequently, military power in Zimbabwe has grown progressively over the years due to the military's increasing political power and economic autonomy so that its dependence on elected government has lessened over time. The source of this power has partially been based on allowing the military to build business empires through redistributive nationalist policies. It is argued that the more economic autonomy the military gains, the less answerable it is to the civilian oversight, a prerequisite to democratic transition and consolidology desperately needed in Zimbabwe.

CONTEXTUALISING A DDS CONSTRUCTION

There is an increasing din of voices calling for the transformation of CMR and the construction of a democratic developmental state in Zimbabwe (Moyo, 2013). At continental level, the past failures of the development paradigms, including nifty neo-liberal market orthodoxy policies, have led heterodox thinkers to argue for the return of the state into the development arena. This emerging heterodox thinking has subsequently dusted the concept of the East Asian model of developmental state. However, unlike the classical authoritarian developmental state, the emerging scholarship is advocating a DDS that is pluricentric and people-centred, and that embraces civilian supremacy over military commandism in the governance of public goods. Ndlovu-Gatsheni (2011) describes this kind of 'a state as one that is capable of working to fulfill the democratic and developmental aspirations of the majority of the people within its borders'.

A DDS is characterised by a number of defining features. First, a DDS is viewed as a state that allows its citizens to enjoy civil liberties, citizen participation, citizen empowerment, citizen ownership, political legitimacy and public accountability (Moyo, 2013). Simply put, a DDS is a state that prioritises human security, socioeconomic development, and democracy with social content (Edigheji, 2010). Second, a DDS is conceived as a type of state that is defined in terms of networked infrastructure, possession of effective and functioning technology, existence of functioning education and health systems, accumulated high national income, and a diversified economy (Mkandawire, 2010; Evans, 2010). Third, a DDS is characterised by visionary leadership, independent bureaucratic elite, embedded state, development coalitions and constitutionalism (Amuwo, 2008; Evans, 2010, Mkandawire, 2010). Fourth and final, a DDS is conceived as post-Washington Consensus, where the state is central but not the sole actor in development planning, and where social inclusivity is institutionalised as part of governance of the public sphere. In short, a DDS is a reconstructed and reconfigured state that prioritises both democracy and development as contrasted to autocratic developmental states of the East Asian model of the 1980s and 1990s.

From a more practical perspective, the main objective of a DDS is to broaden citizen participation and make governments responsible and responsive in an environment in which citizens enjoy broad civil, political, social and economic rights (Edigheji, 2010). It can therefore be posited here that a successful DDS is characterised by strong institutions that foster predictability, accountability and transparency in public affairs; free, fair and credible electoral process; capable and credible public institutions such as the judiciary, the police service, and anti-corruption commissions. The now-expired Inclusive Government of Zimbabwe had expressed its intention to build a DDS in the backdrop of its Medium Term Plan (2011-2015). While addressing a civil society conference on 25 November 2013 in Bulawayo, the national chairman of ZANU-PF who is also a Senior Minister of State in the President's Office, Simon Khaya Moyo, pointed out that the ZANU-PF-led government of Zimbabwe had adopted the notion of a 'Social Democratic Developmental State' as its development model. This remains to be seen since there is no mention of the said model in the most recently adopted economic blueprint: the Zimbabwe Agenda for Sustainable Socio- Economic Transformation (Zim-Asset, 2013-2018).

The project of constructing a successful DDS is more urgent and compelling in Zimbabwe today because of the current multifaceted development and governance challenges. In recent years, Zimbabwe has been paralysed by economic melt-down, inconclusive and disputed electoral outcomes, incessant political strife and partisan gridlock, rampant corruption, and recurring political squabbles. Available evidence implicates the executive-military alliance as largely responsible for these lingering economic, political and social problems in Zimbabwe (Masunungure, 2011; Chitiyo & Rupiya, 2005). While the July 2013 elections which marked the end of the Inclusive Government (2009-2013) may have been granted a seal of approval by the Southern African Development Community (SADC) and the African Union (AU) observer missions, the new government is suffering from a crisis of legitimacy after the leading opposition, the Movement for Democratic Change (MDC), and countries such as USA, UK, Canada and Australia, refused to accept the results, citing massive rigging and the alleged role played by the military establishment in tampering with the electoral process.

In the context of this discussion, the notion of a DDS insists on military subordination to its civilian leadership and, by extension, to democratic processes of authority and control, resting ultimately on the freely expressed opinion of unfettered electorates in choosing officeholders. Evidence abounds that, unchecked and unaccountable, military institutions often prey on the most vulnerable members of society, hampering daily struggles for survival and other basic freedoms. As acknowledged by Ndlovu-Gatsheni (2011) 'the continuing struggle is over the nature and type of the state that will not be a menace to the people but a facilitator of economic development and provider of freedom and security'.

It is argued that the current military forays into public affairs are detrimental to public accountability and principles of democracy, and hence to the institutionalisation of a DDS. Okwadiba Nnoli (n.d.) was right when he observed that:

> ... the military and democracy are in dialectical opposition. The military can never engender democracy because it is the antithesis of democracy in regard to its norms, values, purpose and structure. The military addresses the extreme and the extraordinary while democracy addresses the routine, the military values discipline and hierarchy, democracy freedom and equality. The military is a taut chain of command while democracy is anarchy of diversity. Democracy presupposes human sociability, the military its total absence, inhuman extremity of killing the opposition. The military demands submission, democracy enjoins participation. One is a tool of violence, the other a means of consensus-building.

Viewed from this perspective, modern, capable and democratic states are poised to emerge from democratic systems and socially inclusive processes. In Zimbabwe, the prospects for a successful DDS project will be a function of new CMR. So far evidence has discredited the notion that East Asian-style developmental dictatorships are desirable. Rather, new readings of traditional developmental states indicate that they (Asian models) were fostered not by pure authoritarianism but by the rise of more accountable rule-based institutions that controlled corruption and limited the arbitrary power of government (Diamond, 1997). Moreover, the sustainability of an authoritarian developmental state is debatable, particularly in the light of the Asian crisis of the late 1990s. In recent years, the authoritarian developmental states of Egypt, Libya and Tunisia collapsed under the weight of demands for freedom and democracy from the ordinary citizens.

In response to the demand for regime change by opposition political parties and civil society in Zimbabwe, the executive-military diarchy adopted a battery of redistributive nationalist policies aimed at creating a social base for the ruling party. These policies included radical agricultural reform, indigenisation and economic empowerment. In giving priority to these goals, the ruling executive-military alliance gave the people the feeling that they were taking a more direct role in the economy. These nationalist-inspired economic development approaches have proved to be antagonistic to democracy but amenable to regime survival and security.

Moreover, the implementation of these policies took place against the backdrop of violence, intimidation, abuse of people and civil rights, and denial of competitive democracy. All this was championed by the military in cahoots with war veterans, youth militia and ZANU-PF. This contribution is therefore doubtful of the feasibility of a successful DDS in Zimbabwe in light of current CMR, even though its desirability is not contestable. Yet the country can learn from the experiences of Botswana and Mauritius, which are widely touted in literature as successful DDSs in Africa. South Africa, Ethiopia, Uganda and Ghana are also aspiring to construct DDSs.

MILITARISATION OF THE POLITICAL ECONOMY

The prospect for a successful DDS in Zimbabwe is in doubt, in part because of the existing structure of CMR which is inimical to the democratic participation of the citizens in the economic and political public spheres. Due to its particular role during the liberation struggle, the military is given a privileged status as guardian of hard-won independence, national integrity, and sovereignty. As a consequence, the military has seen its missions profile diversify and increase over time. As explained earlier, the military has become heavily engaged in political decision-making, commercial activities, social development and civic projects. Clearly, the diffusion of the military sector comprising security agencies such as the military, police, prison and intelligence services into the political economy of the country is problematic to the construction of a DDS. Specifically, practices such as militarisation of state institutions, state capture, and neo-patrimonialism are counterproductive to the incubation of a successful DDS.

Available evidence indicates that Zimbabwe has experienced a phenomenal rise in the number of military officials in the spheres that are traditionally non-military. This incursion into the political economy has been gradually expanded and consolidated since the dawn of independence in 1980, but accelerated over the past two decades. The military establishment is now involved in most major institutions of the state and formal policy-making structures and processes of government. It has ostensibly become a significant part of the state bureaucracy and many top military commanders have teamed up with politicians and business people to form political and economic interest groups, advancing into lucrative business ventures such as diamonds, platinum and gold mining; agro-based industries; hunting and conservancies; transport; and farming (Zimbabwe Institute, 2008). From the 2000s onwards, the executive-military alliance considered itself to be pursuing the redistributive nationalist policy that had been bequeathed to it by liberation history. This belief ostensibly allowed and entitled the alliance to claim to embody the interests of the state as a whole. Specifically, the Fast Track Land Redistributive Programme (FTLRP) appeared to be intended to provide the wherewithal to expand the government's patronage network to the regime's dwindling support base, including the military.

It has now become a common practice in Zimbabwe for the core military generals and commanders to serve as members of the cabinet, state bureaucracy, parliament and state-controlled entities. For instance, serving and retired military officers have been appointed to key local government, foreign service positions, Zimbabwe Election Commission (ZEC), National Railway of Zimbabwe (NRZ), Grain Marketing Board (GMB), and National Parks and Wildlife (Rupiya, 2004; Chitiyo & Rupiya, 2005; Kebonang, 2012). This increased militarisation of state institutions has led to the military taking control of an expanding range of decisions and actions, from political strategy to the formulation and implementation of economic policy and election strategy, for the ruling party, ZANU-PF. While some observers may argue that the military carry their discipline into these economic sectors and thus should contribute to their success, evidence indicates that these sectors and activities are more complex and require more than military training, which could be accounting for the high failure rate of military-led economic activities.

Apart from the Ministries of Defence, Security and Home Affairs, the Ministry of State Enterprises and Parastatals was one of the most heavily militarised in Zimbabwe. There are 78 state enterprises and parastatals, each with a board composed of approximately ten members, meaning that there are approximately 800 board members (military officers) presiding over public entities in Zimbabwe. As the minister responsible for the state enterprises and parastatals, this author met almost all the board members who introduced themselves as retired brigadier so and so, retired air commando so and so, etc. Most of the chief executive officers were also either former army, police, intelligence or war veterans. Certainly, the co-option of military officers into government posts greatly strengthened the influence and participation of the military in running the country's public affairs. Regrettably, though, the majority of state enterprises and parastatals in Zimbabwe are characterised by odious debts, mismanagement, skills flight, and poor performance, and none have declared dividends over the last ten years. Admittedly, the military forays into civilian life that could have diffused a sense of discipline and efficiency have been no more successful. Instead, discipline, punctuality and carrying out instructions efficiently are offset by a lack of flexibility and creativity (Khan, 2011).

Invariably, Zimbabwe is currently under the *de facto* control of a group of military oligarchy who refer to themselves as the JOC (Chitiyo, 2009; Chitiyo & Rupiya, 2005). Each member of this unit has played a substantial role in Zimbabwe's history of military violence (Williamson, 2010). As mentioned earlier, the members of the JOC are engaged in a wide variety of economic activities, including service, agriculture, housing, mining, manufacturing industry and informal trade. Initially, most of these companies were privately owned, until they were forced by government (through empowerment and indigenisation laws) to enter into joint ventures with the ruling elite in which the later holds majority stakes (51%), profits and other compulsory payments such as community share ownership schemes. As acknowledged by Naidoo (n.d.), 'the military has been the very institution of power and force that allows states to confiscate private property and abuse the rights of their citizens and thereby become the primary source of insecurity for the people'.

Moreover, JOC members have considerable discretionary power at their disposal and they are accountable only to President Mugabe. This takes place outside the formal military bureaucratic channels. Cabinet, which is formally invested with executive power, has increasingly become a rubber-stamping organ that endorses policies and policy ideas generated by the military establishment. The classic example was in 2005 when the controversial Operation Murambatsvina was launched without the knowledge and sanction of the cabinet (Zimbabwe Institute, 2008; Rupiya, 2013). The other military-style operations launched by the securocrats include, among others, Gukurahundi, Third Chimurenga, Operation Tsuro, Operation Makavoterapapi, Operation Sunrise, Operation Maguta, Operation Garikai, Operation Chikorokodza Chapera, Operation Akudzokwi, Operation Chimumumu, and Operation Restore Order II (Chitiyo, 2009). As noted by Maroleng (2005), with such power, the military officials perceive themselves to be more than just the custodians of Zimbabwe territorial integrity and sovereignty from the external threats, but also as some type of praetorian guard that must safeguard ZANU-PF'S political dominance.

Viewed from this perspective, the Zimbabwe military retains enormous clout in political decision-making. As mentioned earlier, it has informally assumed control and oversight of public policy, merged issues of security with politics, played the role as an agency for defining security, and has constrained civilian authority. In this sense, the military sector deems itself the bulwark of the nation, and the bastion that is qualified to define and defend national interest, sovereignty and national integrity. Although formally an elected civilian government, serious reservations exist with regard to the extent to which the government of Zimbabwe is able to control the JOC, or, if it rather functions as a mere civilian window-dressing tutelage (Williamson, 2010). The real danger is that the JOC has transmogrified into a semi-permanent feature of CMR in Zimbabwe. Some prominent scholars have come to the conclusion that the military has formed a state within a state.

Evidently, the main impediment to the construction of a DDS in Zimbabwe is neo-patrimonialism practiced mainly by the executive-military alliance. There is no doubt that the executive-military nexus in Zimbabwe has been and continues to be controlled and sustained by a system of patronage network. Ownership of Zimbabwe's assets resides largely with the executive-military alliance and ZANU-PF party loyalists. The military establishment in Zimbabwe is bestowed with favours by the state, such as luxurious cars and other financial and material incentives aimed at buying their loyalty. Other rewards for the military have included bigger military budgets and other avenues to accumulate wealth through the selling or renting influence, bribery, corruption and extortion. Between 2000 and 2008, land grabbing was the main mechanism for building and sustaining economic dominance by the military. This land grab has now been transformed into a social welfare programme to ensure comfortable retirement, particularly for the senior military officers, and to ensure the economic future of their progeny. All this was motivated by the desire of the executive-military alliance to retain power through clientelism, making military commercialism one of many financial supports for the domestic regime (Dietrich, 2000).

Likewise, the seizure of the Marange diamond fields in 2008 should be understood in the light of Mugabe's need to secure the resources necessary to maintain the loyalty of the military establishment (Masunungure, 2011). The companies that operate in the diamond fields are controlled by the military. Profits from military commercial activity allow for the augmentation of the military apparatus and provide swank lifestyles for the generals

(Dietrich, 2000). More generally, the use of patronage to allocate resources in Zimbabwe has allowed state security officials and the political elite to be super-rich (Kebonang, 2012). Almost invariably, the provision of rewards and opportunities have entrenched the military more deeply in the structure of power, giving them a personal stake in upholding the authoritarian system in Zimbabwe. In this disproportionate drawing of resources, the military represents a constraint on the economy and the wellbeing of the rest of Zimbabweans.

Retrospectively, some analysts have argued that Zimbabwe's military involvement in Mozambique in the 1980s and the DRC in the late 1990s have been part of the military incursion into business and the economy. These military deployments have functioned more to provide cover for the enrichment and personal economic activities of the military and party officials (Scarnecchia, 2005). Campbell (2003) was right when he observed that, for the military and politicians at the helm of the ruling party, the DRC war in particular presented an opportunity for military entrepreneurs to find new areas for commerce, mining and super-profits. It is generally believed that the military commanders now own mining claims which were given to Zimbabwe as part payment of the role played by the Zimbabwe National Army (ZNA), together with Angola, Namibia and the DRC, in stopping the invasion of the DRC by rebels backed by Uganda and Rwanda. These mining claims have never been declared and the proceeds are believed to be shared among the members of the politico-military oligarchy. Thus, a small number of military officers, political elites, and President Mugabe's family and friends, have a monopoly on key government contracts and licences, which led to the concentration of economic and political power in their hands, and to widespread institutionalised corruption. Thus, as observed by Dietrich (2000), corporate-military business ventures have been created for the financial benefit of military officers and other cronies of state leaders, rendering the military apparatus a commercial asset.

Evidence also indicates that the barons behind the highly informalised economy in Zimbabwe are senior military officers (serving and retired). This situation is clearly marked in the gold-panning sector. Most of the gold panners are either workers of the militricians or they sell their products to the military at very low prices in return for their continued panning trade. As a result of a directive from the JOC, gold panning has recently been decriminalised, and a law to formalise gold panning is under consideration by the ministry of mines and mining development. In short, the elites within government, military, and ZANU-PF have accumulated much of the country's wealth and assets through abuse of authority, corruption and clientelism. The classic example of neo-patrimonialism in Zimbabwe surrounds war veterans. This quasi-military force has benefited from the government largesse, receiving payments, pensions and land in order to gain their support for the regime. Further, opportunities were created for the military to profit from criminal activities, including tacitly approved road blocks where motorists pay spot fines for a variety of traffic offenses. It cannot be further from the truth to argue that the military dabbles in politics in Zimbabwe for venal interests.

As part of the patronage network, over 4 000 members of the army were absorbed by the GMB as part of Operation Maguta between 2002 and 2006. These members of the force were incorporated into parastatals, presumably so that they could be paid from both the parastatals and the army. Similarly, the NRZ absorbed about 2 000 members of the military. In this way, the army was cushioned against the low salaries at the height of economic recession of the 2000s in Zimbabwe. This was against a background of large army desertions and disgruntlements. While seemingly useful in the short term, this approach had the opposite effect in the long run, perpetuating and increasing the militarisation of state institutions.

In 2010, the inclusive government of Zimbabwe, through the Ministry of Public Service carried out a pay roll and skills audit of the public service. The Minster of Public Service, Professor Mukonoweshuro, was from the Movement for Democratic Change (MDC-T). A professional audit firm, Ernst and Young India, established that there were over 70 000 ghost workers in the public service in Zimbabwe. Most of these ghost workers were either military officers deployed in various government ministries and departments in order for them to earn twice, or were graduates from youth training centres deployed to drum up support for ZANU-PF during the life of the inclusive government.

In the 2012 national census, the army wanted to smuggle in 15 000 of its members to be part of the 31 000 enumerators. This author was the acting Minister of Finance at the time, responsible for the national census programme. The plan to use the army was thwarted and only 600 army officers were allowed to participate in the 2012 census in order for them to count in the barracks and cantonments where civilians are not allowed for security reasons. There were supposedly three reasons why the army wanted to take control of the national census: firstly, to earn some allowances; secondly, to manipulate the figures for the purposes of the elections; and thirdly, no national programme of that magnitude could be allowed to take place in the country without the involvement of the army. The army was supposed to be seen to be in charge of the country.

Not surprisingly, military officers have arm-twisted erstwhile civilian elites to recognise them as national heroes at death. Thus, between May 2013 and August 2014, nine senior military commanders were declared national heroes and were buried at the national shrine. These were; Major General Javan Maseko (buried on 24 May 2013), Deputy Director of CIO Elias Kanengoni (27 May 2013), Retired Air Commodore Michael Karakadzai (25 August 2013), Brigadier General Misheck Tanyanyiwa (8 December 2013), Retired Lieutenant Colonel Harold Chirenda (9 January 2014), Brigadier General John Zingoni (21 May 2014), Retired Colonel Stanely Urayayi Sakupwanya (6 July 2014), and Major General Elliah Bandama (17 July 2014) (Moyo, *forthcoming*). In the past, the conferment of national hero status was reserved mainly for the political elites in ZANU-PF and a few army commanders at the level of service chiefs. This recent recognition of the late military officials as national heroes buried in the national shrine is reflective of the military institution's new economic and political status.

Given the extent of militarisation of politics, economy and society, it is evident that the military has been the most powerful institution in Zimbabwe since the 1980s, but more-so in the 2000s. The long years of authoritarian nationalist rule under President Mugabe have left a legacy: a coercive and corrupt political and economic culture. This legacy continues to plague the economy and sustain a sense of deep mistrust of ZANU-PF-led government. In short, ZANU-PF has used neo-patrimonialism as a method of controlling the military at the expense of the poor majority in Zimbabwe. Thus, ZANU-PF-led government is more concerned about appeasing the military sector that, in turn, protects the interest of the ruling elite through coercion and intimidation. This essentially forecloses any chances for public accountability, citizen participation, citizen ownership and democratic governance, yet these factors are foundational to the institutionalisation of a DDS.

RELATING THE MILITARY TO THE MARXIST-LENINIST PARTY

The ruling party, ZANU-PF, subscribes to the Marxist-Leninist ideology, where the party is viewed as the sovereign, acting as the chief arbiter of values, authority relations, institutional arrangements, political practices, and policy (Perlmutter & LeoGrande 1982). From its place at the pinnacle of politics, ZANU-PF acts as integrator by setting public policy and assuring that other institutions follow through faithfully with its implementation. Under these circumstances the ruling party and the military are organically linked in the party-state relations. The sum total of this system is alienation of opposition political parties and other stakeholders that are viewed as hostile to the ruling party. In this context, the army acts as the tool for enforcing government policy, and protection of the ruling party and the regime.

Works by Zimbabwe scholars such as Brian Raftopoulos, Sabelo Ndlovu-Gatsheni, James Muzondidya, John Makumbe, Lloyd Sachikonye, Martin Rupiya and Alois Mlambo indicate that the executive-military alliance has been practicing the politics of exclusion against civil society and opposition political society since independence in 1980. ZANU-PF in alliance with the military establishment believes that they are the only ones entitled to rule Zimbabwe, and that their victory in 1980 marked the end of history of all struggles. This observation has been reiterated by Masunungure (2011) who has observed that:

> The top ZANU-PF political generation and its allies in the military/security establishment have an 'end of history' perspective of the liberation struggle and the achievement of independence in 1980. The attainment of Uhuru through a protracted liberation struggle against settler colonialism marked the end if all struggles and the triumph of ZANU-PF was the last triumph. 1980 marked the victory of light over darkness, and in this line of thinking any other struggle in Zimbabwe would be tantamount to an attempt to bring back darkness. This leads ZANU-PF to brag that it delivered democracy and therefore there cannot be any other democratic struggle.

Apparently, Zimbabwe's military sector has long been a willing and effective midwife of ZANU-PF's political ambitions. They see themselves, first and foremost, as servants of the ruling party, rather than servants of the state and the people of Zimbabwe (Ndlovu-Gatsheni, 2008). It appears that all high-ranking members of the security forces are expected to be members of ZANU-PF. 'As it stands today, the military is only led by those who passed through the nationalist liberation war and who are thoroughly indoctrinated with ZANU-PF nationalist ideology' (Ndlovu-Gatsheni 2006:77). In a way, Zimbabwe is a party-state that conforms to the notion of partocracy. Masunungure (2011) defines a party state as follows:

> A party-state means the ruling party is fused to the state; party and state structures at all levels are conflated ... in the party-state duality, the party is supreme over the state. All formal organs of the state – including the military and security services – are closely linked to the party without being officially integrated into it.

The ultimate goal of the executive-military alliance and the party-state is to stifle pluralism by imposing a single shared sense of identity based on the rhetoric of nationalism, sovereignty, liberation struggle and patriotism. This forced identity is always accompanied by an attitude of belligerence, coercion and repression against anyone who does not express loyalty to the memoirs of ZANU-PF. This approach to governance effectively denies effective citizenship and further robs people of their right to hold the government accountable for its failures, a phenomenon which has negative impact on the process of constructing a DDS since it opposes people rule and people-centred development, and denies the citizenry full enjoyment of human security. What is clear is that, in Zimbabwe, state-society relations have not been characterised by deep and horizontal comradeships running across interactions of ruling elite and the governed (Ndlovu-Gatsheni, 2011). As a result, the ordinary citizens remain shut out of economic benefits. It is argued that the practice of privatising the public space as a preserve of the executive-military oligarchy is not consonant and amenable to democratisation and development. Instead, it stifles the necessary broad-based, open and honest dialogue involving the development coalition that is imperative for the construction of a DDS.

It is also a matter of public truth that Mugabe and his party have previously lost elections to Morgan Tsvangirai and the MDC, but the military sector has not allowed the will of the people to prevail. Such subversion of the will of the people has had a multiplicity of ramifications, such as the erosion of confidence in government, and the withering away of political legitimacy, which, in turn, has diminished the state's capacity to extract domestic and international sources. Consequently, Zimbabwe is currently going through a difficult period of economic downturn, unemployment, de-industrialisation, brain drain and abject poverty. In the run-up to the 2002 presidential elections, security chiefs publicly stated that they would not salute politicians who did not possess liberation war credentials, a sentiment that has subsequently been repeated before all presidential and parliamentary elections in Zimbabwe (2005, 2008 and 2013). Thus, ZANU-PF allows elections in order to suggest legitimacy, but refuses to be ousted by popular vote.

Certainly, Zimbabwe holds elections whenever they are due, as provided by the constitution and electoral law, yet the elections are fraudulent and ZANU-PF uses violence and intimidation to influence the results. It is not surprising that the manner in which the military is perceived to have acted during the 2000, 2002, 2005, 2008 and 2013 general elections has been regarded as evidence of Mugabe's corrupt relationship with the military. It is argued here that the military did not intervene in domestic politics in its own right, but rather because it is one of the instruments of power controlled by the political elite. To this end, Williamson was right when he observed that the unleashing of the power of the armed forces to quell political opposition is detrimental not only to civilian control, but, consequently, also to prospects for democracy and development. Regrettably, this has resulted in the erosion of political legitimacy in Zimbabwe. Yet political legitimacy is one of the central tenets of democracy and a pillar of a successful DDS.

Apparently, in the July 2013 harmonised elections, the military sector was allocated a quarter of the seats by ZANU-PF. Thus, in the current parliament, the military is overly represented. Among the several retired generals who are now members of parliament are the former assistant commissioner, Oliver Mandipaka who only retired from the police force after winning elections in July 2013, and Joseph Chinotimba, who is the vice-chairman of the Zimbabwe National Liberation War Veterans Association (ZNLWVA). Moreover, the current Parliamentary Portfolio committee on Defence, Security and Home Affairs, constituted after the July 2013 national elections, has 21 members, of which 16 are from ZANU-PF and all are former members of the military establishment (police, army, air-force, prison service, and war veterans). The other five are members of the opposition MDC. This simply means that the oversight role of the Parliamentary Portfolio Committee on Defence, Security and Home Affairs over the military establishment has already been functionally and structurally lobotomised and weakened.

This assessment contends that the long history of executive-party-military alliance has disastrous effects, not just on the coherence, efficiency and discipline of the army, but also on the institutionalisation of the norms and values of a DDS. Ideally, a DDS is nurtured within a framework of maximalist democracy that is socially inclusive. Minimalist forms of democracy characterised by state capture are not conducive to public participation in policy formulation and implementation. In fact, the long-term potential for effective governance is sacrificed as the military stunts the development of civilian capacities to rule, while offering, instead, its version of praetorian rule lacking the accountability essential to a DDS. In this context, an important constraint for the building of a DDS is the military specter in the political economy. Zimbabwe needs to transform its CMR, lest the country remains a failed transition, driven by military objectives to the neglect of development, democracy and accountability, and unable to change direction because of neo-praetorian and neo-patrimonial practices.

PROFESSIONALISING CMR

To build a successful DDS, Zimbabwe will have to demilitarise its state institutions and political decision-making processes. It will also need to dismantle the political management system that formed the backbone of the CMR under the Mugabe authoritarian nationalist regime; and create robust, credible and functioning civilian institutions of accountability. Moreover, to restore the military to its primary function of defence requires rolling back the military's economic autonomy, founded on equitable treatment of military and non-military bureaucracies, based on the constraints imposed by the economy (Khan, 2011). The creation of such architecture will require time and ongoing research to develop, but it does have practical implications on the construction of a DDS. This section reflects on the roles that can be played by political leadership, bureaucrats, legislature and civil society as possible social transformative forces that can both civilianise CMR and drive the project of constructing a DDS in Zimbabwe. The assessment illustrates the breadth of the battery of reforms that can be implemented to improve CMR and, in this way, serves as a demonstrative model for developing democratic civilian control in that country.

Political leadership

It is argued that the application of democratic control of the military requires a competent political leadership to initiate it. Theoretically and conceptually, political leadership is viewed as a chief interlocutor of state processes and institutions (Moyo, 2013). It is charged with responsibility to ensure equitable distribution of power, efficient allocation of resources and effective expansion of human capacities. In other words, effective political leadership facilitates the development of mutual relations between the state and the citizens. Arguably, the idea of a DDS presupposes citizens as subjects, co-shapers of their own development destinies, and not as periodic voters or passive recipients of government services delivered to them. In this regard, the notion of effective public leadership recognises the values of sound CMR that would facilitate the interface between state and society. More importantly, DDS requires political leaders who understand the critical importance of public accountability, transparency, democratic participation and political legitimacy. The current politico-military leadership in Zimbabwe is oriented at winning votes every five years; self-aggrandisement and wealth accumulation; regime security at the expense of human security; and leadership for absolute and contested power. There is therefore a need for leadership transformation and political will as the prerequisites for the purposes of democratising CMR in Zimbabwe.

Viewed from this perspective, the new National Constitution which came into force in March 2013, should be used as a framework for mediating a new relationship between society and the military. Political leadership should utilise the constitution in laying the foundation for the construction of a successful DDS in Zimbabwe. For instance, Chapter 11, Article 208(2-4) of the constitution stipulates that:

> (2) Neither the Security Services nor any of their members may, in the exercise of their duty (a) act in a partisan manner; (b) further the interest of any political party or; (c) prejudice the lawful rights or freedom of any person; (d) violate the fundamental rights or freedoms of any person (3) Members of the Security Services must not be active members or office bearers of any political party or organisation (4) Serving members of Security Services must not be employed or engaged in civilian institutions except in periods of public emergency.

These constitutional provisions have set a new foundation for the transformation of CMR in Zimbabwe. However, there has never been a shortage of progressive constitutional, institutional or policy framework for the democratisation of CMR. In fact the old constitution, Defence Act, and the National Defence Policy have all been laced with the notion of 'civilian supremacy' (Chitiyo & Rupiya, 2005). Yet political will on the part of the executive-military leadership to implement the letter and spirit of the law has been lacking in Zimbabwe. The current crop of political and military leaders is regime-security fixated and caught up in the liberation conceptual envelope that prioritises the use of a barrel of a gun as a source of power. Notwithstanding this leadership paradigm, the new constitution provides the political leaders a fig leaf to absolve itself by democratising CMR. Ndlovu-Gatsheni summed it up well when he observed that the constitution 'is one of the fundamental pre-requisites for the burial of the past authoritarianism and a necessary condition for the entrenchment of a new genuine, people-centred, pluralist and democratic consensus in Zimbabwe'.

The democratisation of CMR in Zimbabwe can benefit from a battery of regional institutions such as the AU's Conference on Stability, Security, Cooperation and Development in Africa (CSSCDA), the New Partnership for Africa's Development (NEPAD) and the African Peer Review Mechanism (APRM) instruments that contain a number of objectives, principles and standards aimed at promoting democracy and good political governance (Mangu, 2008). Thus, it will be important for Zimbabwe to accede to the APRM in order for it to benefit from the process.

It is argued that leadership for common good and personal leadership character of magnanimity is most needed now in Zimbabwe to ensure successful transition and enforce functional democratic governance in CMR. Its task is to progressively democratise the coercive apparatus as part of a broader process of popular participation and democracy in the society (Campbell, 2003). Succinctly put, a DDS is possible in Zimbabwe provided political leadership commits itself to the process of dismantling the matrices of the coloniality of power, including democratisation of CMR; genuine civilian authority over the military; and authentic citizen participation in the affairs of the state. As observed by Ndlovu-Gatsheni (2002), 'this should be coupled with a courageous and bold adjustment of the existing inflexible nationalist ideology consistent with global developments, while at the same time not sacrificing local needs and demands of Zimbabweans'.

Bureaucratic elite

Over and above competent political leadership, available evidence indicates that an efficient and well-coordinated bureaucracy is central in the project of constructing a DDS. This bureaucracy should be autonomous, independent and must have administrative and technical capacity to set national goals. As acknowledged by Evans (2010), effective bureaucracy is crucial for the functions of a modern state because of the requirement that such a state be sufficiently autonomous to craft national development strategies without being captured by sectional interests. Apparently, as mentioned earlier, the state bureaucracy in Zimbabwe has been invaded by both serving and retired military officers. Most of these military officers have been deployed as permanent secretaries and directors in government ministries, departments, public service commissions, and public entities; and in constitutional commissions such as the ZEC, Human Rights Commission, Anti-Corruption Commission and the National Reconciliation Commission. Chitiyo (2009) has observed that 'the embedding of serving or former security services personnel has resulted in service personnel being sandwiched between institutional cultures of politicisation and militarisation to the detriment of professional values'.

It should however be made clear here that there is nothing essentially amiss with former military personnel working in the civil service, but there is everything wrong if these officers are appended to government departments as part of clientelism and the state-party nexus. This contribution argues that bureaucrats should cease being an extended bureaucracy of ZANU-PF; should exhibit and maintain ethics and professionalism; restore hope, trust and confidence in the people; and operate on the golden principles that governments come and go but the civil service remains (Forje, 2009). The new national constitution provides a framework for the public service to reinvent itself.

If Zimbabwe is going to reconstruct the state, it will need to have public servants who are skilled, experienced, competent and independent from interferences of political party players. The policies designed must be responsive to the needs of the people, and sensitive to regional and global dynamics. The current policies such as 'empowerment and indigenisation' and 'land reform', while sounding good, were designed by the executive-military alliance for the purposes of regime survival rather than for really empowering and emancipating ordinary Zimbabweans. In fact, the majority of the benefactors of these policies are the senior army commanders, police bosses, intelligence chiefs, war veterans, youth militias and the nationalist ruling elite, as well as the ruling party loyalists, for their role in regime survival. To create conditions favourable to the construction of a DDS this contribution argues that 'the security of the state must cease to be privileged over other forms of security such as human security, social security and security from arbitrary power' (Ndlovu-Gatsheni, 2002). Moreover, as important as the military's separation from politics is, so is the accompanying separation of the military from the economy (Khan, 2011). As noted earlier, there is evidence that the militarisation of economic life is inefficient and crowds out other stakeholders in a DDS project.

Legislature

It is an undisputed tenet of democracy that parliament, being the body representing the public, making or shaping laws, and exercising oversight over every element of public policy, including the military or security sector in general, is a critical factor in the process of transforming CMR. The role of parliament regarding CMR is well defined by the 2013 National Constitution. Certainly, parliament in Zimbabwe pronounces the existence of the security sector and is responsible for approving defence budgets proposed by the executive (Chitiyo, 2009). At least in theory, through budget allocations, parliament has the most potent weapon of controlling the manner in which the executive directs the military. In this regard, the institution of parliament has a constitutional mandate to demand accountability and transparency, and determine policies of the security sector services (Dhoro, n.d.). Currently, however, this check and balance is non-existent as parliament is totally controlled by the ruling executive-military alliance with 73% majority. Arguably, for the DDS to be consummated in Zimbabwe, loyalty of the military must be secured to institutions including parliament, and not just the executive.

As observed by Rupiya (2005), the National Defence Policy correctly identifies cardinal principles of democratic control of armed forces including the defence force's subordination to civilian authority; civilian responsibility for the formulation of defence policy with the technical assistance of the military; civilian responsibility for the political dimensions of defence policy; military execution of defence policy, non-interference of government and politicians with the operational chain of command; and non-interference of the government and politicians in the application of the code of military discipline. These norms and values of CMR have been further entrenched in the constitution, which stipulates that 'the state must adopt and implement policies and legislation to develop efficiency, competence, accountability, transparency, personal integrity and financial probity in all institutions and agencies of government at every level and in every public institution'(Chapter 2, Article 9). In this regard, a parliament-initiated dialogue is a prerequisite in building trust between the military and the generality of the citizenry, which currently views the security as a destroyer rather than a facilitator of democracy and development in Zimbabwe (Chitiyo, 2009).

Civil society

Civil society is one of the critical players in modern society. Ideally, civil society acts as a bulwark against the power of the state; challenging abuses of authority; monitoring human rights and strengthening the rule of law; and enhancing the overall quality of the democratic process, educating citizens about their rights and responsibilities, and building a culture of tolerance and civic engagement; incorporating marginal groups into the political process and enhancing their responsiveness to societal interests and needs; providing alternatives means, outside the state; and building a constituency for economic as well as political reforms (Diamond, 1997). Undoubtedly, civil society enhances the practice of responsible governance, public accountability and transparency. A lack of responsible governance, public accountability and transparency creates a dangerous trend toward the politicisation of the army, the militarisation of public institutions and abusive use of the military sector by the ruling oligarchy. Such a situation undermines Zimbabwe's long-term economic and political stability, and disrupts the construction of a successful DDS. Ndlovu-Gatsheni (2002) was correct when he opined that 'this century does not belong to the warlords and their militaries ... it belongs to civil society'.

The role of a civil society in the DDS building project should include representing the interests of citizens; articulating citizen interests to decision makers; influencing policy decisions based on the interests represented; and exercising oversight to ensure government compliance with adopted policies (Mkandawire, 2001; Edigheji, 2005; Gumede, 2009). Moreover, linkages need to be built between the military and the civil society sector to enable the military to hold a rational calculus towards domestic political and social order, which would enable it to promote professionalism within its own institutions. In other words, there is a need for the military to reconstruct its own dialogue with civil society. Ndlovu-Gatsheni (2002) argues that what Zimbabwe needs is not coercion derived from military might, but consensus framed around governance, democracy, human rights, human security and economic stability and prosperity. To the extent that civil society can contribute to these different democracy-building processes, it can also help to ensure the transformation of the CMR in Zimbabwe. It is only reforms designed and executed in this way that appear capable of patiently and incrementally bringing forth strong institutions that will lay down the foundation for the institutionalisation of a DDS. Until Zimbabwe is able to address these issues satisfactorily, the effort towards constructing a DDS will remain elusive and an exercise in futility.

Admittedly, stable CMR does not happen overnight, especially in countries like Zimbabwe where the liberation legacy still holds fast. Clearly, what is desperately needed in Zimbabwe is not coercion derived from military might, but consensus framed around the pertinent issues of governance, democracy, human rights, human security and economic stability and prosperity. In this sense, it is important to begin an open discussion within the military, and between the military and citizenry, on what they see as the primary roles of the security sector in Zimbabwe, and to gauge mutual responsibilities and expectations (Chitiyo, 2009). Until that occurs, the principles and practices advanced in this assessment will continue to be received politely, but there is little chance that they will be applied in the short- to mid-term, and, risking being cynical, thus there is little hope that a true DDS will be achieved.

CONCLUDING REMARKS

The chapter set out to examine the implications of CMR on the project of constructing a successful DDS in Zimbabwe. It was noted that the collaboration between the executive and the military for short-term political goals has been detrimental to both democracy and economic development. It was also argued that the militarisation of state institutions and politicisation of the military were not consonant and amenable to economic reforms and democratic transition. On the contrary, these twin processes stifle citizen participation, public accountability and political legitimacy based on popular consensus. To this end, the disproportionate claim of the resources by the military and political elites would have to end for a DDS to take root. Thus, the constitution which came into force in 2012, presents an opportunity for Zimbabwe to rethink and repurpose its CMR. In this regard, the ZANU-PF-led government has an arduous task of turning the constitutional guidelines into practical instruments for implementation by various state institutions, including the military sector. In doing this, it is crucially important to strike a balance between the strengths of the classical Huntington objective control and the reality of subjective CMR highlighted in this analysis. In short, CMR will need to be transformed in line with Zimbabwe's practical and historical realities if a DDS is to be successfully incubated in that country. Since all these problems cascade from coloniality, it is suggested that there be a sustained and comprehensive decolonial therapy, involving decolonisation of being, decolonisation of knowledge, and decolonisation of power – not only within the military sector, but also across the whole gamut of society in Zimbabwe. It is hoped that this contribution will bring a new perspective on the relationship between the democracy, development and military arenas. Further research needs to study more intensely how CMR in countries that gained their independence through an armed struggle can be transformed in such a way that they contribute to democratic consolidology and, by implication, support the institutionalisation of DDSs. The existing body of literature has given insufficient thought as to how to achieve this.

REFERENCES

Amoako, K.Y. 2011. 'The critical role of capable states in driving Africa's economic transformation agenda'. Paper presented on Governance Academy Day, 26 October 2011, Maputo.

Amuwo, A. 2008. *Constructing the Democratic Developmental State in Africa.* Johannesburg: Institute for Global Dialogue.

Campbell, H. 2003. *Reclaiming Zimbabwe: The exhaustion of the patriarchal model of liberation.* Cape Town: David Philip Publishers.

Chitiyo, K. 2009. The Case for the Security Sector Reform in Zimbabwe. Occasional Paper, RUSI.

Chitiyo, K. & Rupiya, M. 2005. 'Tracking Zimbabwe's political history: The Zimbabwe Defence Force 1980-2005' in Rupiya, M. (ed.). 2005, *Evolutions and Revolutions: A contemporary history of militaries in Southern Africa.* Pretoria: ISS.

Cleary, L. n.d. 'Lost in Translation: The Challenge of Exporting Models of Civil-Military Relations' in PRISM, 3(2).

Croissant, A. et al. 2012. *Breaking With the Past? Civil-military relations in the emerging democracies of East Asia*, Singapore: East-West Center.

Dhoro, E. n.d. *Reviewing the Debates on Security Sector Reform in Zimbabwe and Locating the Role of the Legislature in the Reform Process*, Parlzim/RD/4.2.4/6RE.

Diamond, L. 1997 'Rethinking Civil Society: Toward Democratic Consolidation' in *Journal of Democracy*. 5(13).

Dietrich, C. 2000. 'The commercialism of military deployment in Africa' in *African Security Review*, 9(1). Available at http://www.issafrica.org/pubs/ASR/9No1/commercialism.html. Accessed 26 September 2014.

Dikeni, L. 2012. *South African Development: Perspectives in Questions: The Conflict Nature of People, Environment and Development*. Johannesburg: Real African Publishers.

Ebo, A. 2005. *Towards a Code of Conduct for Armed and Security Forces in Africa: Opportunities and challenges*. Geneva Centre for the Democratic Control of Armed Forces (DCAF).

ECA. 2011. *Economic Report on Africa 2011: Governing Development-the role of the state in economic transformation*. ECA.

Edigheji, O. (ed.) 2010. *Constructing a Democratic Developmental State in South Africa: Potentials and challenges*. Cape Town: HSRC Press.

Evan, P.B. 2010. 'Constructing the 21st century developmental state: Potentialities and pitfalls' in Edigheji, O. (ed.) *Constructing a Democratic Developmental State in South Africa: Potentials and challenges*. Cape Town: HSRC Press.

Fakir, E. 2005. *The democratic state versus the developmental state: A false dichotomy*. Isandla Development communiqué 2.

Fayemi, K.J. 1998. 'The future of demilitarisation and civil-military relations in West Africa: Challenges and prospects for democratic consolidation' in *African Journal of Political Science*, 3(1).

Gumede, W. 2009. *Delivering the Democratic Developmental State in South Africa*. DBSA Working Paper Series No.9, 2009.

Gumede, W. 2010. *South Africa as a Developmental State in the Making*. Johannesburg: University of Johannesburg.

Hendricks, C. 2009. *Security Sector Reform in Zimbabwe: What, Why and How?* Policy Brief No.1, June 2009, ISS.

Huntington, P.S. 1957. *The Soldier and the State: The theory and politics of civil military relations*, Cambridge, Mass: Vintage Press.

Kebonang, Z. 2012. 'Of politics and anarchy: Zimbabwe's 2008 run off presidential elections in context' in *The Open Political Science Journal*, 2012: 5.

Khan, S.R. 2011. *The Military and Economic Development in Pakistan*. Amherst College.

Kundishora, H. n.d. 'Contradictions between postcolonial coercive redistributive mechanisms and global competition'. zimfinalpush7.blogspot.com. Accessed 22 May 2014

Leftwich. A. & Hogg, S. 2007. *The case for leadership and the primacy of politics in building effective states, institutions and governance for sustainable growth and social development*, Developmental Leadership Program.

Luqman, S. 2011. 'The faltering prospect for stable civil military relations in Africa's emerging democracies' in *International Journal of Politics and Good Governance*, 2(23).

Maroleng, C. 2005. *Zimbabwe: Increased Securitisation of the State*. ISS.

Masunungure, E. 2011. *Zimbabwe at the Crossroads: Challenges for Civil Society*.

Melber, H. 2012. 'The Legacy of Anti-colonial Struggles in Southern Africa: Liberation movements as governments'. Paper presented to the Conference on Election Processes, Liberation Movements and Democratic Change in Africa, Maputo, 8-11 April 2012.

Mkandawire, T. 2001. 'Thinking about developmental states in Africa' in *Cambridge Journal of Economics*, 2001: 25.

Mkandawire, T. 2010. 'From maladjusted states to democratic developmental states in Africa' in Edigheji, O. (ed.) 2010. *Constructing a Democratic Developmental State in South Africa: Potentials and challenges*. Cape Town: HSRC Press.

Mlomo, M.G. 2001. 'Civilian-military relations in Botswana's developmental state' in *African Studies Quarterly*, 5(2).

Moyo, G. 2013. 'The Quest for a Democratic Developmental State in Africa: Assessing public participation and public leadership in the context of the APRM', Unpublished PhD thesis submitted to the National University of Science and Technology (NUST).

Moyo, G. (forthcoming) *The Rise of Competitive Authoritarianism Contextualised Within the Chimurenga Ideology and Gukurahundi Policy: The Tyranny of the executive-military alliance*. In press with the *Journal of Southern African Studies*.

Moyo, J.N. 1993. 'Civil society in Zimbabwe' in Zambezia, 1993: XX(1), University of Zimbabwe.

Musavengana, T. 2011. *Security Sector: No transition without transformation*.

Naidoo, S. n.d. *The Role of the Military in Democratic Governance in Africa: The need to institutionalise civil-military relations*.

Ndlovu-Gatsheni, S.J. 2002. 'Dynamics of the Zimbabwe Crisis in the 21st Century'. Paper presented at the 7th Congress of the Organisation Social Science Research in Eastern and Southern Africa (OSSREA) held in Sudan, 14-19 December 2002.

Ndlovu-Gatsheni, S.J. 2002. *Reaping the Bitter Fruits of Stalinist Tendencies in Zimbabwe*. ACAS Bulletin 79: Special Issue on Zimbabwe Crisis. Available at http://www. concernedafricascholars.org/bulletin/issue79/Ndlovu-gatsheni/. Accessed 3 August 2014.

Ndlovu-Gatsheni, S.J. 2011. 'Fiftieth Anniversary of Decolonisation in Africa: a moment of celebration or critical reflection'. Third World Quarter, 33(1). Available at http://www.tandfonline.com/loi/ctwq20. Accessed 12 June 2014.

Ndlovu-Gatsheni, S.J. 2012. 'Coloniality of power in development studies and the impact of global imperial designs on Africa'. Inaugural lecture delivered at the University of South Africa, 16 October 2012.

Ndlovu-Gatsheni, S.J. 2013. *Coloniality of Power in Postcolonial Africa. Myths of decolonisation*. CODSRIA, Dhakar.

Nnoli, K. n.d. 'The military, civil society and democracy in Africa'. Paper presented to DPMF Conference.

Noyes, A. 2013. 'Securing Reform? Power Sharing and Civil-Military Relations in Kenya and Zimbabwe' in African Studies Quarterly, 13(4).

Ogbazghi, P. 2011. 'Personal Rule in Africa: The case of Eritrea' in *African Studies Quarterly*, 12(2).

Onslow, S. 2013. *Zimbabwe and Political Transition*. The School of Economics and Political Science, London.

Perlmutter, A. & LeoGrande, W.M. 1982. 'The Party in Uniform: Towards a theory of civil-military relations in communist political systems' in *The American Political Science Review*, 76(4).

Rupiya, M. 2004. 'Contextualising the military in Zimbabwe between 1999 and 2004 and beyond' in Raftopoulos, B. & Savage, T. 2004. *Zimbabwe: Injustice and Political Reconciliation*. Institute for Justice and Reconciliation, Cape Town.

Rupiya, M. 2005. 'Tracking Zimbabwe's political history: The Zimbabwe Defence Force from 1980-2005' in Rupiya, M. (ed.). 2005. *Evolutions and Revolutions: A Contemporary History of Militaries in Southern Africa*.

Rupiya, M. 2013. *Zimbabwe's Military: Examining its veto power in the transition to democracy, 2008-2013*. African Public Policy and Research Institute.

Scarnecchia, T. 2006. 'The Fascist Cycle in Zimbabwe, 2000-2005' in Gaitskell, D., Schmaker, L. & Simon, D. (eds). *Journal of Southern African Studies*. Routledge, Taylor and Francis Group.

Williams, R. 1998. *Towards the Creation of an African Civil-Military Relations Tradition*. African Association of Political Science.

Williamson, J.I. 2010. 'Seeking Civilian Control: Rule of law, democracy, and civil military relations in Zimbabwe' in *Indiana Journal of Global Legal Studies*, 17(2).

Zimbabwe Agenda for Sustainable Socioeconomic Transformation (Zim-Asset, 2013-2018). 2013.

Zimbabwe Institute. 2008. *The state of civics in Zimbabwe*. Zimbabwe Institute.

Zinyama, T. 2011. 'The Complexity of Democratic Transition: The Zimbabwe Case, 1999 to 2011' in *International Journal of Humanities and Social Science*, 2(12).

Chapter 10

Tracking Lesotho's Sixth Military Coup, 30 August 2014: What has changed?[1]

by Martin Rupiya and Mpho Mothoagae

The politics of Lesotho continue to be intertwined with its raucous security cluster infighting. This dynamic poses a long-term threat to the country's political stability – characterised by violence and assassinations with impunity.[2]

The Southern African Development Community's (SADC's) odd man out, Lesotho, on 30 August 2014, experienced its sixth successful military coup since the first one in January 1970 by Chief Leabua Jonathan. This time round, the coup has turned out to be different, depicting an event against indictment for grand corruption, and possible arrest and incarceration of political elites. Curiously, when the coup occurred, it was not condemned by the SADC in line with existing African Union (AU) unconstitutional removal of government guidelines. Why? This moderation appeared to further embolden the *putschists* who proceeded to create an army within the Lesotho Defence Forces army.' Operating in the fluid and complex Lesotho political system and the inexplicable SADC conflict resolution matrix, after the 28 February Election, the politico-military faction was propelled to become the now been legitimated in the new state. Further emboldened, the new politico-military administration has continued the intolerance, violence and assassinations with impunity, succeeding to force into exile all the key political opposition players. With the United Nations (UN), the AU and others expressing alarm and condemnation, the SADC, almost belatedly, issued an unprecedented *communiqué* on 3 July, effectively reducing the sovereignty and independence of the new state. The crisis, in all its political, socio-economic and security aspects is now confronting three actors: the regime in Maseru, the opposition in exile, and the SADC. But what does the future hold for Lesotho in the next five years in the hands of the now democratically elected *putschists*?

INTRODUCTION

Of the seemingly relatively stable SADC, the mountain Kingdom of Lesotho continues to be the odd-man out, perennially seized with deep, political and military crises since the first military coup in January 1970. At that time, Prime Minister, Chief Leabua Jonathan, and leader of the Basotho National Party (BNP), launched the first coup after losing 35 to 23 to Dr Ntsu Mokhehle, of the Basutoland Congress Party (BCP). Soon afterwards, Jonathan unleashed the police and the military to brutalise the political opposition, forcing the leadership to flee the country by 1974. A half-century later, nothing has changed; the culture of intolerance, violence, assassinations with impunity and the forced expulsion from the country of the political opposition, has come to characterise Lesotho's political landscape. (Mills, 2015; Little, 2015; Makoa, 1996; Weisfelder, 1967).

On 30 August 2014, following seeming irreconcilable differences that had culminated in the political rupture of the governing coalition government, the Deputy Prime Minister, Mothetjoa Metsing, leader of the Lesotho Democratic Congress (LDC), working closely with the then recently dismissed Chief of Defence, Lieutenant General Tlali Kennedy Kamoli, launched a military coup and succeeded in deposing the fragile leadership of Prime Minister, Dr Thomas Motsoahae Thabane, leader of the All Basotho Convention (ABC). Kamoli had been dismissed by Thabane the previous day, 29 August 2014 and Brigadier Maaparankoe Mahao was promoted to Lieutenant General and appointed the new Chief of Defence. This most recent military coup revealed a pattern where factions of political parties and military officers collude and coalesce into entities that are ready to seize power as an acceptable route to capturing and retaining state power.

The execution of the coup was a public secret, known and anticipated, with neighbouring South Africa monitoring the situation. Hence, when the military units started moving, South African intelligence operatives were able to evacuate the beleaguered Thabane an hour before his residence was attacked. In practice, the execution of the military coup followed a classic template, with some specific local dimensions (Little, 2015). After switching off the main power grid and plunging Maseru into darkness, similar switches were also sprung, terminating all radio and television communications frequencies from the country. Immediately afterwards, military units, in hard driving armoured personnel carriers, targeted the prime minister's residence and those of the police and army commanders, forcing Thabane to flee into South Africa via the nearby town of Ladybrand. In tow were his most trusted cabinet and political coalition partner, Thesele Maseribane, leader of the BNP, as well as the Police Commissioner, Khothatso Tsooana, and the newly installed Chief of Defence, Mahao, effectively decapitating the executive and the commands. Next, the mobile units 'captured,' disarmed and ransacked the police general headquarters in Maseru, and seized and disarmed two other urban police stations – Maseru Central and Mabote – before spreading countrywide. In the process of looking for some files, the military shot and killed police Sub-Inspector Mokheseng Ramahloko, responsible for the weapon armories (Jordan, 2014).

By the next day, over 250 assorted weapons had been taken from the police. Meanwhile, the human resources operational structure and the physical infrastructure of the Lesotho Mounted Police Service (LMPS) were taken over by the military. Disarmed police details were forced to shed their official uniforms and go into hiding or flee into nearby South Africa. (Country Watch, 2015). The deputy police commissioner and country Interpol representative issued an official statement for the police to remain out of sight until the situation calmed.

By capturing the police, the military left the country without any policing for several weeks. In parallel, the *putschists* targeted nearby government buildings succeeding to force into either hiding or exile an estimated 150 senior officials, the majority of whom ended up on a hastily constructed 'refugee tent-city' in South Africa. Again, the effect of the coup completely paralysed the public sector. Clearly, the military coup had been conducted, with the support of a select few trusted officers and units within the Lesotho Defence Force (LDF), allowing for the secretive lighting strike against the executive, government and police (Little, 2015).

The August 2014 military coup was the sixth successful dislocation of an elected government in Lesotho and is viewed as having 'undemocratically, shifted power following the ousting of the coalition government.' (Country Watch, 2015; Jordan, 2014). Furthermore, the subsequent transformative impact of the coup on the LDF, appears to have not been fully appreciated, at least by the SADC, and yet the full implication will only become evident in time.

But why did the coalition government, established in June 2012, confirm the cynical predictions that this administration merely represented the 'anti-Mosisili sentiment', with little hope of long-term survival?

Curiously, when Thabane survived the machine gun and rifle fire onslaught, reaching Pretoria and briefing the SADC that he had been ousted in a military coup, the usual AU protocols against the undemocratic removal of an elected government were not adopted. The said protocols include: the existing provisions of the AU's Lome Declaration of July

2000; the provisions of the African Charter on Democracy, Elections and Governance (ACDEG); Article 30 of the Constitutive Act, which also provides the authority to intervene under Article 4, adopted in 2003 amongst protocols that go back to the June 1997, Harare Declaration of the Organization of African Unity (OAU) (Omotola, 2011). In the case of Lesotho, the SADC simply decided to continue taking the sub-regional lead without publicly acknowledging developments on the ground. As one analyst pointed out, in such instances, the 'SADC deprives itself of the political instruments necessary to help address deep conflict situations' (Pallotti, 2013).

Against the background of muted condemnation of the coup by the SADC, already engaged in attempting to address the political crisis in Lesotho following the June suspension of the National Assembly in Maseru, the sub-regional body failed to acknowledge the reality of the brash entry of the military into the political crisis. During the Extraordinary Summit after the coup, the SADC appointed South African Vice President, Cyril Ramaphosa, as the main negotiator, and provided security aides for Thabane and his key officials, including Police Commissioner, Khothatso Tsooana, to return to Maseru and engage all stakeholders. The objective for the SADC was to bring about 'constitutional normalcy' without antagonising those who had now captured the state and its coercive institutions. As we shall see, this proved to be detrimental in finding a lasting solution, while allowing tacit support for the consolidation of the belligerents.

In the period immediately after the August coup, the SADC's early benign reaction appeared to embolden the *putschists* who remained free to engage without sanction. On 3 September, Ramaphosa arrived in Maseru and engaged with all parties, with Thabane and Tsooana in tow; all being guarded 24/7 by Namibian and South African security units. What the SADC had been able to achieve in the initial reaction was to deny the *putschists* external recognition, but it was unable to remove them from practically holding the elected government to ransom. Stated differently, the negotiations did not dislodge the *putschists* although political legitimacy remained with Thabane. This precarious political position was to continue until the elections of 28 February 2015. Meanwhile, acting under the naïve sense of legitimacy as the elected representatives of the coalition government, once the SADC returned with the executive and commanders, both Tsooana and Mahao started calling for the arrest and detention of those who had committed treason – specifically Metsing, who had announced that he was in charge, and Kamoli who had planned and executed the event. The new Chief of Decence, Mahao, was reduced to calling for external assistance, 'including military assistance', to reign in the rebel commander (Motsamai, 2015). Frustrated and unable to achieve this, the SADC's answer came from the South African Minister of the Department of International Relations and Cooperation (DIRCO), Maite Nkoana-Mashabane, who pointed out that the SADC preferred negotiations rather than the military option that was being suggested.

Sensing danger, the dismissed Kamoli marshalled 'his' force out of the capital, Maseru, in the second week of September, relocating some 60 km away, deep in the Sedibeng mountains. A former chief of intelligence, Kamoli took with him the Military Intelligence Unit, the 40-strong Special Forces led by Brigadier Ramanka Mokaloba, and over 200 soldiers, armed with artillery, mortars and anti-air guns, as well as almost all the small arms weapons from the LDF armouries, where he established an almost impenetrable defensive and offensive position. This blatant division of the LDF into a faction that supported Kamoli and his political masters, effectively ruptured the institution, leaving behind a shadow of the LDF that was unable to confront him. Furthermore, this flaunting of civil authority by the rebel force was taking place in the presence and full view of SADC mediators, who continued to work with a semblance of the legitimate coalition government. More importantly, while Kamoli returned from the Sedibeng Mountains to engage in South African-SADC inspired talks, his force was not dismantled and remained intact. There were also no calls from the SADC to disband the clearly partisan force before the February elections. Never in the history of Lesotho had something like this happened – the creation of an army within the army – an entity that had clear diverse and partisan political affiliation and had surreptitiously organised a coup, proceed to gather all weaponry, take up an offensive/defensive position within the territorial confines of the country, and fail to be challenged by the SADC. This was unprecedented and is a development that remains unmatched in the troubled history of Lesotho. Against this, Ramaphosa continued to engage Kamoli in the broader political and security dialogue that was taking place, while the latter commuted between Sedibeng Mountains, Maseru and even Pretoria. The result of that engagement was quick to emerge.

On 2 October 2014, Ramaphosa was able to reach the political Facilitation Declaration with all the political parties. This provided agreement on just two aspects: agreement to re-convene parliament, limited to discussing only two items: that of arranging for the modalities of holding an election and, secondly, authorising the finances required for that purpose. Three weeks later, on 23 October, he was able to secure the Maseru Security Facilitation Agreement. The latter was a loose arrangement reached between the confrontational military commanders, Kamoli and Mahao, and the Police Commissioner, Tsooana, to stand back from the political and electoral process until after the snap election scheduled for 28 February 2015. In the security agreement, Tsooana was directed to go to Algiers, Algeria, and left in November 2014, while Mahao went to Juba, South Sudan, during the same month. However, while Kamoli was supposed to travel to Kampala, Uganda, he refused to go and remained behind. His reason for not travelling was that the coalition government had blocked his salary and he was therefore not prepared to cooperate. Against this, the SADC appeared to have no capacity to enforce compliance.

Furthermore, Kamoli's army exhibited all the traits of not being under the authority of the elected civilian authority during the interim period. Alagappa (2001) acknowledges the Weberian notion of the state maintaining monopoly over the legitimate instruments of violence as its key features. However, he then proceeds to identify the difficult challenge of:

> ... prevent[ing] the coercive institutions from dominating the state and society ... ensure that state coercion is used in service of public interest, not for private and partisan purposes.

On 13 February, the army wrote to government, 'advising' that it was prepared to launch countrywide patrols in defence of Lesotho's national security. Alarmed, the coalition government urgently wrote back seeking to question the veracity of the army taking such action without consultation or authority. In attempting to deliver the hastily written response, the corporal guarding army headquarters refused to accept the letter, citing that this was after duties could only be accepted the following day. For the umpteenth time, Thabane rushed to the SADC in the South African capital, Pretoria, to report the threatening measures.

The SADC responded by holding yet another Extraordinary Summit at which the body authorised that the LDF would be confined and quarantined to barracks until March, and called for the deployment of 475 police, drawn from the 12 mainland-based countries on the continent, to be on the ground within a few days in Lesotho. This phase created an opportunity to address the seemingly endemic role of the military in politics in Lesotho. First, the confinement to barracks could have been followed by the swift disarmament of the partisan forces responsible for the obvious insecurity in the Kingdom since August 2014, and secondly, such decisive action could have laid the foundation for establishing a new and democratic force with SADC facilitation and assistance. However, this opportunity was allowed to pass and what followed as the final transformation of the LDF and its relationship with the rest of Basotho society is likely to haunt the SADC and the African continent for a long time to come.

The final dimension appeared soon after the Ntsu Democratic Congress led by former prime minister, Mosisili, won the 28 February poll and established a seven-party coalition that included his former secretary-general and now leader of the LDC, Metsing. For the *putschists*, the reappointment of Metsing as deputy prime minister was significant, and appeared to confirm the fact that the coup was now being embedded and enjoying legitimation after the February poll. There was further political grounding in the next appointment announced by Mosisili. This was to appoint the beleaguered Monyane Moleleki to become the new Minister of Police. In the same breath, Mosisili dismissed Tsooana, viewed as a protégé of Thabane and the ABC. In doing this, the stage was set to establish a new and compliant police force following the forceful dismantling of the existing one.

Even as this was taking place, at the end of March, the SADC announced its departure and closure of its representative office in Maseru, heralding mission accomplished. However, the political and security situation was set to worsen, with Lesotho's culture of intolerance, violence and assassinations with impunity continuing. The period from May to June witnessed unceremonious departures of frightened political leaders, senior civil servants, lawyers, witnesses, and media, with some citizens losing their lives in brutal assassinations that were not investigated. In May 2015, over three days, political opposition members including Thabane (ABC), Maseribane (BNP) and Keketso Rantso, leader of the Reformed Congress of Lesotho (RCL) were forced to flee the country, fearing for their lives. Rantso related a frightening experience that eventually forced her to escape. Concerned with the security situation, Rantso employed a security guard at her residence. On 26 May, during the night, armed people arrived and chased off the guard and tried to force entry into the house. Disturbed by the commotion, she raised an alarm by telephone, resulting in local people gathering and coming to her rescue. This resulted in a temporary retreat by the armed men and, taking advantage of this, she immediately fled across the border into South Africa.[3] In parallel, on 17 May 2015, a well-known businessman, supporter and funder of the ABC, Thabiso Francis Alex Tsosane was shot and killed by an unknown gunman. The matter was not investigated in spite of appeals and written submissions that included a very public intervention by Rantso.

During this turbulent period, in retrospect, on 14 May, attention turned towards the military, with the reinstatement of Kamoli to his post of Chief of Defence and the demotion of Mahao to Brigadier, as well as the reinstatement of the charges that he had been facing since February 2014. Soon afterwards, Kamoli launched the most extensive, Stalinist-type, purge of the Officers Corps. Conducted under the cover of a special operation, officers were accused of having committed mutiny and collaborating with Mahao during the period September 2014 and May 2015.

The operators sought out the officers, at home, in their offices and elsewhere, and kidnapped, tortured and incarcerated them. Within two weeks, over 56 officers had been arrested. Almost all were taken to the bitterly cold military camp at Sedibeng. Sedibeng Barracks has become notorious with military atrocities, including extrajudicial killings, according Hofstatter and Jika (2015). Made to disappear for days, most would resurface at the Makoanyane Barracks, a military intelligence camp, before being taken to court, bruised and bleeding, in leg irons and handcuffs, transported on the back of pick-up trucks and guarded by balaclavad, gun-bearing soldiers. While in the hands of the military, as evidence was later to emerge, officers were subjected to extreme abuse, and asked to relate their role in the mutiny, according to a former soldier and now lawyer representing the victims (Hofstatter, 2015). Clearly the officers targeted are those that did not participate in the coup and remained behind when Kamoli and his entourage created a fortress at Sedibeng in the second week of September 2014. They were viewed as 'loyal to Mahao' during his short reign when the SADC was in town.

Worse was to follow. On 25 June 2015, three LDF vehicles that appeared to have been trailing Mahao, 30 km from Maseru, blocked his exit from his farm in Makame and then shot him.[4] Whether he died on the spot or later is a matter before the SADC Commission of Inquiry led by Judge Mphaphi Phumaphi. This incident, in broad daylight and before witnesses, caused consternation and evoked international outrage, culminating in strong statements of condemnation issued by the UN and the AU.

Alarmed and somewhat embarrassed, the SADC called an urgent Extraordinary Summit, after which it issued the 3 July *communiqué* that has far reaching implications. More importantly, the July *communiqué* also followed numerous and successive interventions between June 2014 and when SADC closed its offices in Maseru at the end of March 2015. This time round, also guided and goaded by the alarming adverse report submitted to the summit by the appointed facilitator, subsequent decisions have far-reaching consequences, bordering on suspending Lesotho's sovereignty and casting aspersion on the professionalism of the LDF. In practice, the summit established an Oversight and Early Warning Committee for increased intervention; called on the government to create a conducive political and security environment and allow the return of fleeing, leading political opposition members senior, civil servants, police and military officers; established an Independent Commission of Inquiry into the 25 June 2015 assassination of the former military chief, Mahao by the LDF; and, worse, called for the immediate stop to the purging of senior officers in the special operation.

But what explains the inexorable deteriorating trajectory of the crisis in Lesotho, even after repeated South African and SADC intervention since 1993? Why has the military assumed an increasingly decisive political role in the fluid, complex and technically democratic environment of the kingdom? To this end, to what extent has the crisis transformed the military that is aligning itself with the contemporary political agenda? And finally, how significant has the intervention of the SADC been?

This discussion is concerned with evaluating the nature and impact of civil-military relations (CMR) on the African continent more broadly and, in this case, using the events in Maseru and the interventions adopted by the SADC as a case study. In examining the context of the sixth military coup in Lesotho, the aim is to provide an understanding of the factors at play so that the research informs intervention mechanisms of the AU and SADC, even as Lesotho continues on its inexorable downward trajectory characterised by a rapidly deteriorating political and security environment.

ARRANGEMENT AND ARGUMENT

After extensively detailing the coup itself, the following sections provide background and a brief discussion of the aftermath of the SADC's 3 July 2015 *communiqué*.

Since independence in 1966, the state in Lesotho has remained weak and fragile, susceptible to being captured, at regular intervals, by coalitions of intolerant and exclusive, political, traditional and military factions concerned with reigning and power retention, and prepared to vanquish the 'other' with impunity. This is in spite of the introduction of multiparty democracy in 1993, in which elections have been reduced to Roger Southall's famous description of Lesotho elections as 'rigged or *de rigeur*' – simply going through the motions, but failing to imbibe democratic notions. This was the first event that witnessed the SADC's first intervention into the Lesotho crisis, forced to work with the then apartheid South Africa, but concerned with bringing about stability in the mountain kingdom. It is therefore clear that the politico-military factions seizing power in Lesotho are concerned with the capturing and retention of state power, and reliance on military force in this quest has become almost intractably integrated in the political intercourse. In other words, in the minds of key political elites in this country, military coups have become an acceptable route to state power. In practice, this has created overly partisan state institutions, especially those responsible for the monopoly of force. Furthermore, the same political elite, from either side, once ensconced into power, has exhibited that it is imbued with no serious national developmental commitment and vision. In practice, Lesotho exhibits marked impoverishment, characterised with 'active poor' amid alarming unemployment levels from the international and regional collapse in commodities and minerals prices. However, external intervention by South African and SADC has not been able to dissuade the Basotho away from their winner-takes-all, mendacious attitude.

BACKGROUND TO THE COUP

The major conflict drives leading to the military coup began with developments in the ruling LDC, characterised by leadership succession battles as the country approached the scheduled May 2012 general election. On 28 February 2012, Mosisili took the usual step, historically taken by congress leaders unwilling to relinquish power, of launching a new party, the Ntsu Democratic Congress. This left the LDC in the hands of Metsing. As the election approached, there was therefore bad blood between Metsing and Mosisili.

Meanwhile, the 26 May election result reflected a stalemate in which no party was able to claim independent victory. Instead, the political parties were reduced to negotiating with like-minded parties. Ultimately, this brought together the first coalition government in Lesotho made up of strange bedfellows led by Thabane of the ABC with 30 seats, joined by Metsing of the LDC with 26 seats, and Maseribane of the BNP with five seats, constituting a wafer-thin 61-seat majority in the 120-seat parliament. It may be remembered that Thabane had also split from the LDC in 2006 to establish the ABC. Hence the two leading political leaders in the coalition were perceived to have angst towards the now official opposition leader, Mosisili.

The second feature of drives culminating in the military coup was the government policy and focus adopted by Thabane, who launched a high risk strategy of attempting to root out deeply embedded corruption while, in parallel, undertaking state and institutional reforms. The state reform agenda targeted foreign affairs, the judiciary, the election commission, and senior officials in the public sector, police and the armed forces among others. In January 2013, Thabane appointed a new police commissioner while establishing an anti-corruption agency.

On the anti-corruption drive, evidence was not hard to find of corrupt practices by officials of the previous regime. The anti-corruption campaign identified former LDC stalwarts as chief culprits. Among the most prominent was Metsing, former Minister of Finance, Timothy Thahane, and Minister of Minerals and Natural Resources, Mopanye Moleleki, who were close aides to Mosisili. As to the nature and extent of the corruption under the successor to the coalition during the preceding 15-year reign of Mosisili and the LDC, various independent reports alleged deeply embedded and state sanctioned corruption in the management of the Lesotho state. These reports are confirmed by successive government reports that have unearthed serious corruption by state officials and other commercial players (*Report of the Public Accounts Committee: 8th Parliament Auditor-General Report 2008/09, 2012/13 & 2014*). The government reports also refer to the state of affairs characterised by negligence, bribery and theft, resulting in millions of Maloti (Lesotho currency) lost through corruption. The same reports also noted the rot in the public sector, stemming from highly politicised appointments in the public sector. From 2006, the reports speak of a state patronage system providing luxury cars, including Land Cruisers, to officials for use on both official and private activities.

However, within months, this campaign began to suffer a stillbirth, fiercely resisted by the former political elite and highly politicised public-service state officials (Bertelsmann Stiftung, 2014). In fact, by default, this made a strong case for completing state reform in order to infuse a sense of national service in the public sector. More specifically, anti-corruption investigations had also located large and regular deposits made into Mesing's bank accounts between February 2013 and April 2014. When confronted with the evidence, Metsing could not offer an explanation and, instead, launched a vitriolic attack on what authority the state had used to access his private affairs.

With the anti-corruption campaign continuing without relent, a third drive emerged: that of the role of the military in the highly charged political context. It is significant that, during the election campaign, Mosisili had accused Thabane of being a nationalist in disguise, prepared to take people to court if he won the election. In January 2014, grenades were thrown at the residences of the prime minister's partner and that of the Police Commissioner, Tsooana, which resulted in some deaths. Subsequent investigations revealed that eight of the armed group had been drawn from the LDF military aides allocated to Metsing and that they had used his vehicle in mounting the attack (Motsamai, 2015; Jordan, 2014, 2015). This was viewed as a warning, a shot across the bow, designed to get the prime minister to back off.

However, when the police tried to follow up and question the soldiers, Kamoli refused to make available the alleged perpetrators. This defiance was viewed as insubordination and spurred Thabane to urgently consider replacing the leadership of the armed forces as part of his state reform agenda. Kamoli faced treason, murder and insubordination charges.

The debate appeared to reach the military ranks when Captain Hashatsi addressed 38 Special Forces members on 14 January 2014, referring to the MoAfrika programme and that, as long as he lived, no piece of paper would be allowed to remove Kamoli from office (Hashatsi's address to the Commission of Inquiry, 21 February 2014). Brigadier Mahao got wind of the address and remonstrated Hashatsi for dabbling in politics. A few days later, the matter was reported to the authorities; Mahao was suspended by Major General Motsomotso, and charges laid against him. The political power struggle had now entered the military ranks.[5] In retrospect, from this period on, Mahao was a marked man in the military. Meanwhile, Thabane was convinced that appointing Mahao would allow him to transform the institution while advancing his state-reform agenda.

By late 2013 and early 2014, the political coalition was dissolving. In June, Metsing announced that he and the LDC were leaving the coalition. Furthermore, under the anti-corruption threat, Metsing and Mosisili had managed to find each other and reached an agreement where they would be future political partners. In order to stop the anti-corruption drive and its obvious outcome, the two parties sought to launch a vote of no confidence in parliament that would remove Thabane from power. This democratic parliamentary act would have brought down the coalition.

However, Thabane pre-empted the parliamentary process when he deftly blocked this by proroguing parliament for nine months. Frustrated and facing possible arrest and detention, it is safe to argue that, from this point on, Metsing and Mosisili began the earnest plot of removing Thabane by force, including supporting a military coup. The trigger for the well-laid but publicly known plans occurred on 29 August 2014, when Thabane was dismissed and Mahao was appointed. This was the last straw. The under-pressure political class was confronted with the stark choice of either facing jail time, arrested by the new commanders installed by Thabane in the police and the armed forces, or resorting to military options.

In the background to the coup, the four key dimensions of a weak and fragile coalition government that emerged from the 26 May 2012 elections was but an aberration of the internal ructions over political succession within the ruling LDC. The fact that Thabane, himself a former LDC member until 2006, was able to form a majority of one in order to form the new government, demonstrated the fragility of the new regime. However, relying on this limited political legitimacy, Thabane embarked upon a high-risk strategy, attempting to root out corrupt tendencies while reforming the state. The resistance was palpable, coming from the political elite and the whole public service that had enjoyed largesse over the last decade-and-a-half under the LDC leadership. Soon it was predictable that the project would collapse. SADC intervention appeared only limited to massaging the egos of all stakeholders, unconcerned and appearing unwilling to tackle the more hard issues of condemning the illegitimate removal of an elected government by force, and looking aside as that force consolidated itself in open confrontation with the state.

THE AFTERMATH: POST 28 FEBRUARY CONSOLIDATION OF PUTSCHISTS AND IMPLICATIONS

The period since the SADC's 3 July 2015 *communiqué* and this research does not provide sufficient distance for assessing the true implications of what has transpired since 30 August 2014. Some of the pointers are still emerging in the SADC Commission of Inquiry, and will need time and distance for analysts to digest and comprehend before drawing its implications. In spite of this limited handicap, however, a few areas can be cited in which the 30 August 2014 coup reflects differences to the previous five coups between January 1970 and September 1994.

There is a new and legitimate administration, complete with its partisan force, in power in Lesotho for the next five years. In CMR, the key political appointment of Moleleki to head the internal security portfolio while suspending Tsooana and embarking upon the fresh reconstitution of the 'defeated' old mounted police is instructive. For now, it is also clear that the relationship between armed institutions and society is not harmonious, with a series of deaths and arrests crudely carried out outside of the constitutional laws, at least in the eyes of the SADC. The same is true of Mosisili's reinstatement of Kamoli, openly challenging Thabane and his supporters, leading to the former refusing to return from exile in South Africa. In this way, Mosisili has embedded political divisions while increasing the security of his faction at the direct expense of all others, whether in or outside the country. He also turned his attention to foreign deployments within months of taking power. The result has been that several representatives previously appointed by Thabane have been summarily recalled. It is also true that Mosisili has embarked upon extensive transformation of the state and its institutions within Lesotho, designed to consolidate power and exclude all remnants of the coalition era. The willingness to use force has remained central. To this end, the notion of the use of the military to seize and hold state power has been reinforced in Lesotho yet again.

CONCLUSIONS

This background is policy-oriented research aimed at providing an analytical version of what confronted the SADC's unprecedented 3 July *communiqué* on the crisis in Lesotho. It is therefore focused on the coup of 30 August 2014 carried out by the recently dismissed Kamoli. This is likely to inform the process beyond the *communiqué* as the SADC's intervention deepens to include early warning political and security oversight and dealing with the evidence emerging from its Commission of Inquiry into the circumstances surrounding the death of Mahao.

The discussion began with a historical perspective linking the current coup to the previous five that have occurred since January 1970, making the country prone to coups and susceptible to groups of officers considering the option. In 2012, when a coalition government was installed, this was a demonstration of the further weakening of central government, but was itself the result of internal fighting within the ruling LDC for purposes of political succession. Armed with a narrow political mandate, the post 2006 LDC and leader of the ABC, Thabane, embarked on a high-risk dual strategy of attempting to root out corruption while reforming the state. While the evidence was not hard to find, its likely impact on the political elite, some of whom were members of the coalition. This development also identified the culture of negligence, bribery and theft that government annual audits presented in parliament had found of the whole management of the public sector. The same state documentation had also found that human resource appointments in the public sector followed equally corrupt practices, resulting in a highly politicised public service. It was therefore not surprising that Thabane's new administration was faced with sector-resisting change and refused to embrace the new inquiries. Soon, this political programme poisoned the fragile coalition, further threatened by the appointment of Tsooana in January 2013, who appeared ready to follow up and arrest culprits. This development also set the police apart from the army, led by Kamoli, a former intelligence chief and later the Chief of Defence appointed by Mosisili. In May 2014, the government was facing political revolt, leading to the initial entry of South Africa and the SADC in attempts to mediate relations between the antagonists. In June, with Thabane determined to continue with his governmental policy, Metsing announced his departure from the coalition while reaching a rapprochement with his old enemy and official opposition, Mosisili. Given their numbers, the two planned to push for a vote of no-confidence in parliament that would bring down Thabane. Sensing danger, the latter moved quickly to prorogue parliament for nine months, while speeding up investigations and the potential to make arrests. To effect this, Thabane also needed to remove Kamoli, which he did on 29 August 2014, and appointed Mahao in his place. This was the last straw for both the political actors and military leaders who had begun to act in tandem.

The next day, 30 August 2014, Kamoli launched a military coup. The impact of the long-heralded and expected coup was dramatic. With South African security officials' assistance, Thabane was able to cross the border into nearby South Africa only hours before the attack. In tow were his commanders, other political leaders of the coalition, such as Maseribane, and an estimated 150 senior public-service officials. This resulted in the disintegration of the police as a formed unit, as well as government. A few days later, the SADC intervened, deploying Ramaphosa as lead negotiator. It is important to note that South Africa and the SADC deliberately refused to publicly condemn the coup, perhaps hoping to continue to have leverage with the *putschists*. In the period September 2014 until the elections held on 28 February 2015, two agreements facilitated the interim process: the first agreement was to consider a snap election as a way cut of the crisis and, three weeks later, on 23 October, a security agreement between the contending commanders of the military and the police, Kamoli, Mahao and Tsooana. The latter agreed to step aside and allow the political process to take its course. Whereas Mahao and Tsooana complied, Kamoli refused and, in fact, used the period to further entrench his hold of the dominant faction within the LDF. Kamoli was able to rip out the heart of the LDF and leave behind a mere shell. With the SADC located in its offices in Maseru, no action was taken to remonstrate this highly confrontational act of defiance towards the elected coalition government. Pressed for a military response by Mahao, the SADC responded that they preferred a negotiated solution. This stalemate within the country continued until the elections of 28 February. However, in early February, with the election weeks away, Thabane ran to the SADC, trying to dissuade the army from undertaking countrywide patrols. The SADC responded by deploying 475 police officers from its 12 land-based member-states. After the elections, the SADC withdrew at the end of March 2015.

This withdrawal opened a new page in the Lesotho crisis, characterised by violence, threats to lives of opponents and assassinations with impunity. In May, the new government of Mosisili and Metsing appointed a new minister and commander of the police, dismissing Tsooana. Next, Mahao was demoted, while Kamoli was reinstated as Chief of Defence. Thabane, Maseribane and Rantso were forced to flee Lesotho and seek refuge in South Africa. The assassination of Tsoasane poisoned the political environment in the country, and the subsequent purge of the Officer Corps effectively changed the command structure of the LDF.

What has become clear is that the coup of 30 August 2014 has become embedded in the state structures of the new regime, elected on 28 February 2015, and become legitimate. Secondly, there has been extensive security sector reform of a partisan nature, ending with the appointment of Moleleki, a former minister facing potential charges during the anti-corruption campaign after being put in charge of the police.

As the SADC finds itself back in Maseru, it is faced with a situation where all the political opposition are in forced exile and the local force is one that launched the unconstitutional change of government in August 2014. It will be interesting to see how the situation is going to evolve over the next five years.

NOTES

1   The first coup was conducted by Jonathan Leabua in January 1970, after Ntsu Mokhehle of the BCP had won the election. The latter was later forced into exile by 1974. Jonathan suspended the Constitution. The second coup took place on 20 January 1986, when Leabua was removed by Major General Justin Lekhanya; in the third, in April 1991, Colonel Elias Ramaema deposed Lekhanya in a bloodless coup. The fourth coup took place from 19 August 1994 until 14 September 1994, when King Letsie III, urged on by the military, suspended the constitution and dissolved parliament, replacing it with a 16-member governing council of senior military and police officers. On 14 September

Secretary-General Ahmed Salim Salim intervened along with Moses Anafu. In September 1998, the fifth coup forced Botswana, Zimbabwe and South Africa to intervene to establish an interim political authority.

2   Van Staden, 2015; Makoa, 1996.

3   These political leaders, senior officials of the coalition government and uniformed forces personnel are still 'hiding' in South Africa.

4   Whether he died on the spot or later in Makoanyane Barracks military hospital is a matter before the current SADC Commission of Inquiry headed by Botswana Judge, Mphaphi Phumaphi.

5   In just over a year, when the SADC Commission of Inquiry started sitting, Hashatsi appeared before it, now with the lofty rank of Lieutenant Colonel, and refused to answer questions on whether or not he was present at the scene when Mahao was shot. The judge chairing the session then pointed out to him that he was a suspect.

REFERENCES

Alagappa, M. 2001. *Coercion and Governance: The declining political role of the military in Asia*. Stanford: Stanford University Press.

Al-Jazeera News Service. 2014. 'Army targets Government Buildings, Police, Radio and TV', 31 August 2014. Available at http://www.aljazzera.com. Accessed 30 June 2015.

Bertelsmann Stiftung, 2014. 'BTI 2014 Lesotho Country Report'. Available at http://www.bti-project.org. Accessed 30 June 2015.

Clapham, C. 1996. *Africa and the International System: The politics of state survival*. Cambridge: Cambridge University Press.

Clapham, C. 2000. 'Rethinking African States' in *African Security Review* (ASR), 10(3).

Country Watch. 2015. *Lesotho 2015 Country Review*. Available at http://www.countrywatch.com. Accessed 30 July 2015.

ENCA News 24. 2015. 'Lesotho on edge after killing of its former army commander', 28 June 2015. Available at http://www.enca.com/africa/lesotho-edge-after-killing-its-former-army-commander. Accessed 9 July 2015.

Hofstatter, S. & Jika, T. 2015. 'Reign of terror grips Lesotho' in *Sunday Times*, 5 July 2015.

Humphrey, B. 2014. 'Lesotho army appears to fracture' in *Lesotho Times*, 21 September 2014.

Jordan, M.J. 2014a. 'Op-Ed Assassination in Lesotho: Blood on SADC's hands too' in *Mail & Guardian*, 31 August 2014.

Jordan, M.J. 2014b. 'Lesotho wrestles with corruption' in *Mail & Guardian*, 12 December 2014.

Jordan, M.J. 2015. 'Ominous rumblings from Lesotho army ahead of elections' in *Mail & Guardian*, 13 February 2015.

Little, A.T. 2015. 'Coordinating, learning and coups' in *Journal of Conflict Resolution*, SAGE, 2015. Available at http://www.jcr.sagepub.com. Accessed 30 July 2015.

Makoa, F.A. 1995. 'Coup fails dismally: King scores morally' in *Light in the Night Extramural Studies Newsletter*. National University of Lesotho.

Makoa, F.A. 1996. 'Political instability in post-military Lesotho: The crisis of the Basotho nation state?' in *African Security Review*, 5(3).

Makoa, F.A. 2013. 'Beyond the electoral triumphalism: Reflections on Lesotho's coalitions, government and challenges' in *Strategic Review for Southern Africa*, 36(1).

Mills, G. 2015. 'A fractious lot: Anatomy of (another) coup in Lesotho' in *Daily Maverick*, 3 July 2015. Available at http://www.dailymaverick.co.za. Accessed 30 July 2015.

Motsamai, D. 2015. 'Elections in time of instability: Challenges for Lesotho beyond the 2015 poll'. Issue Paper, 3 April 2015. Institute for Security Studies.

Ntsukunyane, L. 2015. 'Mahao knew he was going to die: Family' in *Lesotho Times*, 2 July 2015.

Pallotti, A. 2013. 'Regional cooperation in Africa: SADC and the crisis in Zimbabwe' in *Strategic Review for Southern Africa*, 35(1).

Robinson, J. 2002. 'States and Power in Africa by Jeffrey Herbs: A review essay' in *Journal of Economic Literature*, Vol. XL, June 2002.

SADC. 2015a. 'Extraordinary summit of double troika', *SADC Communiqué*, 20 February 2015.

SADC. 2015b. 'LDF quarantined to remain in barracks until 31 March 2015'; *SADC Communiqué*, 3 July 2015.

Skiti, S. 2015. 'Politicians exiled in SA live in fear' in *Sunday Times*, 5 July 2015.

Southhall, R. & Fox, R. 1999. 'Lesotho General Elections 1998: Rigged or *de rigeur*?' in *Journal of Modern African Studies*, 37(4).

Weisfelder, R.F. 1967. 'Power struggle in Lesotho' in *Africa Report*, Vol. 21.

Zihlangu, B. 2015a. 'Family of assassinated former Lesotho military commander demands answers' in *Lesotho Times*, 2 July 2015. Available at http://www.lestimes.com. Accessed 30 July 2015.

Zihlangu, B. 2015b. 'LDF now a lawless ghetto' in *Lesotho Times*, 8 July 2015. Available at http://www.lestimes.com. Accessed 30 July 2015.

Zihlangu, B. 2015c. 'Lekhetho Ntsukunyane, Lesotho's PM under fire at SADC summit' in *Mail & Guardian*, 19 August 2015.

Chapter 11

Conclusions

by Martin Rupiya

This CMR study is concerned with, firstly, raising awareness of the state of power relations between the state (executive), parliament (legislature), the institutions of coercion and societies in the 54 African Union member-states. Secondly, this book seeks to motivate for the study of the multi-disciplinary subject of CMR by civil society groups – a subject deliberately placed in the ghetto, denied resources and due academic attention by occupying powers. There was no reason for those sitting around the table at the 1884 Berlin Conference to consider establishing faculties in the study of repelling the violence and armed institutions that they were deploying to subjugate the continent. Only in the final stages of the colonial period did the metropolis countries consider engaging the new governments and their token militaries, providing limited training and equipment. It is instructive to note that, just before Nelson Mandela and the African National Congress took power in a negotiated settlement in South Africa in April 1994, from 1992, Washington, London, Berlin and Tel Aviv conspired with the outgoing National Party to remove six gun-type nuclear weapons that Pretoria had developed with Western assistance. Hence, while we speak of the dawn of a new era in which African is able to exercise independence of action in the area of CMR and weaponry, this is only true to levels below certain thresholds.

The security studies restrictive stance, which witnessed marginalisation of the discipline, was later taken advantage of and perpetuated by unrepresentative states. Under the auspices of the Cold War, until the 1990s, the one-party state system criminalised political opposition and created forces whose mandate was to dismantle structures of actual and perceived political opposition. Three examples will suffice:

The first is an important one, not necessarily covered in the texts, but carries similar traits and trends. This is the long reign of Chadian President, Idriss Derby, a former pilot, the country's Chief of the Armed Forces and later advisor to the president, who, in April 1989, was forced to flee the country. Returning with an organised force from Sudan in November 1990, by December, he had successfully marched and seized N'Djamena, forcing Hissiene Habre to flee to Senegal. Once in office in the coup-prone state, Derby created structures that included a protection force and a nominal political party, whose purpose was power retention. It is the argument by Daniel Vencovsky's *Presidential Term Limits in Africa,* supported by the Centre for Conflict Resolution's *Africa at Ten Report,* that, during the era of the one-party state between 1960 and 1990, no ruling party lost an election. Furthermore, currently, when a president seeking a third term goes for an election, he normally wins hands down. James A. Robinson states that this is as a result of weak African institutions that then lead to almost predictable state failure. At the heart of these institutions are those responsible for the monopoly of force in a state.

It has also been shown that the overwhelming external architecture of the Cold War, when lifted during the Winds of Change African independence era, did not completely end the participation of former colonial powers in the defence and security arena of member states. In the Central African Republic case study, the departing French neo-colonial stranglehold on foreign policy, economic and monetary control, strategic minerals exploitation policy and defence has been well argued. Furthermore, the case studies on Benin and the Central African Republic have confirmed this phenomenon. Paris remained responsible for recruitment, training, equipment and paying local forces, and used this at regular times to unseat an unwilling incumbent in the presidency. After the country experienced six military coups, the last one between Francois Bozize and Michel Dodjotia, the CMR chaos added a new layer, that of Islamisation and the introduction of militia groups mainly drawn and supported by Chad.

The second example is that of Eritrea, a promising new nation that fought its liberation struggle with allies in Ethiopia. Isaias Afwerki was chair of the Eritrean Peoples Liberation Front (EPLF) from 1973 and, in April 1993, Eritrea won its independence, supported by the new Ethiopian regime of Meles Zenawi in Addis Ababa. Soon afterwards, the EPLF established the Peoples Front for Democracy and Justice, with a view to transform from a liberation movement to one that would lead on development, peace and stability. However, this was not to be as the country was soon engaged in a protracted war with Ethiopia. To date, after nearly 42 years at the head of the Eritrean people, the country has the highest number of refugees attempting to jump off the North African, Libyan coast of the Mediterranean to Europe. Why? Because the country has failed to provide hope to millions of youth and it is the only state on the continent that requires active young people to seek exit visas. In order to maintain his hold over the years, Afwerki has created a brutal force, able and willing to repress citizens.

The third and final example is Togo, a country that has become a fiefdom of the Eyadema's since Silvanus Olympio attempted to establish a small army in 1962 and concentrate resources on sevelopment. Among others, Etienne Eyadema had a one-on-one with Olympio on 24 September 1962, who remained firm in his intention to keep military expenditure to a minimum. Aggrieved, the returning French soldiers, who included Etienne Gnassimbe, Emmanuelle Bodjolle and Kleber Dadjo, conspired to launch the first military coup on the continent. This was just months before the formation of the OAU in May. During the early hours of 13 January 1963, the disgruntled returning soldiers launched a ferocious assault on the presidency, who was later found shot dead just feet away from scrambling into the US Embassy in Lome. Eyadema admitted that he was part of the coup plotters who attacked government buildings and arrested the cabinet. Staying in the shadows briefly, he stepped forward in 1967 and removed the interim president, Nicolas Grunitzky. In keeping this brief, but identifying relevant CMR implications, Eyadema was to run Togo until his untimely death on a medical rescue plane over Tunis, *en route* to Paris for treatment. Meanwhile, in the 38 years in power, Eyadema had created an ethnic, *Kabre* force against the perceived Southern Togo *Ewes*, supporters of the late Olympio. On hearing of his demise, the army closed the country's borders – blocking the constitutional successor, the Speaker of Parliament, Fambare Outtara Natchaba, from returning. In parallel, he summoned parliament to meet and pass constitutional amendments, leading to the installation of the late president's son, Faure Gnassimbe Eyadema on 5 February. In this, Togo was witnessing the action of a politically inspired military as the legacy bestowed by Eyadema on the nation.

The sub-regional body, ECOWAS, reacted, led by the then Nigerian President, Olusugun Obasanjo, arguing for Togo to follow its constitution on the question of succession. Peeved and fearful of being routed, the military retreated strategically and, on 12 February, Faure theoretically left the presidency to run a one-man election – against the son of the first president, Gilchrist Olympio, who had been in exile and been unable to return until a few weeks into the campaign. The result, aided by the advantages of the incumbency, were almost predictable. On 24 April, Faure won the election and was installed into office.

After ten years and two terms in office, Faure Gnassimbe proceeded to change the constitution in order to run for a third term. This drew spirited protestations, strikes, riots and school boycotts. With a determination akin to his father, Faure, supported by the Togolese Armed Forces, shot and killed over 1 000 people, while 40 000 fled for their lives into neighbouring Benin and Ghana. Others have argued that the sub-regional countries hosting the refugees have been complicit in the perpetuation of the politico-military crisis in Lome and Togo generally. This has now split the country in half, with Kabres from the North lording it over the Southern Ewes. As we have begun to coin the phrase in the texts, Togo represents one of the most graphic 'stable coup' countries that have added extended presidential term limits. In Togo, it is easy to see what the context is when we ask the question: What have the Eyademas organised the Togolese state to achieve? Maintain power retention and internal repression of the *Ewes*, while sustaining the access and patronage system of the Kabres? And most importantly, as has been widely reported, maintain a high-level intelligence operation, in collaboration with hosting countries, of surveillance of Togolese refugees in the camps in neighbouring Ghana and Benin? If one were to argue that these dimensions are what the state in Togo has been geared to achieve, one would not be far off the mark.

Again, ECOWAS and the AU have been unable to stop this monarchical rule of over the 50 years of the Eyademas in Togo, representing one of Africa's most tragic CMR case studies. This is instructive in research and future comparative research and options, critically evaluating the role of sub-regions in assisting hapless citizens in righting the wrongs in their societies. Certainly the determination and impact of the civil society groups in Burkina Faso has been a unique development, unmatched by other surrounding countries in West Africa.

In writing conclusions on the challenges facing state formation and nation building on the African continent, we cannot help but pass comment on the current dynamics in Ouagadougou, capital of Burkina Faso. One of the causes of the second coup by General Gilbert Diendere leading the former special forces created by Blaise Compaore, the Presidential Security Guards (RSP), is that, in the transformation from dictatorship to democracy, the interim authority of President Michel Kafondo has called for the dismantling of the RSP and the barring of all officials associated with the 27-year coup and subsequent repressive reign by Compaore from contesting the upcoming election.

There are some interesting dimensions reflected in this case study. Diendere, for example, is participating in a third military coup having operated with Thomas Sankara and Compaore in the 1983 coup, and then, assisting the latter to remove Sankara four years later, in 1987. This makes Diendere a local Burkinabe coup specialist. During the 27-year reign of Compaore, Diendere and the RSP operated as an army within an army in the Burkina Faso National Force. Furthermore, this habit did not die with the hasty departure of Compaore in November 2014, when he was deposed. This makes a strong case for African citizens to call for the rapid dismantling of a dictator's personalised units when they leave power and, as an alternative, motivate for the reposition of the hitherto marginalised national forces at the centre. The operational ethos, equipment, higher pay and allowances afforded the RSP compared to the regular army, speak of an institution created, not for national security but for personal protection and purposes of power retention at all costs by the long-reigning Compaore. In a recent event, they burst into a Cabinet meeting and took the interim president and prime minister into custody, demanding no action on their continued existence as a special force. When the public reacted with anger and demonstrations, the RSP opened fire, killing ten people and wounding hundreds. This is the second important CMR point: identifying the willingness of this force to shoot and kill citizens viewed as political opposition. This goes back to the nature of the state under Compaore and the fact that the RSP is, generally, exclusively drawn from one ethnic group. This is a force that is then provided with partisan focus and mandate, in which they regard the local population and political opponents as the enemy. In doing so, Compaore established skewed CMR, while effectively dividing the armed forces. Before the end of his many terms in office in November 2014, Compaore, in subtle ways, directed parliament to change the constitution and extend his rule. The surprise was the existence of what has now been recognised as a rare and vehemently determined civil society made up of workers, trade unionists, political parties and youth activists, known as the *Balai Citoyen* who called for mass protests. In November 2014 when parliament sat to consider Compaore's directive, depicting weakness and the possibility to comply, Ouagadougou's civil society did the unthinkable and burnt down the parliament buildings. In most dictatorships, parliamentarians have been found to be ready to comply, extremely weak-willed and given to delivering the constitutional changes with little resistance. Fast forward to 16 September 2015, when Diendere and the RSP violently broke up a cabinet meeting, arresting the president and prime minister: the Speaker of the National Assembly, Sheriff Sy, immediately announced that, in line with the constitution, he was now the country's president and called for their unconditional release. This theatrical action, in the face of extreme danger, resulted in masses joining the protest on the streets, and the RSP responding by killing ten and wounding hundreds, but failed to intimidate the protestors.

This short introduction provides a salient example of what the African continent has been facing since the collapse of global international security frameworks, such as the era of slavery and mercantilism; the period of imperialism and colonialism that covered the five-month 'Scramble for Africa' Berlin Conference in 1884/1885. This provided the basis for the armed Chartered Companies to invade the continent.

WHAT IS NEW IN AFRICA'S CMR PARADIGM?

What is certainly new is the opportunity to undertake research and analysis, with home grown experts and faculties, about the history, nature and evolution of the continent's CMR. We have a number of states that can invest in this area and establish mutual disciplines that begin to feed into this much neglected area, while providing opportunity for new expertise and science to grow. Furthermore, what is also new is the partial lack of interest or loss of appetite in the physical occupation of the continent soon after the devastating events in Somalia that witnessed warlords killing and dragging US servicemen on the streets of Mogadishu. While the vacuum created at the time has been accused of leading to the genocide in Rwanda in April 1994, the fact remains that, today, the opportunity of the majority of African states and civil society to begin contemplating serious and dedicated work on better understanding CMR is in our hands. What is still missing is the realisation that we have seen in Central and Eastern Europe, where a cottage industry around the New Research Agendas led by Anthony Cotty and his colleagues emerged. It is also true that in Asia, Muthiah Alagappa's *Coercion and Governance: The Declining Political Role of the Military in Asia* has begun to make similar positive statements based on research and analysis. What is also new are the demands induced into political systems by the introduction of multiparty democracy following the end of the Cold War. Although initially confused by John Williamson's, later much maligned Washington Consensus, the mandarins in the World Bank and the International Monetary Fund attempted, by sleight of hand, to use this as a platform to inform and guide the management of economies in the developing world. The sleight of hand also included putting forward Samuel Huntington's dated *The Soldier and the State: The Theory and Politics of Civil Military Relations* and Morris Janowitz's *The Professional Soldier: A Social and Political Portrait* until disabused of their theoretical content by Peter D. Feaver's *The Civil Military Relations Problematique: Huntington and Janowitz*, in which it became clear that the former was responding to the challenges of CMR within the US and the latter, fluent in German, had been useful in conducting exit interviews of participants coming out of World War II. Both works do not constitute the comprehensive theory of CMR, with aspects that differ from country to country based on history, culture, ethnic composition and other attributes. African countries have to come up with their own texts that explain and suit their subjective and objective conditions in order to better understand and explain their circumstances. Its quick demise after the originators recanted on liberal economic theory has cleared the way, somewhat, for Africa to begin the much needed balanced process of creating a state structure designed to serve the interests of the majority. For now, as the case studies attempt to show, there has been little imaginative thinking on the key question: What is a state organised to achieve? Most polities and their political elite have not taken time to sit and debate and then come out with a mutually agreed objective(s) for which a state is then organised to compliment private sector and other civil society groups to deliver.

Establishing credible CMR as part of state formation is a complex undertaking for which the majority of African civil society has been left out so far. Perhaps now is the time to build local and continental skills that begin to address this subject. In defining balanced CMR, the discussion has looked at the interplay of the roles, checks and balances of a constitution; an elected executive-civilian authority in a democracy whose power is renewed at the polls every five years generally; a functioning parliament that has the sole responsibility of allocating resources and undertaking the accountability checks on the executive; the creation of national institutions responsible for the monopoly of force and accountable to the executive; an informed civil society, including a think-tank organisation – a phenomenon currently missing on the continent; and tertiary institutions that conduct unrestricted research and analysis on the discipline. If this is not done, then the acceptance of weak, fragile and ready to collapse states scattered throughout the continent will continue to exist.